DRAWING

THE LINE

AT THE

BIG DITCH

Drawing the Line

OTHER BOOKS BY ADAM CLYMER

Edward M. Kennedy: A Biography

The Swing Voter in American Politics (coauthor)

Ronald Reagan: The Man, The President (coauthor)

at the Big Ditch

THE PANAMA CANAL TREATIES AND THE

RISE OF THE RIGHT   Adam Clymer

UNIVERSITY PRESS OF KANSAS

Published by the
University Press of Kansas
(Lawrence, Kansas
66045), which was
organized by the Kansas
Board of Regents and is
operated and funded by
Emporia State University,
Fort Hays State University,
Kansas State University,
Pittsburg State University,
the University of Kansas,
and Wichita State
University

Library of Congress Cataloging-in-Publication Data

Clymer, Adam.
    Drawing the line at the big ditch : the Panama Canal
Treaties and the rise of the Right / Adam Clymer.
    p.   cm.
    Includes bibliographical references and index.
    ISBN 978-0-7006-1582-7 (cloth : alk. paper)
    1. Panama Canal Treaties (1977) 2. United States—
Foreign relations—Panama. 3. Panama—Foreign
relations—United States. 4. Panama Canal (Panama)—
History—20th century. 5. United States—Foreign
relations—1977–1981. 6. United States—Politics and
government—1977–1981. 7. Carter, Jimmy, 1924–
8. Reagan, Ronald. 9. Conservatism—United States—
History—20th century. 10. Presidents—United States—
Election—1980. I. Title.
    JZ3715.C58 2008
    324.973´0926—dc22   2007045716

British Library Cataloguing-in-Publication Data is available.

Printed in the United States of America

10 9 8 7 6 5 4 3 2 1

The paper used in this publication is recycled and contains
50 percent postconsumer waste. It is acid free and meets
the minimum requirements of the American National
Standard for Permanence of Paper for Printed Library
Materials Z39.48–1992.

In memory of my mother,

Eleanor Clymer, who was always writing,

but is now only fifty-six books ahead of me.

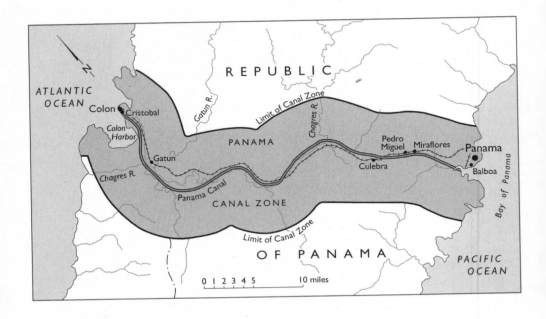

CONTENTS

" PLUCK AND LUCK CONQUERED ALL "

A CANAL FOR THE AMERICAN CENTURY

The conservative movement in America that produced the presidencies of Ronald Reagan, George H. W. Bush, and George W. Bush grew out of the ruins of the glorious lost cause of Barry Goldwater, especially the people drawn into politics to support him at the grass roots in 1964. Its intellectual heritage lay in the writings of Friedrich von Hayek, Russell Kirk, Whittaker Chambers, and William F. Buckley Jr. It stood for less government, less regulation, lower taxes, and a firm, even pugnacious posture toward powerful nations, especially the communist bloc.

The movement came to power for many reasons, ranging from the substance of its arguments to the new politics of Christian conservatives to the personal contrast between the optimistic Reagan promising a "shining city on a hill" in 1980 and the Jimmy Carter who seemed adrift in difficulty. But the *occasion* of its success was the generous and wisely self-interested decision by the four presidents who came before Reagan, that the United States should turn the Panama Canal over to Panama.

At the beginning of what *Time* would later call "the American Century," the United States defeated jungle and disease to build the Panama Canal, the greatest engineering work in the history of the world. Throughout that century, American schoolchildren would read of the heroism and determination of the work, if only glancingly of the American military intervention that created a pliant Panama. As one popular 1928 text put it, "American pluck and luck conquered all. The grand dream was realized. In 1913 the waters of the Atlantic and the Pacific were united." And so the idea of giving it up, understood and accepted by Lyndon B. Johnson, Richard M. Nixon, and Gerald R. Ford and acted on by Carter, seemed wrong to a majority of Americans, chagrined by the now inescapable realization of defeat in Vietnam and resentful of a challenge from a tiny country the United States had sired, or at least midwifed.

From the midseventies to the early eighties, the Canal question, consistent with but hardly central to conservative concerns, revitalized a Right that had grown sullen with the presidencies of Nixon and Ford. The Canal issue kept

Reagan's insurgent candidacy in 1976 alive, leaving him a victor in narrow defeat, poised for victory in 1980.

The Canal issue won conservative Republicans enough Senate seats to give Reagan a Republican majority, a helpful Senate leader, and friendly committee chairmen when he took office in 1981.

It also provided vitality to the conservative movement, with an issue that transcended its ordinary frontiers and an entrée to workers suspicious of its traditional pro-business instincts.

This overlooked turning point in American political history was hardly an inevitable movement of tectonic forces. It depended heavily on the actions of a handful of interesting people who made decisions that they did not have to make, often to their political disadvantage.

Gerald Ford, an accidental president to begin with, did not have to risk taking on an issue with no political appeal.

Reagan, more worried about big government and the Soviet Union, did not have to disagree with conservative friends like Buckley and John Wayne. In his case, the choice was the politically popular one. But, as he asked aides after treaty negotiators laid out the final details, "What if they're right?" that the Canal's operation was best secured by giving it away.

Carter, new to Washington and to international affairs, did not have to decide to make the Canal his first foreign policy priority.

In the Senate, Robert Byrd and Howard Baker, the majority and minority leaders, did not have to abandon their previous instinctive if casual commitment to perpetual U.S. control of the Canal nor, in Baker's case, of any realistic hope for the 1980 Republican nomination for president, and push Carter's treaties to ratification.

The backlash to their success created political candidates like Gordon Humphrey and John East. The airline pilot and the obscure professor would not have existed as public men, let alone United States senators, without the Canal issue. And while skilled political operatives like Richard Viguerie and Terry Dolan might have found another opportunity, the Canal and its aftermath made them central to American politics for a critical time.

I

A canal through Panama, connecting the Atlantic and the Pacific oceans and saving thousands of miles compared with journeying around Cape Horn, was an idea with origins in the days of Spanish exploration of the New World. It gained appeal because of the California gold rush of 1849. The French, led by Ferdinand de Lesseps, builder of the Suez Canal, tried from 1882 to 1889, failing physically on the scene and financially in Paris. The United States used the gunboat *Nashville* to dislodge the restive province of Panama from Colombia in 1903, recognized the new nation two days later, and then essentially imposed a one-sided treaty on Panama to gain the authority to build a canal and maintain control of it and any part of Panama the United States wanted.

In the United States, the history of the Canal was the history of excavation and construction, overcoming repeated mudslides and fabricating locks and dams thousands of miles away that fit perfectly once shipped to Panama, and conquering yellow fever and malaria. The heroic names remembered for that triumph were President Theodore Roosevelt and Colonel George W. Goethals, the engineer who saw the project through, and Colonel William C. Gorgas, who ran the campaigns to exterminate the mosquitoes that spread disease.

But if there was one name that resounded in Panamanian history, and with no heroism attached, it was that of Philippe Bunau-Varilla. An engineer in the failed French effort and a part owner of the rights granted by Colombia to construct the Canal, Bunau-Varilla tried from St. Petersburg to Paris to

Panama Canal Construction, circa 1913 (Library of Congress, USZ62-51996)

Washington to find resources to see that the Canal was built. After the Colombian Senate, in August 1903, unanimously rejected a treaty under which the United States would pay $10 million to build a canal, Bunau-Varilla worked with would-be rebels in Panama and with Roosevelt and Secretary of State John Hay to consummate the rebellion as the *Nashville* and the head of the U.S.-owned Panama Railway kept Colombian troops away from the capital of Panama City. Then, under authority he had demanded from the rebels, the Frenchman negotiated a new treaty, even more favorable to the United States than the failed pact with Colombia.

In fact, some provisions written by Bunau-Varilla were more favorable to the United States than the draft that was prepared by Secretary Hay, who had started by expanding the projected Canal Zone from 10 kilometers (6.2 miles) in width in the pact with Colombia to 10 miles. The Frenchman's version also

Drilling at the Culebra Cut, 1909 (Library of Congress, USZ62-75161)

gave the United States a permanent right to take any lands and waters outside the zone that it needed for the Canal—a provision that led to developing a number of American military bases.

Finally, his version gave the United States "in perpetuity" the near equivalent of sovereignty over the Zone, saying: "The Republic of Panama grants to the United States all the rights, power and authority within the zone mentioned . . . which the United States would possess and exercise if it were the sovereign of the territory within which said lands and waters are located to the entire exclusion of the exercise by the Republic of Panama of any such sovereign rights, power or authority."

Although Roosevelt and William Howard Taft, his secretary of war and successor in the White House, agreed that the provision gave the United

States something slightly less than real sovereignty, over time the distinction faded away in the United States until the debates of the 1970s revived it. In the Canal Zone, during the construction period and afterward, Americans lived well with cheap housing and a low-priced commissary. In 1941 John Gunther, whose best sellers explained the rest of the world to Americans, wrote in *Inside Latin America* that the Canal Zone "is as much a part of the United States as Omaha, Nebraska." A popular textbook for seventh and eighth graders published in 1950 said flatly, "The Canal Zone is United States territory."

While the new Panamanian government briefly objected to the treaty terms, it could do nothing about them because it depended on the United States to maintain its independence from Colombia. But there was another problem that surfaced promptly: the Americans looked down on the Panamanians. In a book published to celebrate the opening of the Canal in 1914, Willis J. Abbot wrote that "they hate us." He said, "The real, unexpressed reason for the dislike of the mass of Panamanians for our people is their resentment at our hardly concealed contempt for them." He said that a typical American—"with a lofty and it must be admitted a rather provincial scorn for foreign people"—looked down on all Panamanians. "From his lofty pinnacle he brands them all, from the market woman with a stock of half a dozen bananas and a handful of mangoes to the banker or the merchant whose children are being educated in Europe like their father are 'spiggotties.' " He said the word was derived from the "speaka-da-English" cry of a hack driver. The resentment occasionally boiled over, as it did on July 4, 1912, when Panamanian policemen shot and killed three unarmed U.S. Marines and arrested and beat others after being called to a whorehouse to break up a fight. That superior attitude did not go away. One children's book published in 1945 spoke of the "colossal ignorance and inertia of the Isthmian population" and said, "Natives of the country were indolent and undependable." During the debate over the treaties, Zonians argued that the Panamanians were too backward to run the Canal.

The anticolonialism that the United States championed during World War II began to be felt in Panama, with students at the fore. In 1947, they rioted against an agreement to extend temporary wartime base rights well outside the Zone. The National Assembly then voted unanimously against the pact. The president of the National Assembly, Harmodio Arosemana Forte, explained, "Nobody will vote for bases when he can look out the window and see ten thousand boys sharpening their knives." U.S. forces cleared out of the bases in three months. The New York Times reported that an underlying reason for the disturbances was the pay scale in the Zone, under which, for example, American teachers were paid three times as much as Panamanian teachers.

In 1955 the United States promised to establish an equal pay scale in the Zone. But Congress passed employment legislation only after Panamanian students, asserting their country's sovereignty, planted Panama's flag at fifty points in the Zone in May 1958. An official Canal spokesman told the New York Times the incident was ridiculous.

No one called the next flag incident ridiculous. President Dwight D. Eisenhower's brother Milton, a Latin American expert, had urged after the 1958 incident that Panama be allowed to fly its flag in the Zone. But nothing was done until waves of students celebrated Panamanian independence day on November 3, 1959, by trying to force their way into the Zone with flags. Rebuffed by Canal Zone police, they tore down the American flag at the U.S. embassy in the city of Panama and raised a Panamanian flag in its place. Rioting followed, American cars were burned, and U.S. companies' offices were wrecked. U.S. troops took over the defense of the Zone's border with Panama. There were thirty injuries but no deaths.

President Eisenhower, though he called the riots "puzzling" at a news conference, worked to accommodate Panama over the next several months. His own service in the Canal Zone in the 1920s had convinced him the original treaty was unfair. He told another news conference in December that "the question of the flag has never been specifically placed before me, but I do in some form believe we should have visual evidence that Panama does have titular sovereignty over the region." That angered the House of Representatives, which, in February 1960, passed a resolution against the idea of flying Panama's flag in the Zone. Eisenhower waited until September, when Congress was out of town, to order Panama's flag flown, together with the American flag, in a highly visible corner of the Zone (named for James Shaler, the railroad superintendent who kept the Colombian troops away in 1903), just across from Panama's legislative building. The Pentagon had objected that allowing the flag to be flown, the New York Times reported, would become a "wedge for a drive to oust the United States altogether." Before that, in April 1960, Eisenhower ordered wage increases and new housing for Panamanian workers in the Zone.

In September 1961, Panama's president, Roberto Chiari, wrote President John F. Kennedy to ask for a series of revisions to the 1903 treaty, calling it the result of "rapid collusion" between Hay and Bunau-Varilla, "which threw the new Republic of Panama, bound hand and foot, at the mercy of the Government of the United States." Kennedy took six weeks to answer and said he had ordered a "complete re-examination" of the issues. That was not enough for Chiari, who went to Washington the next June. He pressed those demands, especially the need to replace the "in perpetuity" clause of the 1903 treaty with a date on which U.S. control would end. Kennedy told Chiari he would not consider basic changes in the treaties, but a memo prepared by his aides and Chiari's a few days later did say "a new treaty will have to be negotiated." Both sides agreed to set up a commission to examine problems. Its one accomplishment was an agreement to fly both nations' flags at selected points in the Canal Zone. The commission was disbanded at Panama's insistence in August 1963.

★ The American decision to surrender control of the Panama Canal really began to take shape on January 10, 1964. Chiari told Lyndon Johnson, who had become president after Kennedy's assassination on November 22, 1963: "What we need is a complete revision of all treaties which affect Panama-US relations because that which we have at the present time is nothing but a source of dissatisfaction which has just now exploded into violence which we are witnessing."

They were talking because of anti-American rioting that would kill four Americans and twenty-four Panamanians. The rioting began on January 9, 1964, two days after American high school students hoisted the Stars and Stripes at Balboa High School. The school was not one of the seventeen sites authorized for joint flag displays. On the ninth, Panamanian high school students marched into the Zone to protest the absence of their flag. They were surrounded by American students. Taunts were exchanged, then pushing and shoving. The Panamanian flag was torn, and police made the Panamanian students leave the Zone. The students smashed windows and cars on their way. Then thousands of students and others poured into the streets, as a radio commentator spurred them on with accounts of brutality against Panamanians. President Chiari and the National Guard stayed aloof, doing nothing to halt the disorder, then suspended diplomatic relations to protest U.S. gunfire, and Chiari complained to Johnson that despite his meetings with Kennedy, "not a thing has been done to alleviate the situation."

Johnson's response was firm. He insisted that calm had to be restored before any other matters were considered. But then, he said, "We will look at the facts and try to deal with the problem. . . . We will carefully and judiciously and wisely consider both viewpoints and reach an area of agreement." That comment, in a telephone call made public three decades later, did not show in his current posture. He would brag to his friend Senator Richard Russell of Georgia that "being firm with them caused them to cave."

But within a few months the Johnson administration concluded, as Mark Atwood Lawrence put it, "that ceding some rights in the Canal Zone, far from a sign of caving in to America's leftist enemies, would in fact help reduce the danger of radicalism in Panama by strengthening the rightist oligarchy that had served U.S. interests for decades." On March 21, 1964, Johnson said he wanted talks concerning "every issue which now divides us, and every problem which the Panamanian Government wishes to raise." On April 3, he announced the restoration of diplomatic relations and the appointment of Robert Anderson, a fellow Texan and former secretary of the Treasury, as a special ambassador. And on December 18, he announced a plan to build a new sea-level canal and said the United States would pursue "an entirely new treaty" on the existing Canal that "should recognize the sovereignty of Panama." Conscious of the political risks, Johnson had assured himself of Eisenhower's support for that statement after sending a CIA agent to meet the former president's train in Chicago and clear the announcement with him.

It took not the few months Johnson expected but until the summer of 1967 before new treaties were agreed on, under which U.S control would end no later than 2009. A major element of the negotiations dealt with the idea, which Eisenhower and Kennedy had encouraged and Johnson adopted wholeheartedly, of building a new canal at sea level, possibly using atomic bombs to do the digging. It would not necessarily be dug in Panama, but perhaps in Colombia, or Nicaragua.

But those treaties never went anywhere. The Panamanian political opposition said they gave Panama too little; congressional Republicans and the *Chicago Tribune*, which broke the details of the treaty before the administration was ready, said the pacts gave away too much. Johnson did not submit them to the Senate, and a Panamanian presidential election in May 1968 went to Arnulfo Arias. Arias was a critic of the treaties, which never went before Panama's National Assembly, either.

A military coup that autumn ousted Arias after less than two weeks in office and put Lieutenant Colonel Omar Torrijos Herrera, a high-ranking officer of the National Guard, Panama's mixture of an army and a national police force, in charge. He survived a countercoup the next year and made himself a general. Believing the United States was behind the coup, he was reluctant to deal with Washington. For his part, newly elected president Richard Nixon had Vietnam, Russia, and China on his mind and gave little attention to Latin America and none to Panama.

But the State Department worried that without moving forward, disruptions even worse than those of 1964 were probable. Secretary of State William P. Rogers, largely overshadowed by Henry A. Kissinger, the national security adviser, sought out Panama's foreign minister at a Washington meeting of the Organization of American States to assure him the United States wanted a new dialogue, and talks were renewed in April 1971. But for some time, nothing much happened; the United States' position seemed harder than it been during the Johnson administration, as it insisted first on a treaty with no date in it ending U.S. control of the Canal, and then on a treaty of very long duration. This was unacceptable to Panama, recalling the U.S. position under Johnson, but its negotiators had little that they were allowed to propose as an alternative.

Instead Torrijos was pushing to get international support. He arranged to have a UN Security Council meeting held in Panama in March 1973. The United States had to veto a resolution, demanding, "without delay," a new "just and fair" treaty that would "fulfill Panama's legitimate aspiration and guarantee full respect for Panama's effective sovereignty over all its territory." No nation voted with the United States; even Great Britain abstained. That meeting got Kissinger's attention. He and Nixon decided to look past the resolution itself and recognize they had a serious problem. In May, Nixon told Congress it was time for the United States and Panama "to take a fresh look at this problem and to develop a new relationship between us—one that will guarantee continued effective operation of the Canal while meeting Panama's legitimate aspirations." That summer a new U.S. negotiator was chosen to replace Anderson, who had been inactive since Nixon took office. He was Ellsworth Bunker, a veteran diplomat who had just returned from six years as ambassador to South Vietnam.

After a new set of talks that winter, Kissinger, by now also secretary of state, flew to Panama to sign a set of "principles" with the foreign minister,

Juan Antonio Tack. Signed on February 7, 1974, they promised to replace the 1903 treaty with one providing a prompt end to U.S. control of the Canal Zone, a greater share of Canal profits for Panama, and a promise that Panama would join in the administration and defense of the Canal. It promised the United States the use of "lands, water and airspace" necessary to operate and defend the Canal. Most important, the document promised to abrogate the 1903 treaty and replace it with one having a fixed termination date. "The concept of perpetuity will be eliminated," it said.

Over those ten years, Presidents Johnson and Nixon knew that any major change in the status of the Canal would provoke serious political opposition at home, though not of a particular ideological cast. With other problems facing them, from war to impeachment, they spent no political capital trying to prepare the American people to accept their belief that this national treasure would be best preserved not by a continuation of colonial rule but by cooperation on terms modern Panama could accept.

But on February 7, 1974, even as only one major newspaper, the *Los Angeles Times*, considered the Kissinger-Tack agreement a front-page story, the opposition stirred. Strom Thurmond, the very conservative South Carolina Republican, told the Senate the principles "invite disaster." The same day, Representative John Murphy of New York, a Democrat, told the House that Kissinger was undertaking "a course of action which borders on insanity." An even more insistent voice was that of Representative Daniel J. Flood, a Pennsylvania Democrat, who had been inspired over the Canal by meeting ex-president Theodore Roosevelt as a child. Flood had vast knowledge of the Canal's history and an intense fear that communists would take it over. He had warned Johnson, the day the first American flag was raised at Balboa High School, that the problem was that the United States has been yielding "to politically and communistically motivated and ever increasing demands of Panama, at times featured by mob violence." He repeatedly sought meetings with Nixon to warn against "surrender of sovereignty." Nixon did not see him.

The opposition was not just talk. Senator Thurmond followed up on March 29 by introducing a resolution "in support of continued undiluted United States sovereignty over the United States–owned Canal Zone on the Isthmus of Panama." He proclaimed, "We own it. We bought it. It is ours." Thirty-four senators sponsored the resolution, or enough to block ratification of any new treaty, if they all stayed in office and stood firm.

" NO CONSTITUENCY TO HELP "

PRESIDENT FORD NEGOTIATES

2

Of all the political leaders involved in the Panama Canal treaty issue in the 1970s, Gerald Ford probably came to it best prepared. He had sailed through the Canal in World War II on the USS *Monterey*, a light aircraft carrier, and had seen the engineering marvel firsthand. Although as a party leader he had denounced the treaties negotiated under Johnson, in his years in the House of Representatives he had encountered and disliked both the colonial mentality of the Americans in the Canal Zone and the die-hard resistance to any change in status from such colleagues as Representative Daniel J. Flood, the flamboyant Pennsylvanian with a twirled waxed mustache and a black cape. Flood, later convicted of corruption, had suggested the impeachment of President Eisenhower for allowing the Panamanian flag to fly in the Zone. Most important, before Ford became president upon Richard Nixon's resignation and had to make decisions himself, he had been kept informed about the negotiations over the Canal that had begun under Lyndon Johnson and were moving ahead again.

As vice president, Ford met with American diplomats in March 1974, offering political advice drawn from his years in the House. He told Ambassador William J. Jorden that "there is no constituency to help you" and urged Ellsworth Bunker, the chief Canal negotiator, to keep the issue quiet for the balance of 1974 and to make 1975 the year of decision. Ford next met with Panama's foreign minister Juan Antonio Tack in April, warning him of likely congressional opposition to change but agreeing heartily when Tack told him, "The best security for the canal is to have friends on both sides of it."

Ford had bigger issues to deal with when he became president on August 9, 1974: inflation, relations with the Soviet Union, and, most of all, what to do about Nixon's desire for a pardon. But he was never allowed to forget about Panama. Just five days after Ford took office, Senator Strom Thurmond, the South Carolina Republican, wired him, "urgently" seeking a meeting on issues of "great importance to our party and nation." Tom Korologos, a White House congressional relations aide, sent the president talking points that noted, "Thurmond is worried that we are going to give the canal away." After the meeting, Thurmond's worries were spelled out in a letter he wrote Ford:

In recent weeks the government of Panama has been drifting rapidly to the left . . . the General himself is isolated from all but radicals and Communists. . . . our negotiations for a new canal treaty are fundamentally in error. More than one-third of the Senate—thirty-five senators—have sponsored Senate Resolution 301 against the surrender of U.S. sovereignty in the Canal Zone. Any loss of control of the Canal would be extremely detrimental to our vital interests, especially in Latin America. We should make it clear that U.S. vital interests are not negotiable.

But Henry Kissinger's commitment to a fixed date for turning over the Canal was the hand left for Ford to play. Nixon had picked Ford to succeed Vice President Spiro Agnew in 1973 when federal prosecutors forced Agnew's resignation for taking bribes. Ford was a conservative Michigander, with a 10 percent score in the leading vote rating of the time, published by the liberal group Americans for Democratic Action. But he was practical, not ideological, and an internationalist, with what a biographer, Yanek Mieczkowski, wrote was "for a midwestern representative . . . an unusually extensive exposure to diplomacy." Ford got into politics as a war veteran repulsed by the isolationism of an incumbent Republican congressman. Ford beat him in the 1948 primary. Ford was a strong party man and rose steadily until he became minority leader in 1965.

Some in Nixon's camp thought the choice of Ford would protect Nixon from impeachment over scandals that had begun to unravel with the Watergate break-in of 1972. To them, plain old Gerry Ford did not seem like a president. But nothing could save Nixon, not even Ford's loyal speeches in his defense, as a special prosecutor and Congress closed in on the president. On August 9, facing certain impeachment by the House and conviction by the Senate, Nixon resigned. Ford became president shortly before noon and caught the country's hopes perfectly when he said, "Our long national nightmare is over. Our Constitution works; our great Republic is a government of laws and not of men. Here the people rule." It was the most inspiring speech this decent, solid, but never charismatic politician would give.

That very day Secretary Kissinger cabled a message to Panama's leaders, assuring them that the change in presidents "will not affect in any way the negotiation which we have begun to draft a new, modern treaty governing the Panama Canal." Kissinger said that he had agreed to continue as secretary of state, and "One of my highest priorities as I continue in my responsibilities will be to press ahead with the negotiations in order to conclude a new treaty promptly." That message, one of dozens sent to reassure leaders from Spain's Francisco Franco to the Soviet Union's Leonid Brezhnev, was taken with particular significance in Panama and seen to reflect Ford's commitment as well as Kissinger's.

Bunker went back to Panama in the fall, and negotiations resumed and made progress in putting detailed flesh on the bones of the Kissinger-Tack principles. The United States agreed to abolish the Canal Zone government as soon as the treaty took effect and to put a prominent Panamanian in a ranking position with the Panama Canal Company, the entity that ran the Canal itself. In November Bunker cabled Kissinger that he believed a treaty could be negotiated by March 1975, in time to keep it from becoming an issue in the 1976 campaign. Optimistic about both negotiations and U.S. politics, he wrote, "My own feeling is that a treaty, if strongly supported by the Administration, can be moved through the Congress without the very great difficulty which some predict."

Conservatives began to notice, not just professionals like Senators Thurmond or Jesse Helms of North Carolina, but ordinary citizens. Bob Morgan, a North Carolina Democrat elected in 1974, had been in the Senate only a few weeks when Frank Coxe of Asheville wrote him: "From the standpoint of our national defense the Canal is absolutely essential. Please ask any navy man. We have become so obsessed with the idea of being loved by everyone that I'm afraid some of our State Department people may urge us to do something irreversible and wrong and I do hope the Senate will take a justifiably tough attitude in not giving up one bit of our contract for the operation of the Canal."

Ford and Kissinger were aware of the political opposition, though perhaps not of how deeply it resonated. On May 12, 1975, after hearing Kissinger tell of the need for a new treaty, Ford asked, "Will the Thurmonds and the Floods go crazy?" Secretary Kissinger replied, "Yes. I think there are no terms they would accept."

Still, the toughest talks in 1975 did not involve the administration and its political opponents. Nor were they between the United States and Panama.

The arguments were within the U.S. government, essentially with the State Department on one side and the Defense Department on the other. The issues were how much of the Canal Zone could be turned over promptly to Panama, and how long a new treaty should last. Bunker was still operating under instructions issued by Nixon that a new treaty should last at least fifty years— terms he knew Panama would never accept.

In February Bunker sought new negotiating instructions to allow him to negotiate down to twenty-five years of continued operation and defense of the Canal, and to be much more forthcoming on the question of turning land and water over to Panama. The Pentagon resisted. And at a May 15 meeting of the National Security Council, Bunker told President Ford that success in negotiations depended on "flexibility on two issues: duration and land and waters."

Kissinger backed Bunker's assessment of what Panama would or would not accept. He said the negotiating instructions in force prevented exploration of what Panama would accept. And he warned of the consequences of failure: "Internationally, failure to conclude a treaty is going to get us into a cause célèbre, with harassment, demonstrations, bombings of embassies. . . . There will be an uproar in Panama. . . . It will be an armed camp and spread rapidly through the Western hemisphere. It will become an OAS issue around which they will all unite. Then it will spread into the international organizations."

James R. Schlesinger, the secretary of defense, weighed in and stated he opposed any new treaty. Foreshadowing the set of emotions that developed later when the treaties had been negotiated, he said, "When the U.S. shows strength and determination, it receives respect. When it recedes from its position, it whets appetites. . . . If we are tough in the Canal, they will yield. In recent years the U.S. has not shown enough of this quality."

William P. Clements, the deputy secretary of defense, tried to calm the dispute, saying, "I don't think there is any problem about Defense and State coming to some reasonable solution: working out the details is easy." But he also suggested that Panama could be satisfied for a time with "minor concessions."

Ford, who disliked Schlesinger and would later fire him, had mostly listened or asked questions, but now he weighed in and gave his subordinates a sense of where he came from on the issue:

> I've had some experience with the Panama Canal, going back as early as 1951 when I was a member of the House Appropriations Subcommittee that had jurisdiction over the Panama Canal. At that time I had the temerity to look at the sinecures that some of the civilian employees of the canal had acquired, such as rents, which I think were $15 a month, and a raft of other gratuities that few other people working for the Federal government received. I objected and sought to decrease these benefits. I was met with an onslaught from a highly organized group which I hadn't anticipated.

He went on:

> That is the most highly organized group of American employees I know. They have a vested interest in the status quo. This is a group that gives the public the impression of what we should be doing down there.
>
> We are not going to decide this issue on these grounds. They ought to know it. The Army gets its information from them and they infect it with their views. But they're not going to decide this.

Nothing had been settled when on June 27 Kissinger told Ford that the Defense Department was working against him in Congress, supporting an effort to prohibit any negotiations. "Whatever you decide, it should not be a formal decision not to proceed with the negotiations. That would cause a real blowup in Latin America. Were it not for the 1976 election, I would recommend we go forward. It will turn into a Vietnam-type situation. If there are people killed, we will be in a colonialist situation."

On July 23, another National Security Council meeting began like a replay of the May session. Kissinger warned again that Latin countries would make a "cause célèbre" of a failure to agree, and that Bunker could get nowhere under existing orders. Schlesinger, who had a Ph.D. in economics and often gave the impression of thinking himself the smartest man in the room, opposed a treaty, saying the question of duration did not really matter, because once an eventual turnover was agreed to, the Panamanians would kick the

President Ford and Secretary of State Henry A. Kissinger in the Oval Office, August 14, 1974 (Gerald R. Ford Library)

United States out when they wanted to. And Ford complained that Americans in the Zone "have a sinecure down there which they don't want to give up."

But Clements, a rough-hewn Texan who had made a fortune in the oil business and could not stand Schlesinger, now sided clearly with Kissinger against his nominal boss. He said, "The world we live in today is not the world of Teddy Roosevelt." Kissinger in his memoirs called this split "an almost unprecedented occurrence at an NSC meeting." Air force general George Brown, chairman of the Joint Chiefs of Staff, said the chiefs could accept a Clements proposal to give up operation of the Canal in twenty-five years and defense rights in forty. Personally, he said, he would rather not have any treaty to give up the Canal. But, he said, "We are committed and you can't be half-pregnant. We are committed through proposals made earlier. . . . Everyone who has communicated to us about this is dead-set against it, but we're already started down the road and we can't back out now." Brown, who commanded respect in the army and navy, also conceded that the Pentagon was insisting on keeping more land and water than it really needed.

It took almost four more weeks to produce a formal decision and a revised set of negotiating instructions. National Security Decision Memorandum 302, issued by Ford on August 18, allowed Bunker to discuss ownership and defense of the Canal as separate matters. As to ownership, it said the earliest acceptable date for a handover would be December 31, 1999. As for rights of the United States to defend the Canal, Ford said negotiators "should seek to obtain a minimum of 50 years, but are authorized to recede to no less than 40 years." On the question of lands and waters, Bunker was allowed to offer just a little more than before. Bunker was directed to resume talks promptly, but the memorandum clearly recognized that his new negotiating authority might not be enough. The memorandum said, "If agreement is not possible on the basis of these offers, the United States negotiators should request further instructions from the President." That August 18 order also said "the United States Negotiators should seek to obtain Panama's agreement that negotiations will remain confidential so that the Panama Canal issue will not be injected into the domestic political process in the United States in 1976."

That was essential to Ford because he had decided to run for president. He had previously planned to retire after the 1976 elections, but that was when he was in Congress, and thought he would never be Speaker of the House. He liked his new job. Besides, when Ford looked at potential successors, he was dismayed. As he wrote in his memoirs, he thought Reagan had a "penchant for offering simplistic solutions to hideously complex problems," failed to listen to opposing arguments, and did not work very hard.

At that May 12 meeting where Ford and Kissinger talked about how foreign policy and politics had to be coordinated, Kissinger stressed, "This election is one of the most crucial ever." Ford replied, "Look at the alternatives. Reagan would be a disaster," to which Kissinger responded, "He is incompetent."

So they tried to figure out a way to make progress abroad without confronting the issue at home. Kissinger, whose diplomatic skills far outweighed his sense of American politics, repeatedly suggested that perhaps the treaty would not be an issue if it was not formally submitted to Congress. But the details would certainly have leaked.

It was almost equally important to persuade Panama that further delay was not just stalling. So General Brown, Clements, and William D. Rogers, assistant secretary of state for Latin American affairs, made a sudden visit to Panama. In a September 2, 1975, meeting with Torrijos, Clements sought to get his agreement to the domestic political point in Decision Memorandum 302—that negotiations would be secret to keep the issue out of the 1976 campaign. Torrijos replied that he understood the problems in the United States but wished the Americans would understand that he had political problems, too. As he had told David Binder of the *New York Times* in July, "It seems to me progress has almost been paralyzed; it seems to me that our problem has been replaced by your politics."

What Ambassador Jorden called the "decisive moment" came when General Brown, wearing all his service ribbons, told Torrijos: "General, you have my word as a soldier that we will work for a fair and just treaty. We are going to have problems, but I'm sure we can do it. But we can't do it quickly. I am asking you to be patient a little longer and keep things under control until we can move ahead. Then, I assure you, we'll move." Torrijos replied, "We have come this far, and we can go a little farther. But please not too long. Our patience will not last forever." Rogers said in an interview years later that Brown's direct, straightforward manner and military bearing were "the trick in getting through to Torrijos," as he and Clements had not been able to do. Rogers said Brown made it clear that "the Administration decided it can't be seen to be completing the negotiations. Torrijos took it from him."

Those political fears meant that the Ford administration conducted no more negotiations with Panama after November 1974. But that did not keep the issue out of politics. Earlier in that summer of 1975, the House suddenly adopted a proposal by Representative Gene Snyder, a Kentucky Republican, to prohibit spending any money on negotiating a new treaty. The administration and the Senate—which regarded any House involvement in foreign affairs as institutionally presumptuous—eventually watered down the House ban to a vague sense of Congress statement that the administration should "protect the vital interests of the United States in the Canal Zone."

Governor George C. Wallace of Alabama, wheelchair-bound after an attempted assassination in 1972 but beginning a 1976 try for the White House anyhow, challenged Kissinger at a meeting of the Southern Governors Association in Orlando on September 16. He asked whether, considering "the unfortunate conclusion of the Vietnam war, do you feel the United States can now afford to give up control of the Panama Canal?" (Kissinger's tortured reply spoke of the United States' continuing right to defend the Canal "unilaterally," for the "indefinite future," using two code words that predictably angered the Panamanians without satisfying Wallace.)

Conservative organizations began to push the issue. The ultraright John Birch Society distributed a bumper sticker saying, "Don't give Panama our canal: Give them Kissinger instead!" A company in the Canal Zone urged residents there to get relatives in the United States to urge lawmakers to "save the canal." M. Stanton Evans, head of the American Conservative Union, wrote in the movement's weekly, *Human Events*, under the headline "Giving Up in Panama," that "the U.S. State Department is hard at work these days abandoning American sovereignty in Panama," saying it was using arguments based on "vintage Western guilt complex."

None of the attacks might have mattered in the long run, except for one more factor: Ronald Reagan was running for president.

3

Ronald Reagan became the conservative hope for the future in the ashes of Barry Goldwater's landslide loss in 1964.

"A Time for Choosing" is what Reagan called a nationally televised speech he gave for Goldwater in the week before that election. He conveyed optimism for the future, if only the country could shake its addiction to big government. He warned, "No government ever voluntarily reduces itself in size. Government programs, once launched, never disappear. Actually, a government bureau is the nearest thing to eternal life we'll ever see on this Earth." If the nation could recommit to freedom, rather than reliance on government, he said, the nation was still "the last best hope of man on Earth."

While the speech focused more on domestic issues, it also portrayed an America in decline in the world, willing to settle for "peace without victory." In that October 27, 1964, speech Reagan said liberals' "policy of accommodation is appeasement, and it gives no choice between peace and war, only between fight and surrender. If we continue to accommodate, continue to back and retreat, eventually we have to face the final demand—the ultimatum" to surrender.

That speech changed forever the small-town boy from Illinois who had succeeded in broadcasting in Iowa and movies in Hollywood. As his authoritative biographer, Lou Cannon, put it, "In a half hour of national television, Ronald Reagan had transformed himself from a fading celebrity into the nation's most important conservative politician." Conservatives across the country began talking about the former president of the Screen Actors Guild as a future president of the United States.

But in the aftermath of the Goldwater defeat, a real conservative would have to wait a while for a chance at the White House. Wealthy California Republicans backed Reagan for governor of their state; he ran in 1966, won, and governed effectively. But when Reagan made a belated run at the 1968 Republican nomination, Richard Nixon already had it locked up, and despite Reagan's easy reelection as governor in 1970, his White House ambitions seemed sidetracked by the expectation that Nixon would serve eight years; Reagan would be sixty-five in 1976. Only one president had ever been older when elected; that president, William Henry Harrison, died after only a month in office.

Besides that, while conservatives became increasingly unhappy with a Nixon who went to China, advocated "détente" with the Soviet Union, and imposed wage and price controls, Vice President Spiro Agnew seemed a suitably conservative heir apparent—until he resigned in 1973 when prosecutors charged him with taking bribes.

Then came Ford. When he chose a vice president whom many conservatives (but not Reagan) despised, Nelson A. Rockefeller, conservatives turned back to Reagan, though they often complained he wasn't attacking Ford when they wanted him to.

The moment when Reagan decided to run for president against Ford is not clear. He met John Sears in 1974 to talk about running even before Ford became president. Sears startled Reagan and his camp by predicting that Nixon would soon be out of office. Sears would become Reagan's campaign manager. The pace of meetings picked up the next year. White House aides were warning Ford about Reagan in the spring of 1975, but as Ford admitted in his autobiography: "I hadn't taken those warnings seriously because I hadn't taken Reagan seriously."

In mid-July Reagan asked Senator Paul Laxalt to announce the formation of an "exploratory" Reagan committee. Laxalt, as conservative as Reagan, had become a friend while serving as governor of neighboring Nevada. The "exploratory" device allowed Reagan's backers to raise money. It also meant he did not have to give up the lucrative broadcasts and columns that Cannon estimated brought him $800,000 in 1975.

By the time Reagan was ready to announce his candidacy on November 20, 1975, no one was surprised. The day before, when he telephoned Ford to tell him he would run, Ford said he was "very disappointed." He explained, "I'm sorry you're getting into this. I believe I've done a good job and that I can be elected. Regardless of your good intentions, your bid is bound to be divisive. It will take a lot of money, a lot of effort, and it will leave a lot of scars."

Reagan did not mention Panama the next day when he announced his candidacy at the National Press Club, though Stephen Rosenfeld of the *Washington Post* had noted Reagan's views on it a few days earlier: "The particular security issue he seems to have focused on is the Panama Canal, a natural, alas, for a conservative looking for something with a lot of popular vibrations." The issue was highlighted in a fund-raising letter sent out soon after the announcement. As one example of Ford's failings, he asked, "Can we afford to give control of the Panama Canal to an antagonistic and unstable Panamanian dictatorship?" The Canal issue was used in mailings throughout the campaign.

In his announcement speech, Reagan's only major point on foreign policy dealt with the Soviet Union. He said, "A decade ago, we had military superiority. Today we are in danger of being surpassed by a nation that has never made any effort to hide its hostility to everything we stand for." The speech focused more on Washington's "'buddy' system that functions for its own benefit—increasingly insensitive to the needs of the American worker who supports it with his taxes" and with big government that has become "more intrusive, more coercive, more meddlesome and less effective."

Panama had been on Reagan's mind for more than a year, ever since Jesse Helms, a very conservative North Carolina senator, warned him about it on October 26, 1974. Helms's warning in a Charlotte hotel room, just before Reagan was to speak at a dinner for Helms, grabbed Reagan's attention. (In 1967, when the Johnson treaties were in the news, Reagan had written a treaty opponent, "We've followed the false flag of appeasement.") He had Pete Hannaford, an aide who worked on his syndicated radio broadcasts and columns, research the subject. In a 2005 interview, Hannaford recalled, "What began to happen in '75 was we began hearing from a number of individuals who were opposed to the treaty and professed to have a lot of knowledge about the background of all of this. And some of them did. We began to get quite a flood of material from these people. . . . And Reagan did quite a lot of reading. . . . We did get quite a few people staying in contact, sending us stuff regularly." Reagan and Hannaford did not seek the views of supporters of the treaty directly.

In 1964 when Reagan warned in the Goldwater speech against appeasement, accommodation, and retreat, he was talking about the Soviet Union.

But as longtime aide Lyn Nofziger put it in his own memoir, Reagan "outraged easily on Foreign Policy that involved the United States knuckling under to another nation, whether Panama or the Soviet Union."

What appears to have been Reagan's first public comment came in late April or May 1975. He was an avid reader of *Human Events*, the pre-electronic chat room that enabled conservatives to keep in touch with each other. It reported in its April 26 issue a bizarre Helms charge that Kissinger was about to use an executive order to hand over police, fire, and postal services in the Canal Zone to Panama. Reagan cited Helms's warning in a radio broadcast and said if it happened, "U.S. citizens could be subjected to having all their mail monitored by the head of Panama's G-2 section, Lieutenant Colonel Manuel Noriega, a man not unfriendly to the Cuban Communists." Reagan followed up May 31, on the theme of national power that seemed to matter most to him, in an Atlantic City speech condemning decades of U.S. weakness, in Korea and Vietnam and the Bay of Pigs, culminating in "our seeming willingness to give away the Panama Canal." He asked, "Have we stopped to think that young Americans have seldom if ever in their lives seen America act as a great nation?"

He went at it even harder with a speech to the Veterans of Foreign Wars on August 18 and with a column that appeared in *Human Events* on September 27, 1975. To the veterans, he sneered at negotiations with Panama because "that nation exists only because of us." In *Human Events*, he called the Torrijos government "Marxist," citing as evidence that the tiny Communist Party of Panama, when founded in 1930, wanted to seize control of the government through the military, which had occurred when Torrijos seized power in 1968, and also wanted to gain control of the Canal through negotiations, as Torrijos was doing. He insisted that the 1903 treaty, made shortly after Panama seceded from Colombia with U.S. help, conveyed sovereignty to the Canal Zone to the United States. "The Panamanians seceded because they wanted to participate in the benefits the canal would bring to their part of the world," he explained, "and they identified future success with the United States, having watched the French fail at attempts to build a canal." He scoffed at warnings of possible sabotage of the Canal, saying, "Panama has the highest standard of living in Central America," and its government would not kill the goose that laid the golden egg. Reagan demanded that Congress stand up to the State Department's inclination to surrender.

Reagan's great political gift was rhetoric. Though his career was in movies, he had a good actor's sense of when a line connected with an audience. And he showed this on Panama when he answered a question in Philadelphia on October 21, "I think we'd be damn fools to turn over the Panama Canal to Panama. We built it. We paid for it. It's ours." The *Philadelphia Inquirer* said he got "thunderous applause" for this response to a question after only a mild reaction to his formal speech to a World Affairs Council meeting.

Two weeks later, after meeting with Arnulfo Arias, the elected Panamanian president whom Torrijos had deposed, Reagan added a line about Torrijos, saying on November 3 in Coral Springs, Florida, "We bought it. We paid for it. It's ours, and we aren't going to give it away to some tinhorn dictator."

Early on, the 1976 Republican primary race was poorly run on both sides. Each campaign underestimated the other. Ford and his people thought of Reagan as a feeble opponent, a right-wing dope. Reagan's people ignored the value of Ford's incumbency.

But the Reagan campaign made one monumental tactical blunder. In a September speech, Reagan said the federal government had taken on the responsibilities of the private sector and state and local governments, and then provided specifics of $90 billion worth of federal spending cuts. That offered ammunition that the Ford campaign later skillfully fired at him in town after town in New Hampshire, accusing him of wanting state taxes there to go up because federal money would stop coming.

Although Reagan generally campaigned effectively and drew friendly crowds, the $90 billion misunderstanding put him on the defensive, at least as far as press coverage was concerned. He tried to explain that he had only wanted the idea considered, and that various presidents had said similar things about federal power.

Reagan's campaign was long on generalities, and he was reluctant to say anything negative about Ford. That was both Reagan's nice-guy personality at work and scrupulous obedience to the "Eleventh Commandment," coined by Gaylord Parkinson, California's Republican state chairman during that first Reagan run for governor in 1966: "Thou shalt not speak ill of any fellow Republican."

Reagan usually gave only brief remarks and took questions in what he called "Citizens' Press Conferences." Panama came up occasionally, and he would draw applause with his now-familiar mantra about buying it, paying for it, building it, and keeping it. Reagan himself brought the Canal up only rarely, once in the course of a foreign policy speech delivered to students at Phillips Exeter Academy on February 10:

> Our foreign policy in recent years seems to be a matter of placating potential adversaries. Does our government fear that the American people lack willpower? If it does, that may explain its reluctance to assert our interests in international relations. How else can we explain the government's bowing to the propaganda campaign of the military dictator of Panama and signing a memorandum with his representative signifying our intention to give up control and ownership of the Panama Canal and the Canal Zone?

★ The "placating potential adversaries" sentence was quoted in some major newspapers, but not the reference to the Canal. Reports focused more on the Soviet Union and cruise missiles. Some papers, like the New York Times and the Washington Star, ignored the speech entirely.

Throughout the New Hampshire campaign, the Ford camp tried to portray Reagan as an extremist, a threat to Social Security, and someone who would have "elderly people thrown out in the snow," as Ford's inept campaign manager, Howard (Bo) Callaway, cheerfully put it. At the same time, Ford himself argued that he was a conservative, too, so the only real choice for Republicans was between the one with experience as president and the one without it.

Reagan made another mistake at the end. He stayed out of the state the weekend before the vote, surrendering the political stage. Ford squeaked through, winning New Hampshire by 1,587 votes. Ford's win surprised the press. Even though Hugh Gregg, the former governor who managed Reagan's campaign (and kept Reagan away so as to concentrate on get-out-the-vote efforts), had insisted all along that his man would only come close, the press had relied on earlier public polls and the optimism of Reagan's national staff and made Reagan the favorite. So his 48.6 percent was a "defeat" in a state where Eugene McCarthy's 41.9 percent in 1968 and George McGovern's 37.1 percent in 1972 had been "victories" in Democratic primaries even though their second places were further behind Lyndon Johnson and Edmund Muskie than Reagan was behind Ford.

Even though it was close, Ford was exhilarated by the victory. "What a shot in the arm!" he wrote in his autobiography. "It proved I could win an election outside the Fifth Congressional District in Michigan, and I hoped it would have a springboard effect, hurtling me all the way to a first ballot nomination in Kansas City."

4

For a few weeks, it looked as though Ford's hopes would come true. The next week he won in Massachusetts and Vermont, where Reagan had made no efforts. On March 9 he beat Reagan in Florida, narrowly but clearly. On March 16 he swamped Reagan in the challenger's native Illinois.

The Reagan campaign was broke going into North Carolina's March 23 primary. The plane that brought him there to campaign on March 15 was delayed on the tarmac in Los Angeles until the Washington office was sure enough checks had arrived to pay for the charter.

Republicans prodded by the Ford campaign were urging Reagan to give up. Sears, without Reagan's knowledge, was talking to the Ford campaign about surrender. Bill Buckley wrote, "Ronald Reagan, it would appear, has lost his fight for the presidential nomination." Another conservative journalist, James J. Kilpatrick, mourned, "His role in the '76 campaign is just about played out."

Nancy Reagan had serious doubts. She urged Lyn Nofziger, a longtime Reagan aide, to persuade her husband to give up. Reagan walked in on their conversation in a hotel room and interrupted, saying, "I'm not going to quit. I'm going to stay in this thing until the end. I still think we can win, but even if we don't I can't let down all those people who believe in the things we believe in and want me to be President." But beneath the surface things were changing for Reagan, and Panama was central to the change in ways both planned and unplanned.

The unexpected change came in the retirement community of Sun City, Florida, a little south of Tampa. On Friday, February 27, just three days after New Hampshire, Reagan appeared there before 700 retirees and offered his standard "We bought it . . . " line about the Canal. The audience went wild. To David A. Keene, who was running Reagan's Florida campaign, that was particularly telling because these retirees were from the Midwest, Ford country. He thought they were not particularly aware of the Panama Canal, beyond what they had read about it in school, but instead were frustrated with the complexities of America's place in the world, of why it was difficult or impossible for the United States to do just what it wanted, and this issue seemed simple and clear. In any case, Reagan knew something was working, and he kept on using the "bought it, paid for it, keep it" line. The planned effort, a new speech, was unveiled the next day in Winter Haven, Florida, at a spring training ballpark idled by a baseball players' strike.

The night of the New Hampshire defeat, Dick Wirthlin, the campaign pollster, and John Sears, the campaign manager, worked to find a different, winning strategy. Wirthlin's polls had shown that Reagan's early lead in Florida had vanished and Ford was ahead, and the results from New Hampshire were sure to make things worse. The momentum they had expected New Hampshire to bring to them was now going to Ford instead. They concluded that a more direct argument against Ford was needed, although Reagan's discomfort at that kind of attack made that difficult.

They chose to make the attack over foreign policy, enabling them to aim at the "State Department," rather than Ford personally. The Exeter speech (which Hannaford had written) was toughened. By the time it was delivered, and after Reagan had heard the Sun City reaction, the speech dwelled heavily on the Panama Canal issue: "State Department actions for several years now have suggested that they are intimidated by the propaganda of Panama's military dictator, Fidel Castro's good friend, Gen. Omar Torrijos. Our State Department apparently believes the hints regularly dispensed by the leftist Torrijos regime that the canal will be sabotaged if we don't hand it over. Our Government has maintained a mouselike silence as criticisms of the giveaway have increased."

"I don't understand how the State Department can suggest we pay blackmail to this dictator, for blackmail is what it is. When it comes to the Canal, we bought it, we paid for it, it's ours and we should tell Torrijos and company that we are going to keep it," he said.

There was far more to the speech, and to Reagan's unhappiness with the Ford administration's foreign policy generally, than the Canal issue, but Wirthlin explained the emphasis in an autobiography:

A minor issue such as this might not seem like the rhetorical dynamite necessary to ignite victory. But issues are seldom what they appear. 'Policy' is often little more than voters' values in disguise. What's more, issues are only as relevant as the symbolic meaning they produce. For this reason, the question of who would control the Panama Canal packed a political punch. In the wake of Vietnam, many voters felt America lacked the respect and strength it once enjoyed. For those conservatives who considered America's entrance into Vietnam a mistake, control of the Panama Canal symbolized American autonomy and might. If Ronald Reagan could contrast his resolve to maintain ownership of the Panama Canal against Ford's position, I felt confident the governor's message could gain traction, something we needed desperately.

Reagan's Winter Haven speech got a good response at the midday rally and considerable national attention for both Panama and his promise to replace Secretary Kissinger—which made headlines even though the last newly elected president to keep a predecessor's secretary of state was Martin Van Buren in 1837. But the speech was overshadowed in Florida, where it mattered, by coverage of a visit to the state by President Ford. So Sears and Keene organized a press conference for Reagan's next visit and put out the word that he was making a major attack on Ford.

This time he basically gave the speech as an opening statement, and the March 4 event was carried live by Florida television stations. He kept up the criticism for the rest of the campaign and added a television commercial over the Canal issue, along with one attacking the policy of détente with the Soviet Union.

Even though Reagan was still not attacking Ford by name, he finally seemed more comfortable with some advice Keene had given him before an early January speech in Tallahassee. Reagan asked Keene what he ought to say, and the blunt, thirty-year-old aide replied. "Well, Governor, you have two options: You can go out there and follow the Eleventh Commandment and lose your ass, or you can kick the shit out of Jerry Ford and win this thing." Nancy Reagan liked Keene's attitude, but Reagan had still been reluctant to attack Ford.

Reagan's new approach narrowed the gap in Florida that had opened up after Ford won in New Hampshire. That 1.4 percentage point victory, narrow as it was, meant the Ford campaign could tell Florida voters that their man was a winner. The Ford campaign also charged that Reagan would gut Social Security and spread federal grants around Florida so lavishly that Reagan had a point when he said bands welcoming the president did not know whether to play "Hail to the Chief" or "Santa Claus Is Coming to Town." So Reagan could not catch up. The president won Florida with 52.8 percent of the vote. Illinois was next, and Ford won with 58.9 percent.

The Ford campaign and supportive Republican governors and mayors started calling on Reagan to withdraw from the race. That got his back up, but it also dominated local press coverage as the campaign moved to North Carolina. The Ford operation made a bigger mistake by easing up in its campaigning, as if to make it easier for Reagan to quit. As Bob Teeter, Ford's pollster, acknowledged in a 1997 oral history, "To be honest, we all recognize since then that we made a mistake in not working harder in North Carolina. We made a decision, a decision was made, not to send President Ford back to North Carolina, and Reagan rose up and beat us there."

The Reagan campaign tried something different in North Carolina— a throwback television ad. The first political ads on television in the forties and fifties had featured politicians talking into the camera for up to half an hour, but that had long since gone out of style. With other programs available, viewers generally would not watch a lengthy political show. Besides, Reagan's television producers thought he would appear as an actor reciting prepared lines.

Reagan, who had used television effectively as governor after his spectacular success in 1964, kept asking why he couldn't try that approach again. In North Carolina he had an ally in Tom Ellis, who ran Helms's political operation and was continually at war with Sears, Keene, and the campaign generally. Ellis kept demanding a Reagan speech for television and threatened to produce one himself. The campaign high command gave in after Ellis got Helms to enlist Nancy Reagan in support. Keene recalled Sears saying, "Look, if he is going to lose, let him lose his own way," though Sears contended he was never opposed to a Reagan half hour if it was carefully focused.

The tape they used had been made at a Miami station that offered Ford and Reagan a half hour each to say anything they wanted on the Saturday before the Florida primary. (Ford had declined.) The tape was edited a bit, to remove palm trees and add a fund-raising appeal. That appeal brought in checks each day that paid for the next night's broadcast, and the program was shown, promoted by radio spots, in prime time on fifteen of the seventeen North Carolina television stations, at a total cost of only $10,000 (since advertising rate increases have outpaced inflation, that would have been more than $50,000 in 2008 dollars). The show had Reagan sitting at a table, talking into the camera, and giving what was basically his new campaign speech with its heavy emphasis on foreign policy.

On Panama, Reagan said:

> What are the quiet, almost secret negotiations we are engaged in to give away the Panama Canal? Everyone seems to know the negotiations are going on except the rightful owners of the Canal Zone, the American people. In 1974, Dr. Kissinger signed a memorandum with his Panamanian counterpart, Foreign Minister Juan Tack, which called into question that matter of whether the American people did, in truth, own the canal. Well, we do. The Hay–Bunau Varilla treaty of 1903 gave sovereignty over the Canal Zone to the United States. In 1904 this was upheld by all three branches of the government of Panama and affirmed in 1907 by our own Supreme Court, And yet a February 18 article in *Times of the Americas* quotes Foreign Minister Tack as saying the United States will recognize Panamanian sovereignty over the Canal Zone because both governments have already reached preliminary agreement on a new treaty. Tack gives the president of the United States as the authority for his claim that sovereignty over the canal will be transferred on December 31st 1995. If these reports are true, it means that the American people have been deceived by a State Department preoccupied with secrecy. The Panama Canal Zone is sovereign United States territory just as much as Alaska is, as well as the states carved from the Louisiana Purchase. We bought it. We paid for it, and General Torrijos should be told we are going to keep it.*

---

* Reagan's insistence that the United States was "sovereign" in the Canal Zone was incorrect, as noted previously. It was not, as he contended, American territory like the land acquired by the purchases of the Louisiana Territory and Alaska. One of the simplest differences between the Zone and Alaska, for example, is that when noncitizens have children in Alaska or anywhere else in the United States, the children automatically become U.S. citizens; in the Canal Zone they did not. Walter LaFeber, the Cornell historian, examined and disposed of the question in *The Panama Canal: The Crisis in*

That section lasted only 1 minute and 47 seconds in the 30-minute broadcast, but to both sides, it was critical. J. Brad Hays, a Ford organizer, said the
North Carolina campaign turned on "Sally Jones sitting at home, watching
Ronald Reagan on television and deciding that she didn't want to give away
the Panama Canal." Charley Black, who took over the Reagan operation in
North Carolina at the end, said in a 2004 interview with Craig Shirley that
the Canal had become the "centerpiece of the campaign in the state." In a
2005 interview with the author, Black said, "There were a lot of elements to
the policy, but that was the most emotional. Trying to educate people about
Helmut Sonnenfeldt and Kissinger giving up on Eastern Europe—most people couldn't remember much about that, but they could try to do something
about keeping the Panama Canal, and that was vote for Reagan."

Reagan abandoned his four-by-six-inch cards and spoke passionately and
extemporaneously. He kept hitting the Canal issue. He would ask, "How can
we defend the giveaway of the Panama Canal?" or "What kind of foreign policy is it when a little tinhorn dictator in Panama says he is going to start guerilla warfare against us unless we give him the Panama Canal?" And instead
of emphasizing "we bought it," on the stump, he frequently emphasized the
truly heroic part of the Canal history by stressing, "We built it! We paid for it!
And we should keep it!"

He had help. Helms pushed the issue wherever he went. The American
Conservative Union (ACU) ran 33 newspaper ads and 882 radio spots (taking
quick advantage of a January 30 Supreme Court decision holding unconsti-
tutional a $1,000 limit imposed by the 1974 campaign spending law on in-
dependent political spending) in North Carolina to blunt Ford's argument

Historical Perspective in both its 1978 and 1989 editions. He concluded: "The answer was
clear: the United States did not own the Zone or enjoy all sovereign rights in it." By
1977, Reagan was using the more precise phrase "rights of sovereignty," although allies like Paul Laxalt were still insisting on "sovereignty" itself.

From the Ford (and later Carter) administration's standpoint, the argument for giving up the Canal and the Zone—that the Canal's continued safe operation was best
secured by Panamanian ownership—did not depend on whether the United States
was sovereign or not. But it argued the sovereignty point hard because of the emotion
surrounding giving up territory that was part of the United States. Except for minor
border adjustments, the only time the United States has ever given up sovereignty it
had claimed was when the Philippines became independent in 1946, and that independence had been promised for decades.

Ronald Reagan campaigning in Durham, North Carolina, March 23, 1976
(*The News & Observer*, Raleigh, North Carolina)

that he and Reagan were both conservatives. Citing the Canal issue among others and saying Ford "approved the surrender of the Panama Canal Zone to the leftward-leaning government of Panama," the newspaper ads insisted, "There is a difference." M. Stanton Evans, then the chairman of the ACU, saw the Canal as a simple issue where the contrast could be drawn easily. "It's not like the SALT agreement or the ABM treaty," he said in a 2006 interview. "It was a fairly simple issue in terms of public exploitation." Evans's voice was the voice of the radio ads, which said, "Ronald Reagan would not cave in to Castro, and says American sovereignty in Panama must be maintained. The choice for North Carolina Republicans is clear: continued deficits and the weakness of 'détente' or Ronald Reagan's new initiatives in freedom." With Reagan short of funds, the ACU's $16,000 spending helped.

Going into primary day, Ford was still widely regarded as the favorite. Jim Dickenson of the *Washington Star*, for example, wrote, "The failure of Reagan's challenge, once again, puts the lie to the fond conservative dream that there is a silent conservative majority out there ready to dismantle the New

Deal and return to the days of Calvin Coolidge." Nor was this just the view of reporters like Dickenson or friendly commentators like Buckley and Kilpatrick. "We were staring another defeat in the face," wrote Hannaford, and if that happened, "to continue would be futile." But the Canal and the Ford camp's feeble effort brought Reagan a victory with 52.4 percent of the vote. The Reagan camp was "dumbfounded," recalled Jim Naughton, who was covering Reagan that night in Wisconsin for the *New York Times.* "They didn't expect to win."

5

The Reagan victory in North Carolina transformed the race. Suddenly he was a contender again, and the Panama Canal issue had done it. The next few months would show how much the issue counted. The press immediately recognized his new status. The *Washington Post*'s account of the results, by Lou Cannon, said, "Reagan propelled himself back into the Republican presidential race tonight." Many stories said Reagan was still an underdog, but Jon Margolis's analysis in the *Chicago Tribune* reflected the general press impression: "There's a big difference between being behind and being finished. Reagan was like a fighter who was down on points, pinned against the ropes, and on the verge of being knocked out. In this latest round, however, Reagan is off the ropes and back on his feet." The argument Reagan and Sears had been making that later primaries in the South and Texas would be better ground for him was now taken seriously.

But before Reagan could take advantage of his revitalized status, he needed money. The campaign was deeply in debt. And federal money to match contributions, an innovation that came with the contribution limits of the 1974 Federal Election Campaign Act, dried up on March 22 when the commission that sent out the checks went out of business temporarily after congressional bickering over how to rebuild it to meet a Supreme Court decision. Sears had a bold plan: give up on Wisconsin and put what cash the campaign still had into a half-hour Reagan speech on national television, which could be as effective as the North Carolina half hour, although the immediate goal now was not votes but contributions. After some difficulty in getting any network to sell it the time, the campaign bought a half hour on NBC for $104,000, preempting *The Dumplings*, a program NBC had already announced it would cancel.

Reagan's speech, up against the top-rated evening program *Starsky and Hutch*, did not draw a big audience, and the Ford campaign congratulated itself that the audience was smaller than network newscasts drew. But the broadcast was aimed not at the typical viewer but at conservative true believers, and it hit its target. Reagan used his basic campaign messages: inflation caused by federal spending, the "buddy system" in Washington, and "forced bussing to increase racial balance." He focused heavily on foreign affairs, saying, "Wandering without aim describes the United States foreign policy." And in that section, he spoke for more than a minute about Panama:

> As I talk to you tonight, negotiations with another dictator go forward, negotiations aimed at giving up our ownership of the Panama Canal Zone. Apparently everyone knows about this except the rightful owners of the Canal Zone, you, the people of the United States. General Omar Torrijos, the dictator of Panama, seized power eight years ago by ousting the duly elected government. There have been no elections since. No civil liberties. The press is censored. Torrijos is a friend and ally of Castro and like him is pro-communist. He threatened sabotage and guerrilla attacks on our installations if we don't yield to his demands, his foreign minister openly claims that we have already agreed in principle to giving up the Canal Zone. Well, the Canal Zone is not a colonial possession. It is not a long-term lease. It is sovereign United States territory, every bit the same as Alaska and all the states that were carved from the Louisiana Purchase. We should end those negotiations and tell the general "we bought it, we paid for it, we built it and we intend to keep it."

The March 31 broadcast did not make much news, but it raised about $1.5 million, enough to keep Reagan in the race, campaigning hard in Texas for a May 1 primary and raising the Canal issue at almost every stop. But the speech got under Kissinger's skin, and he ordered the State Department to put out a point-by-point refutation of its "factual errors." One was a flat contradiction of Reagan; the statement said, "The Canal Zone is not and never has been sovereign U.S. territory."

Reagan's campaigning on the issue also got to Ford, who mangled the facts in answering Reagan. In Dallas on April 10 Ford stated, "The United States will never give up its defense rights to the Panama Canal and will never give up its operational rights as far as Panama is concerned." But not only had Ford agreed in 1975 to give up operational rights and defense rights over many years, Ambassador Bunker had revealed just that to Congress only two days earlier.

Bunker testified before the Panama Canal Subcommittee of the House Merchant Marine and Fisheries Committee on April 8 behind closed doors. Under persistent questioning by Representative Gene Snyder, a Kentucky Republican, Bunker said he had been directed in writing by Ford "to give up the Canal Zone over a period of time" and to give up the Canal itself over a "longer period of time."

Snyder telephoned Reagan and then released the testimony and chided the president for changing his mind since he opposed a new treaty in 1967. But Reagan saw a more immediate contradiction. He said in Midland that Bunker's testimony about Ford's instructions "certainly doesn't jibe with his statements even made here in Texas that he was not going to give away the Panama Canal." In Corpus Christi he said, "Well, the Panama Canal Zone is sovereign United States territory. It is every bit as much American soil as is the land, the states that were carved out of the Gadsden and Louisiana Purchases, and as is the state of Alaska. And in my opinion, what we should be saying to that tinhorn dictator is, 'We bought it, we paid for it, we built it, it's ours and we intend to keep it.'"

The contradiction between Ford and Bunker, Sears argued in 2007, enabled Reagan to raise obliquely two alternative ideas that would sound too harsh if stated directly: was Ford lying about Panama, or did he simply not know what was going on and therefore was just not up to the job of president?

The White House quickly backed away from Ford's use of "never." Press secretary Ron Nessen conceded that Ford's comments lacked "precision and detail." Ford knew he had stumbled, telling Kissinger, "I just have to get myself off the hook of using the word 'never' and I also want to demonstrate that Reagan is irresponsible or doesn't understand the issue." So he told a group of Texas editors that negotiations were necessary to prevent a repetition of the "bloody" rioting of 1964, and that he was seeking a treaty that would last thirty to fifty years—a span that Bunker had told him Panama would never accept. That led Reagan to run an ad on Texas stations attacking the contradiction. Reagan then accused the president of yielding to "blackmail" while campaigning in Alabama, and in Georgia Reagan asked: "How could we be contemplating under threats from a tinhorn dictator, threats that he will sabotage the canal, and he will raise guerilla warfare and so forth if we don't give it up?"

Reagan's approach also provoked Panama. On April 16, foreign minister Aquilino Boyd appeared on the CBS Morning News to warn, "I am afraid this is a very explosive situation that we are having in Panama, and people like Ronald Reagan, in a very irresponsible manner, are inflaming patience in my country." He said Reagan was "willfully deceiving" Americans by claming sovereignty. Five days later, Torrijos himself accused Reagan of "irresponsibility." He warned that if a new treaty was not reached in 1977, Panama would be forced to choose "other approaches and other tactics."

An unexpected critic was Senator Barry Goldwater, whose 1964 candidacy had propelled Reagan into national politics. The Arizona senator told a party convention in Phoenix that Reagan was wrong on the Canal negotiations. He appeared on Meet the Press to say Reagan would join him in supporting Ford's position "if he knew more about it," and asked whether Reagan was willing to go to war over the Canal. The Ford campaign made a radio commercial out of a May 4 news conference where Goldwater said Reagan's statements on the Canal "could needlessly lead this country into open military conflict. He has clearly represented himself in an irresponsible manner on an issue which could affect the country's security."

Reagan ignored the complaints. He had found an issue that worked, and he drummed away on it, so effectively that he won all ninety-six delegates at stake in the Texas primary on Saturday, May 1, and then all thirty-seven in Alabama and all eighty-five in Georgia the following Tuesday. He had been expected to win those states, though not to sweep them; he also scored a surprise victory in Indiana that Tuesday, winning forty-five of the fifty-four delegates. He also prevailed in a series of state conventions, and by May 10, the New York Times reported he was ahead of Ford in its delegate count.

As the campaign played out over the next three months, Ford regained the lead. He used the prestige of White House invitations to win over uncommitted delegates. Sears fought to keep the contest close, with a surprise announcement of a vice presidential choice, Senator Richard Schweiker of Pennsylvania, whose moderate to liberal voting record infuriated many of

Reagan's backers. But Sears was gambling, hoping that the choice would shake up the race and at least make Ford check every delegate's loyalty, and at the most that Reagan could use the stunt to bait Ford into making a vice presidential choice of his own before the convention in Kansas City, a move that could cost Ford the loyalty of some of his delegates.

The North Carolinians who had started Reagan on the road back had a different idea of how to upset the Ford applecart. Believing that many Ford delegates were true conservatives at heart, Ellis and Helms wanted ideological fights over the party platform. On issue after issue, as Ellis put it in 2006, "Any place we could put down a peg to the right of Ford, we would." He sent John East, a platform committee member who taught political science at East Carolina University, out "loaded up with foreign policy that we didn't think the Ford people would take," or, as East put it in a 1979 oral history, "challenging the whole Ford foreign policy as too soft, too vacillating, and not sufficient for the challenge we were facing with the Soviet Union and their proxies and minions in the rest of the world."

Sears had been cool to platform fights, which he feared "could lead to fratricidal warfare in the party and sure defeat in November, with Reagan and his supporters getting the blame," as Hannaford wrote in *The Reagans*. So when the Ford camp repeatedly gave ground on issues, the Reagan high command compromised, spurning the more fiery language the Helms camp preferred. There was one general assault, an introduction to the foreign policy plank called "Morality in Foreign Policy"; the Ford camp allowed it to pass on a voice vote despite Kissinger's opposition, and the last chance for a bitter floor fight was gone.

Panama was an example of how neither Reagan's forces nor Ford's really wanted an all-out fight. Helms's North Carolinians proposed the blunt assertion in the "morality" plank that "our foreign policy will recognize that we shall neither give up that which is ours, exemplified by the Panama Canal, nor abandon our friends in order to make new alliances, as exemplified by the Republic of China." That was more than the Ford camp would accept, so it was dropped by the Reagan high command, without telling Helms. The only reference to Panama came in another section, which read: "In any talks with Panama, however, the United States negotiators should in no way cede, dilute, forfeit, negotiate or transfer any rights, power, authority, jurisdiction, territory or property that are necessary for the protection and security of the United States and the entire Western Hemisphere." The loophole there was that Ford, if elected, could have decided that undiluted control of the Canal and the Zone was not essential to U.S. security.

Then all that was left was the roll call vote on the nomination itself. Ford got 1,187 votes and was nominated early in the morning of August 19. Reagan got 1,070.

But the next night Reagan staked a firm claim to the party's future. After Ford had accepted the nomination in one of the best speeches of his life, he invited Reagan to come down from the stands to say a few words from the podium. Reagan reluctantly came, but then stunned the convention with an impromptu version of what had been designed as his acceptance address. Never mentioning Ford, he instead hailed the party platform, called for party unity, and quoted General Douglas MacArthur as saying, "There is no substitute for victory." Reagan was at his inspirational best that night. He spoke of the future, saying that 100 years from now Americans "will know whether we met our challenge, whether they have the freedoms that we have known up until now will depend on what we do here. Will they look back with appreciation and say, 'Thank God for those people in 1976 who headed off that loss of freedom, who kept us now 100 years later free, who kept our world from nuclear destruction'?"

★ Reagan left Kansas City as the front-runner for the 1980 Republican nomination. The Panama Canal issue had rescued his campaign. It conveyed his argument about the U.S. decline simply and clearly, in a way no litany of diplomatic dealings with the Soviet Union or arguments about whose weapons were bigger could ever do.

There is no certainty in the "what ifs" of history. Some of Reagan's intimates think he would not have run again if he had been badly beaten in 1976—as he was about to be before the Canal issue caught fire in North Carolina. And some think he would have run again anyhow and prevailed.

The argument that Reagan would have run again despite a bad defeat in 1976 is an intriguing one. Stu Spencer, who worked for him in 1966 and 1980 and against him in 1976, recalled in 2005 that Reagan "used to say 'the office seeks the man,'" and thought the presidency sought him, starting in 1968. Mike Deaver, Reagan's longtime aide in Sacramento and the White House, made a similar argument the same year: "He believed in destiny. The reason he ran is he really believed he could end the cold war."

Deaver's old partner, Pete Hannaford, is among those who disagreed. In 2006 Hannaford said, "I think had he lost North Carolina it would have been pretty bleak." And he pointed out that Nancy Reagan was demoralized going into that state. If Reagan had been beaten badly in 1976, he said, both of them would have resisted appeals that he try again. Paul Laxalt, who knew Reagan as a contemporary more than did most of the younger campaign aides, recalled that immediately after the national convention, Reagan had been "very emphatic" that he would not run again but quickly changed his mind. But if he had not come to Kansas City as an underdog, but as an also-ran, Laxalt said, Nancy Reagan would have been wary of his being humiliated: "It would have been all over."

And Dick Wirthlin, the pollster, not only agreed that Nancy Reagan would have opposed another try if 1976 had been a dismal failure but pointed out that even if Reagan had tried again despite her, he would not have been the "presumptive presidential nominee in 1980" (as Lou Cannon called him in his book), but would have entered the 1980 race "badly scarred."

There are other voices on both sides of the argument, and the answer is not knowable. Nancy Reagan, who knew Ronald Reagan better than anyone, wrote to me in 2007 to say she did not know, and they had never talked about it.

But my own judgment is that if he had lost North Carolina, Reagan would never have come close to Ford, and probably would not have had the campaign funds to continue the race credibly. If he had soldiered on anyhow, he would have been widely seen as a nagging irrelevancy. Then, if Reagan had emerged from 1976 as a badly defeated candidate, I do not think he would have tried again in 1980. But even if he had, still believing his destiny was the White House, the 1976 defeat would have seemed, like Goldwater's crushing loss in 1964, as proof for a time that someone so conservative could not be elected, and a huge obstacle to winning the nomination.

Not that the conservative movement would have crashed to a stop, for there was much more to it than one man. But it would have had to wait more than four years to triumph.

6

The Ford administration had promised Torrijos that it would settle the Canal issue after the 1976 elections. It did not get the chance. Jimmy Carter defeated Ford and inherited the issue. After reading up on it, he embraced it with enthusiasm, not just with the sense of obligation or necessity his predecessors had felt.

No comparably unknown candidate had won his party's nomination since the Republicans nominated Wendell Willkie in 1940. And Carter, a one-term governor of Georgia who had left office in 1975, was not merely personally unknown to the press and the political establishment; he was very different. The differences started, superficially, with the unpresidential "Jimmy Carter" he used on ballot lines in place of his given name, James Earl Carter Jr., and his identifying himself, accurately, as a Plains, Georgia, peanut farmer, and, extravagantly, as a nuclear physicist. They continued through a southern accent, unfamiliar cadences and emphases on odd syllables, and his way of identifying places he had visited as "Brussels, Belgium" or "Paris, France." His utter self-confidence—"I don't intend to lose"—was striking in a trade where candidates tried to game the press by poor-mouthing their expectations. But his most profound difference from other would-be presidents (and from most of the reporters who tried to explain him to the country) was the depth of his faith and his ease in talking openly about religion, prayer, and being a born-again Christian. That faith and his insistence that he would never tell a lie helped him run against a sinful Washington that had disappointed the nation through Vietnam and Watergate.

When Carter talked about what he would do as president, he promised to simplify the tax code and reorganize the federal government, boring topics to Washingtonians but ideas that appealed to the public. He made some other clear commitments, such as support for national health insurance. On foreign policy his overall message was that the United States should abandon secrecy and strike a posture conveying "the decency and generosity and common sense of our people." As Gaddis Smith wrote, "He proclaimed his belief in the primacy of moral principle over power in foreign policy." That approach reflected his overall, constantly reiterated commitment to a government as "full of compassion and love as are the American people." But while he had his staff list and publish more than 600 promises he made during the campaign, his candidacy was more about character than issues, less about ideological positioning than about geography—in the literal sense of using regional pride to win back southern states that had been going Republican, and in the metaphoric sense of Carter's distance from the Washington he and millions of Americans disdained.

Carter represented the "New South," whose leaders had abandoned segregation and whose Democrats depended on black votes to win. In his inaugural address as governor, he said, "The time for racial discrimination is over," and he hung Martin Luther King's portrait in the Georgia capitol. That record contrasted with that of George Wallace, who was running again, and whose thinly disguised racist appeals had won substantial support from union members in 1968 and 1972. That positioning won Carter support from liberals, notably the United Auto Workers, who might otherwise have preferred a more liberal candidate in the fragmented Democratic field. Moreover, he had a well-thought-out campaign plan and skilled aides, and he worked very hard and won the Democratic nomination.

In the general election, Carter began with a big lead and lost almost all of it. The Ford campaign exploited doubts about putting an inexperienced outsider in the White House, especially to deal with foreign affairs. It made this a target because the Carter record on foreign affairs was blank, aside from some trade trips and participation in the Trilateral Commission. (That discussion group among leaders from Europe, the Americas, and Asia, created by David Rockefeller of Chase Manhattan Bank, made Carter a target for the isolationist Right, though conservatives generally spent more time worrying about whether to make much of an effort for Ford.) Still, Ford put a brake on his own momentum with a bizarre insistence in an October 6 debate that "there is no Soviet domination of Eastern Europe." In the end, Carter squeaked through to victory, and the Panama problem, like many others to which more attention had been given, was his.

Jimmy Carter had never seen the Panama Canal even though he served in the Caribbean after graduating from the Naval Academy in 1946. Indeed, he had never given the Canal much thought until people started asking him about it in 1976 as the issue roiled the Republican race. During the campaign, Carter's public comments on the negotiations were straddles. He sought to sound reasonable and sympathetic toward Panama. But he was running for president of the United States, so it was more important to sound firm, patriotic, even chauvinistic, to Americans. In May, he told Newsweek, "I am not in favor of relinquishing actual control of the Panama Canal or its use to any other nation, including Panama. However, I think there are several things that can be done to eliminate the feeling among the Panamanians that they were excluded in 1903. I would certainly be willing to renegotiate payment terms and be willing to remove the word 'perpetuity' from the present agreement."

People in Panama did not pay much attention to that comment. They were fixed on the Ford-Reagan battle, for, after all, who was Jimmy Carter? But in October, they knew he was the Democratic nominee for president, with a lead in the polls. In that same October 6 debate with Ford, Carter proclaimed: "I would never give up complete control or practical control of the Panama Canal Zone."

Torrijos exploded. He said, "The superficial manner in which the most explosive topic in U.S. relations with Latin America was broached constitutes a great irresponsibility toward the American people." As to Carter's comment, he snapped, "The word 'never' is a word that has been erased from the political dictionary." Panama's unhappiness was also transmitted to the Carter campaign by Sol Linowitz, the lawyer who formerly headed the Xerox Corporation, had served as ambassador to the Organization of American States, and had been working for several years on a privately funded commission to highlight how to improve relations with Latin America. Stuart Eizenstat, Carter's issues director for the campaign, asked him to tell the Panamanians, Linowitz recalled in a 1979 interview, "that Carter has always been devoted to Latin America, that he has a strong sense of kinship with them, that he would never do anything that was not conducive to improved relations between the United States and Latin America, and in the course of our campaigns things get said and instead of getting too upset they should just wait and let the thing take its course, and if Carter is elected, they will be pleased at his reaction."

That warning soothed Panama's foreign minister, Aquilino Boyd, who had complained to Linowitz. But Panama's National Guard showed its continuing annoyance by committing five small, nonfatal bombings in the Canal Zone before Election Day.

After Carter won the election, he was spurred to a decision by Linowitz and the staff director of his commission, Robert Pastor, a doctoral candidate at Harvard, and by Henry Kissinger. Pastor, who had been among Carter's policy advisers for several months, had criticized some of his waffling statements. Then, just before Election Day, Pastor wrote, "A new Panama Canal Treaty is the only item in U.S.–Latin American relations which is of the highest priority in U.S. foreign policy in this period. If a new Administration does not demonstrate a clear-cut intention to negotiate a new treaty and present it to Congress in 1977, then violence is virtually inevitable in Panama, and the repercussions for the U.S. will be widespread." Kissinger met with the president-elect during the transition and described the state of the negotiations and warned that all of Latin America supported Panama's demands, with Mexico even talking about sending troops to back Panama if a conflict resulted.

Before his inauguration, Carter also read the final report of Linowitz's Commission on United States–Latin-American Relations. The report called for a new, equitable treaty and said the Canal problem was "the most urgent issue" in the hemisphere. Carter got the message. In an interview with *Time* published on December 27, he said, "I think the Panama treaty ought to be resolved quite rapidly. That's almost uniquely our responsibility," a comment that attracted little notice, beyond the eighteenth paragraph of a *New York Times* story. In mid-January, as president-elect, Carter met with about fifty members of Congress, including Republican leaders, for an all-day seminar on foreign policy and told them he was going to resume negotiations promptly and hoped to have a treaty by June.

Carter's national security adviser, Zbigniew Brzezinski, hired Pastor on January 8 and told him to have a memorandum on Panama prepared for January 21, the first working day of the new presidency. It was a directive to the State Department and Defense Department to prepare, in a hurry, Presidential Review Memorandum 1 (PRM-1) of the Carter administration. That seventy-eight-page memorandum analyzed negotiating options and gave relatively short shrift to the problems of public and congressional approval. As to public opinion, it noted two-to-one opposition in polls but suggested "much of the opposition is 'convertible'—if a fair treaty is negotiated and effectively presented." As to the Senate, it did suggest that efforts be made to discourage a new Thurmond resolution that would lock senators into opposition when there was a real treaty to vote on. Senator Alan Cranston of California, the Democratic Senate whip, successfully took on that task, and the Thurmond resolution was never introduced in the new Congress.

When that memorandum was considered on January 27, Cyrus R. Vance, the new secretary of state, presided and disposed of the threshold question by agreeing to move forward on the basis of the Kissinger-Tack principles. Linowitz, who by that time had been asked to join Bunker and provide more energy to the U.S. negotiating mission, called that decision "indispensable" because of Panamanian concerns about Carter's campaign statements. Bunker said of the Panamanians, "They're more flexible now than at any time during my negotiations with them. They need a treaty; their economic situation is bad." Bunker and Linowitz were directed to resume negotiations in early February to find out if Panama would agree to let the United States continue to protect the Canal after it was turned over to Panama at the end of the century.

Panama, an issue Carter never raised on his own in the campaign, became the first foreign policy initiative of the new administration, for a variety of reasons. Neither the Soviet Union nor China was ready to move forward on relations with the United States, but the Canal issue was right there to be settled. There was also risk in further delay by the United States. Vance wrote in his memoirs that Torrijos's authority was strong enough to make a treaty, but "if he were rebuffed on the canal issue, a successor government might be either too weak or too radical" to make a deal. As PRM-1 put it, "Delay in a treaty invites violence against the Canal." Or, as Pastor said in a 2006 interview, "Panama couldn't wait any longer. There was a real fear of terrorism. And if terrorism started, then we couldn't get ahead of it, we couldn't be seen as giving in."

For Carter's predecessors, Canal negotiations were driven by the sense that they could enhance the security of the waterway. For Carter, they were also, and more significantly, an opportunity to show a new face of American foreign policy, one that conveyed respect for human rights, small nations, and moral principle.

7

Carter certainly had not planned to make Panama the first foreign issue he tackled. Launching the Mideast peace process had been his first foreign policy priority, but he said in a 2006 interview that Panama had been very important to him, too:

> I wanted to treat Panama fairly. I had studied the issue fairly thoroughly, and I was convinced that it was an unfair original agreement, that was foisted upon the Panamanian people against their will. . . . There was no doubt that I was determined to go through with the Panama Canal, because I thought I could succeed, and I did not anticipate the antipathy and the concerted effort that was aroused around the country against it. I underestimated the opposition.

The opposition started flexing its muscles long before there was a treaty to oppose. Reagan spoke at the annual Conservative Political Action Conference in Washington in February 1977 to denounce negotiating with a dictatorship. In March, Jesse Helms and Representative George Hansen, an Idaho Republican, attacked Linowitz because he was a director of Marine Midland Bank, which did business with Panama. In April, Representative Bob Sikes, a Florida Democrat, warned of growing Soviet influence in Panama, suggesting that Moscow's ambitions were behind the Panamanian demands.

Those were individual voices. There were also, more significantly, organizational efforts. Wes McCune, a Washington journalist who kept tabs on conservatives in a newsletter called *Group Research Reports*, wrote on March 30, 1977:

The organized right-wing . . . is stepping up the campaign. Besides numerous speeches by Congressmen, mostly conservative, three groups are keeping up a din—and raising money to continue it. The John Birch Society took over the Committee on Pan American Policy last summer and has given it added clout. Specifically, it has just produced a filmstrip entitled "Panamania" which begins with "a short survey of America's suicidal foreign policy since World War II" and "focuses a spotlight on the insidious plan to turn over the Panama Canal to the leftist government of Panama."

He also cited efforts by the American Council for World Freedom, "an anti-Communist group led in the U.S. by a group of established right-wingers," and the Council for Inter-American Security, which said it was "launching a concentrated counter-attack to stop these liberals and left-radicals before they succeed."

The American Conservative Union, which had stressed the issue in its 1976 efforts for Ronald Reagan, enlisted Strom Thurmond to raise money for its Panama Canal Task Force in May. In his appeal for money, Senator Thurmond blasted Torrijos as a "strong-arm dictator who maintains close ties with Castro and the Soviet Union." He called the Canal central to national security, saying, "In the event of future hostilities, our security interests could not permit it to be in Communist or pro-Communist hands."

The Conservative Caucus, a newer group headed by Howard Phillips, who had worked in the Nixon White House to dismantle Lyndon Johnson's War on Poverty, started planning in February to build public opposition to any treaty. In June it dispatched its national chairman and "shadow secretary of State," Governor Meldrim Thomson of New Hampshire, to spend two days in Panama. On Thomson's return, he and his fellow "shadow cabinet" officers agreed that economic and military necessities demanded rejection of any treaty to turn the Canal over to Panama, which was run by a "military dictatorship dominated by extreme leftists." Representative Larry McDonald, a Georgia Democrat and an official of the John Birch Society, sent out a fund-raising letter in July, and the Conservative Caucus produced a bumper sticker for its members proclaiming, "Castro . . . Hands Off Our Canal."

The negotiations themselves resumed in February but did not make quick progress. Panamanian delegates felt the United States paid too little attention to Panama's immediate territorial needs, from control of ports to the symbolism of Ancon Hill, the highest point in the Panama City area, situated in the Canal Zone. The American negotiators felt Panama was ignoring its urgent need for some agreed-on device to enable the United States to use force if the neutrality of the Canal was threatened—without which neither the Defense Department nor Congress would go along.

In mid-May the diplomatic logjam was broken. The United States gave ground on a range of territorial issues, and Torrijos agreed in principle to the sort of neutrality treaty the United States required, although the language was vague. As Secretary of State Cyrus Vance wrote President Carter on June 8, "We have agreed to language, which recognizes that the United States, as well as Panama, has legal responsibility to maintain the regime of neutrality. This is the clearest we could obtain, given Panama's insistence on terms which would severely limit unilateral action by the United States in order to maintain the neutrality of the Canal." Carter marked "ok" by Vance's report, but in a few months it would be clear that the vagueness was the gravest problem the neutrality treaty faced in the Senate.

That did not end the negotiating difficulties. The diplomats argued over the bureaucratic arrangements for running the Canal in the years leading up to the eventual handover at the end of the century. Panamanian delegates startled the Americans by asking for a $1 billion payment, a sum Carter rejected in a letter to Torrijos. And even on issues where both sides thought they had reached agreement, new problems kept coming up that had to be examined and often debated. But in the end, with Linowitz's six-month appointment (all that was legal because he would not disentangle himself from his law practice and various corporate boards he served on) expiring that very day, negotiators at Panama City's Holiday Inn agreed on August 10 on a framework for the two treaties—one to turn over the Canal to Panama and the other to ensure it remained neutral and open. The final drafting was not completed until September 4—three days before the pacts were to be signed by Carter and Torrijos in Washington.

Although the negotiations themselves consumed more administration attention, concern abut ratification was never absent. The boldest effort came when Linowitz had lunch with Ronald and Nancy Reagan on April 30 in the Californians' suite at Washington's Madison Hotel. Linowitz's account of the discussion was an optimistic one, concluding that Reagan "did not have a sense of mission" about the Canal, was unfamiliar with many facts about it, and, Linowitz wrote two days later, "was especially uneasy, I thought, when

I kept impressing upon him the danger of the situation and its potentially explosive nature. He remained silent when I asked: 'Would you feel uncomfortable if our unwillingness to negotiate led to bloodshed?' " It seems likely that Linowitz read too much into Reagan's cordiality and not enough into Reagan's expressed fears about perceived American weakness. Linowitz reported that Reagan

> said that he thought "giving up Panama would be another retreat which would lose the respect of the rest of the world." He said he thought we were already without the support of our allies who questioned our willingness to stand up for principles in which we said we believed. . . . Finally, he said that he did not think that it was proper for the United States to be negotiating under a threat of possible violence as he thought we were now doing and that we ought to stand our ground against this crude dictator.

Three weeks later, Reagan wrote Linowitz to say that the United States should not "give up our rights of sovereignty in the Zone" and should not, "at this time, give the appearance of backing down on this particular issue."

Linowitz got a different response when he went to see Howard H. Baker Jr., the Senate minority leader. The Tennessee Republican remained publicly uncommitted on the treaties until January 1978. But after Linowitz briefed him on the negotiations in June 1977, Baker told Linowitz that he was inclined to support them and wanted to help.

After that meeting, and another with Senators Robert C. Byrd and Alan Cranston, the majority leader and majority whip, the administration started conducting regular briefings on the treaty issues for any senators who wanted to come—a project Baker and Byrd encouraged. At least seventy senators took part during the late spring and summer.

The Carter administration was also spending time that spring and summer planning a campaign to build public support for the treaties once they were agreed on. As Joe Aragon, a White House special assistant for Hispanic affairs, wrote two higher-ranking aides, Hamilton Jordan and Landon Butler, on June 7: "Unless a major effort is undertaken to generate public support for ratification of the Panama Canal Treaty by the U.S. Senate, key Senators may find themselves inundated with anti-treaty mail organized by right-wing conservatives. This will make it more difficult for those Senators to support the treaty and will therefore diminish the prospects for ratification." One device they agreed on early was to have a bipartisan citizens' committee to back the treaties, hoping it could counteract conservative anti-treaty efforts. On September 7, the day the treaties were signed, the Committee of Americans for the Canal Treaties was announced in Washington—with a membership including military and diplomatic luminaries of past administrations, union and corporate leaders, former president Ford and David Rockefeller. As George D. Moffett III wrote in his insightful book *The Limits of Victory: The Ratification of the Panama Canal Treaties*, "For one brief moment all of the blue-chip names on the roster of the nation's ruling elite were brought together again." But in fact the committee never raised the resources to have much of an impact, and it did not really start working until two months later.

Carter himself took on a huge role. On August 7, before the treaty was agreed on in Panama, he telephoned or wired all 100 senators to tell them a treaty was imminent but asking them to avoid committing themselves until they had seen the text. As Carter wrote in his diary, "Most of them except a few nuts like Strom Thurmond and Jesse Helms" went along with his request. Both denounced the treaty, and Helms released a poll by the Opinion Research Corporation of Princeton, New Jersey, showing that only 8 percent of the public favored turning the Canal over to Panama, a percentage far lower than indicated by other polls because of different ways of wording the question.

Carter telephoned Ford and Kissinger and had the negotiators brief them. They both endorsed the treaty. He called Reagan and won a promise not to make a definitive statement until he had been briefed by Linowitz and Bunker.

The president called dozens of senators, including outspoken opponents such as Orrin Hatch of Utah, and jotted down notes on their responses. Of his talk with Hatch he wrote, "Don't have votes to ratify. Lean heavily against treaty. Cuban/Soviet influence will keep mind open as possible." Of Dewey Bartlett of Oklahoma he observed, "He is on opposite sides with President— Oklahoma is Against." Of Russell Long of Louisiana, he noted, "If my vote decisive, may help. Otherwise rather go w/ La people. As of now, not supportive." Of Robert Morgan of North Carolina, he wrote, "Inclined to support."

Carter courted Byrd, who had been saying publicly that the treaties faced "an uphill battle." Byrd and his wife, Erma, dined at the White House on August 23 to discuss ratification. Carter and Byrd had a prickly relationship, but this session apparently went well, for Carter then arranged a White House play date for Byrd's grandchildren with Amy Carter, the president's nine-year-old daughter.

He also participated in briefings intended to influence public opinion in Sunbelt states with potentially persuadable senators. Civic leaders from Mississippi and Kentucky came to the White House on August 23; Floridians and Georgians were guests on August 30, when Carter told them he knew that "many well-educated, very patriotic Americans" opposed the pacts, but it was his responsibility to change their minds, "to lead, to educate."

The persuasion did not always work. Carter had hoped to get Barry Goldwater's support, based on what Goldwater had said about the Canal in the 1976 campaign and a letter he had sent Pastor that March indicating he was open to a new treaty because of the threat of guerrilla warfare. On September 2, a White House aide wrote to Henry Kissinger, asking him to talk to Goldwater, saying, "Senator Goldwater has been briefed on the Treaty and has talked with the President. Although he has some concerns, he has indicated his support." But that same day, Goldwater told the Los Angeles Times that though Carter had called him twice, he still expected "the answer will be no." The next week, Goldwater was writing constituents that after reading the treaties, he would oppose them. It was a major disappointment for Carter, who said in 2006, "He would tell me privately that he thought it was the right thing to do, but still I couldn't get him to pledge to vote for it."

Goldwater's support would have been quite a coup; Ronald Reagan's would have been astounding.

Reagan seemed to strain to keep his promise not to take a stand before hearing from Linowitz and Bunker on August 25. He told the New York Times in a Los Angeles interview on August 23 that he did not believe the Joint Chiefs of Staff really favored the pact and said he would "do everything I can" to block ratification if he decided to oppose the treaties. In Atlantic City the next day he called the treaties a "giveaway." Then on the twenty-fifth itself, a few hours after listening to the two diplomats in a friend's New York apartment opposite the United Nations, he attacked the treaties at the annual convention of Young Americans for Freedom, emphasizing that giving up U.S. sovereignty invited Panama to nationalize the Canal whenever it wished.

Finally, Carter entertained Torrijos and seventeen other Latin heads of state or government for an extravagant signing ceremony and state dinner, designed to show how important the treaties were to the entire hemisphere. Byrd and Baker had both suggested this was a bad idea because senators would not be impressed and might be annoyed that the treaties were being signed before senators had been shown the precise texts, but the festivities

President Jimmy Carter and General Omar Torrijos (right) at the signing of the Panama Canal Treaties, September 8, 1977 (Jimmy Carter Library)

dominated the news for several days, like a successful run in an election campaign.

The Carter administration was treating the issue like a political campaign, seeking to build momentum and a sense of inevitability. Agreeing on a treaty after fourteen years was one signal accomplishment, like a victory in the first primary. Then there was the spectacle of Latin American leaders coming to Washington to praise the agreement, which the administration hoped would sway the American public. Jordan, Carter's chief political strategist, or someone close to him told the *New York Times* on August 11 they expected to win public support, at least in a few key states. They read the polls to conclude that because the issue did not affect many people personally, public opinion was "reversible—if we can just get the facts disseminated to enough people," as Jordan put it in October. That would change the Senate, he added confidently if indiscreetly, because "some of these bastards don't have the spine not to vote their mail. If you change their mail, you change their mind."

Carter himself took the view that since the treaties made sense, the American people in their wisdom would come to support them. On August 26, he told a group of editors from out of Washington, "I have a responsibility to be sure that not only the Members of the Senate but the American people know the facts about the current terms of the treaty. My belief is that when those facts are known, the opinion of the American people will change." One step he planned to take soon, he said, was a fireside chat to the nation.

He added, "If I can't sell the American people on the fact that the terms of the treaty are beneficial, then I'll have a very difficult time selling it to the Senate."

8

"It is us, we the people around this table, who are the alternatives to the Democrats—not Bill Brock or the Republicans." That was the motto of a small group of conservatives who would make Carter's salesmanship more difficult than he ever expected. They had breakfast or dinner every week, hosted by Richard A. Viguerie, at age forty-three the kingpin of conservative direct mail. The press often referred to him as the "Godfather of the New Right"; calling him "Postmaster General" might have been more appropriate.

Viguerie and his guests—or most of them—made up what was called the New Right. Regarding compromise as a dirty word, they sought out emotional issues and mounted attacks on officeholders of both parties. To them, most Democrats were liberals, and most Republicans in Washington, such as Brock, the chairman of the Republican National Committee and a former senator from Tennessee, were weak-kneed collaborators.

Most of the organizations had a letterhead and little more in terms of manpower. But their tactics, technical expertise, and instinct for what issues could stir emotions enough to generate checks to New Right groups and letters to Congress helped bring about the polarization of American politics so widely lamented three decades later. Viguerie spoke in the seventies of creating a new party or an independent ticket that could unite various conservative factions such as groups opposing gun control, abortion, obscenity, and the equal rights amendment. That party more or less exists today, with some new hot buttons added, as the Republican Party. Viguerie himself had hoped first to be an engineer, then a lawyer. But as a self-confessed "poor student," the Cajun who grew up in Texas showed more of a knack for politics. He headed Houston's Young Republicans and worked in the Eisenhower campaigns of 1952 and 1956 and John Tower's 1960 Senate race, where he wrote his first fund-raising letter.

After working for Young Americans for Freedom from 1961 to 1964 and learning about direct mail, Viguerie went into business in 1964 and started making money for his candidates, his causes, and himself. He did some work for the Nixon administration, sending out mail to generate support for Supreme Court nominees Warren E. Burger and G. Harrold Carswell. He turned against Nixon because of wage and price controls and the opening to China, and backed Nixon's conservative foe, Representative John Ashbrook of Ohio, in Republican presidential primaries in 1972. Viguerie said he lost $250,000 on that failed effort. Viguerie never worked for Democrats other than George Wallace, whom he helped retire his 1972 campaign debt, thereby accumulating several million new names for future mailings. But he was hardly a dedicated Republican. Viguerie had offered himself as an independent candidate for vice president in 1976 and had spoken warmly of a Reagan-Wallace or Wallace-Reagan ticket.

By the early seventies, the workaholic Viguerie was wealthy, and he began to spend time trying to find ways that he and other conservatives could begin, as he put it, "saving our nation and the world from the liberal leaders and the liberal idea which had almost destroyed us."

Two of the other people at those dinner or breakfast meetings headed New Right organizations Viguerie had been tied to through his fund-raising machinery: Howard Phillips of the Conservative Caucus was better known in 1977 than Terry Dolan of the National Conservative Political Action Committee. Others who attended regularly included Ed Fuelner, head of the Heritage Foundation, and Paul Weyrich, Fuelner's predecessor at Heritage, who was now leading the Committee for the Survival of a Free Congress. They were often joined by Tom Ellis, the political strategist for Jesse Helms, and sometimes by Tom Winter, the editor of *Human Events*, and Rich Williamson, administrative assistant to Representative Philip Crane of Illinois. Crane had succeeded M. Stanton Evans as head of the American Conservative Union and had previously used Viguerie's mailings to win a special election to Congress in 1969.

Richard Viguerie and Tom Winter, often in conflict, enjoy a light moment at a conservative counterinaugural party, January 20, 1977. (Ann Stone)

As Viguerie's comments and history showed, and even though they more often helped Republicans than Democrats, the New Right leaders were hardly committed to the Republican Party. In 1978 Phillips registered as a Democrat to run in the Democratic Senate primary to show his contempt for party labels; he finished fourth with 7.8 percent of the vote. And Dolan once told the *Washington Post*, "The Republican Party is a fraud. It's a social club where the rich go to pick their noses."

But the immediate focus of their discussions was a Democratic president. They played a role in thwarting the Carter administration on issues ranging from the nomination of Theodore C. Sorensen to head the Central Intelligence Agency to various election law changes Carter had proposed. Then they turned to the Canal with a vengeance. As Viguerie recalled in 2006, "It was a big part of our agenda. If there was one issue more than any other that gave impetus and unity to the conservative movement, it was the Panama Canal issue."

While the conservatives thought the treaty was bad for the United States on grounds of both military security and international reputation, perhaps more important, they also thought the issue was good for them. Viguerie said at the time, "It's an issue the conservatives can't lose on. If we lose the vote in the Senate, we will have had the issue for eight or nine months. We will have rallied many new people to our cause. We will have given our supporters an issue, a cause to work for. . . . Now conservatives can get excited about the Panama Canal giveaway and they can go to the polls, look for a person's name on the ballot who favored these treaties and vote against him." Howard Phillips saw the issue as one that would bring Americans who had learned in school of the Canal's glorious history to the conservative movement. Paul Laxalt, Reagan's closest ally in Washington and the liaison between the New Right and Senate foes of the treaty, told the California Republican convention, "This is the best political issue that could be handed to a party in recent years." He predicted it would be "the most significant issue" in the 1978 congressional elections.

Democrats were not their only targets. The idea of creating a new party had been abandoned, so the Republican Party itself was now in their sights. Laxalt explained, "Conservatives will control the party as a result of the Panama Canal," adding, "It's a natural issue to galvanize our people for fund raising and to gear up the troops. It's like manna from Heaven." Phillips said, "I can't think of any other issue that better unites grass roots conservatives than the canal." Gary Jarmin, legislative director of the ACU told Jim Dickenson of the *Washington Star*, "Conservatives see this as a great opportunity to take control of the Republican Party." He asserted, "We should control it because we're the dominant element of the party and without us it would die." Dickenson wrote that the conservatives had a "hit list" of Republican senators, including James Pearson of Kansas, Charles Percy of Illinois, Edward Brooke of Massachusetts, Clifford Case of New Jersey, and, if he voted wrong, Howard Baker of Tennessee.

As Steven F. Hayward summarized it thirty-four years later in *The Age of Reagan*, "Conservative leaders seized on the Panama Canal issue as a means of clobbering Carter. It was a no-lose issue: If they defeated the treaties, they would have a scalp to hang over the mantle. If the Senate ratified the treaties, conservatives would have an issue to use against Carter and the pro-treaty senators in the next election."

There were jealousies among the various conservative organizations, especially on the part of the ACU, which had been founded in 1964 after Goldwater's defeat. Some of its leaders, like Tom Winter of *Human Events*, a vice chairman of the ACU, thought the proliferation of organizations spread available money more thinly. But Crane's connection to Viguerie minimized that friction, and on the Canal issue the organizations worked together.

The first of those joint efforts was a rally on the Capitol steps on September 7, the day the treaties were signed, sponsored by the Conservative Caucus, the ACU, and the Committee for the Survival of a Free Congress. Reagan declined to participate. Instead, he appeared the next day before a Senate subcommittee to complain that the United States negotiated "under repeated threats of violence" and "apparently, made concessions in the face of threats," and the same day spoke more generally about Latin America at the National Press Club.

Without Reagan, the rally featured several congressional opponents of the pacts. Representative Larry McDonald of Georgia, a Democrat and a member of the national council of the John Birch Society who later succeeded Robert Welch as the society's chairman, called the treaties "bipartisan treason." Another Democrat, Representative Gillespie V. "Sonny" Montgomery of Mississippi, said, "As far as I'm concerned, it's like giving away the 51st state." Representative Mickey Edwards, an Oklahoma Republican, argued, "We need the canal, and to turn it over to a left-wing military dictator is to play Russian roulette with the future security of every American." Representative Robert Dornan of California accused Torrijos of "skimming money from whorehouses." Crane attacked the Gallup poll for what he said were biased questions suggesting growth of support for the pacts, and Senator James McClure of Idaho proposed a national referendum on the question. One off-key note sounded when a dozen young men dressed as Nazis tried to join in. The crowd of about 200 booed them, and Dornan dismissed them as "these overweight jerks."

Another collaborative enterprise involved Viguerie, Crane, Williamson, and Reagan in a book, *Surrender in Panama: The Case against the Treaty*. Crane wrote the book, with the help of Williamson and others. Reagan contributed an introduction, which explained that the book covered "all the facts anyone needs to make a reasoned decision about the Panama Canal treaties now before the Congress." That decision, he said, would be to reject the treaties and make it clear "that the United States must retain practical control over the canal for the security of the entire hemisphere."

Viguerie published the book, in 100,000 paperback copies and in hardback as well. It ran 258 pages, with more than half consisting of texts of treaties and testimony. Crane himself, who had a Ph.D. in history from Indiana University, began by insisting that the United States' "proven right to sovereign power" was beyond dispute, and that the "titular sovereignty" that American leaders had said Panama enjoyed meant nothing. He said that if the United States agreed to the treaties and removed its troops, the Canal's only defense could come from "the pathetic rabble" of Panama's National Guard, which would be loyal only to whoever was providing its "salaries and graft." He sneered at "Omar Torrijos and the corrupt, vicious police state he has built in Panama with the help of his Marxist allies."

Crane argued that the Canal was of vital importance to American security, as a way of both controlling the Caribbean and providing for warships to pass between the Atlantic and the Pacific oceans. Moreover, he said, "Surrender in Panama would be one more crucial American step in a descent to ignominy—to the end of America's credibility as a world power and a deterrent to aggression."

But the Right's biggest joint effort came in January 1978, when treaty foes chartered a plane to fly a "Truth Squad" around the country to try to stir opposition to the treaties and to senators who favored them. This effort was not without its problems, since Hubert Humphrey's funeral delayed the start by a day, canceling appearances in Atlanta and Nashville. Then a blizzard kept the plane from a planned stop in Cincinnati.

Another, bigger problem arose long before the plane took off and reflected the distance between the New Right and the Republican Party hierarchy. Reagan had written fund-raising letters for the Republican National Committee, calling the treaties a "line-by-line blueprint for potential disaster." He asked for contributions to the RNC for an Emergency Panama Canal Fund that would "launch an unprecedented campaign to defeat the treaty and elect more Republicans to Congress who will vote against any giveaway schemes." The letter promised the money would be spent to place ads to alert people to the danger and get them to sign petitions against ratification.

The letter raised at least $700,000. But when Laxalt asked chairman Brock for $50,000 to pay the cost of chartering a plane, Brock refused, and Reagan got angry. Laxalt said Reagan was "a pretty hot Irishman" who called Brock a "son of a bitch," unusual language for Reagan. Laxalt said in his 2000 autobiography that he still does not know why Brock refused. But in a 2006 interview, Brock said he told Laxalt and Reagan, who joined in an angry telephone call protesting the decision, that he would not fund any activity that was bipartisan, and Representative McDonald's participation meant there would be at least one nominal Democrat on the Truth Squad. Moreover, he said he explained that he wanted to spend money on a very focused set of objectives, especially the economy, that he thought would help Republican candidates, and the Canal issue was "divisive." Another reason he cited in the 2006 interview was that he did not want to do anything to "advantage one presidential candidate over another," and this issue would help Reagan because it was his. It was clear that whatever had led people to make contributions in response to the Reagan letters, and whatever the Reagan letter had said, Brock was not going to spend money against the treaties and make life harder for Howard Baker, his fellow Tennessean and the Senate minority leader.

That financial problem was solved quickly. Laxalt and the ACU turned to Viguerie, who sent out 5,000 letters that raised $110,000 in two weeks. Viguerie kicked in $5,000 himself, and so did the Conservative Caucus, the American Conservative Union, the Committee for the Survival of a Free Congress, the National Conservative Political Action Committee, Reagan's Citizens for the Republic, and the American Security Council.

The plane carried thirty reporters and a varying collection of conservatives. The first stop, in Miami on January 18, probably paid in publicity for the whole trip's cost of $80,000 to $100,000; each of the three national television networks covered it and devoted about two minutes each to the story. Each featured Laxalt and Senator Jake Garn, a Utah Republican. Laxalt told the audience not to be seduced by talk of reservations and amendments because "the basic gut issue is this. Do we or do we not give away the Panama Canal, and I say no." Garn said the nation should "stand up for our good, old-fashioned values and principles and quit getting kicked around and worried about some tin-horn dictator like Torrijos."

The Miami crowd of about 300 at an airport hotel also heard Laxalt urge them to write to Florida's Democratic senators, Lawton Chiles and Richard

Stone, to warn of the connection between Torrijos and Cuba's Fidel Castro. A retired federal judge in the Canal Zone, Guthrie F. Crowe, warned that if the treaties passed, "it will let Cuba and Moscow proceed with their master plan for takeover of the Caribbean." At the next stop in St. Louis on January 19, an audience estimated by the local paper at "several hundred" heard retired Lieutenant General Daniel O. Graham, a former director of the Defense Intelligence Agency, say he distrusted the support given the treaties by the Joint Chiefs of Staff because Carter would fire them if they disagreed. Senator Bob Dole of Kansas joined the speakers and pleaded, "For once, put our country first."

Reagan himself joined the squad for the next day's appearance in Denver, telling an audience of 400 at a downtown hotel that the treaties were "fatally flawed" and that it was "absolutely hogwash" to claim they were gaining support. Weyrich made the purpose of this particular stop clear when he told reporters they hoped to put pressure on Senator Floyd Haskell, a Democrat still uncommitted on the treaties who was up for reelection that fall. "We feel a definitive show of constituent sentiment might help him clarify his own thinking," Weyrich said. Finally, in Portland, Oregon, on January 20, Crane denounced the costs of the treaty; McDonald said there was an "unholy" alliance of big business, big government, and big labor in favor of it. They were joined by one Charlotte Kennedy, a private citizen who had flown to Portland from the Canal Zone at her own expense to say the Panamanians would be unable to maintain and operate the Canal efficiently.

Their cooperation was not limited to splashy projects. Almost every afternoon, a group of New Right leaders would meet in Laxalt's Senate office, to exchange the latest intelligence on how the eventual treaty votes were shaping up. Paul Weyrich, a former press secretary for Colorado senator Gordon Allott, took a leading role in that effort. Based on that meeting, new efforts would be made. As Bill Rhatican, who worked for Viguerie as a press aide, described the process in 2005, John Laxalt, the senator's brother and a Washington attorney, or Weyrich "would come out of that meeting with new marching orders, or at least new markets for us to market in. So if there was someone from Tennessee who was wavering, or that Laxalt thought was wavering, then direct mail would go into Tennessee and ACU would buy television commercials in Tennessee and whatever else was going on would happen."

9

The Right's attack on the treaties also involved individual efforts by particular organizations, some traditional and some quite innovative.

Partisan newspaper reporting, a journalistic staple since the Revolution, had almost disappeared by the 1970s. But the Right still had Tom Winter's *Human Events*, and that weekly campaigned as hard against the treaties as the "yellow press"— William Randolph Hearst's *New York Journal* and Joseph Pulitzer's *New York World*—had campaigned for war with Spain after the battleship *Maine* blew up in Havana harbor in 1898.

While Winter and *Human Events* did not ultimately succeed as Hearst and Pulitzer had, they still played an important role in developing opposition to the treaties. They publicized a series of provocative statements by Panama's chief treaty negotiator, Romulo Escobar Bethancourt. As he sought to firm up Panamanian support for the treaties, Escobar pandered to student opponents by saying the treaties neither allowed U.S. intervention to protect the Canal's neutrality nor enabled its warships to go to the head of the line in an emergency.* Major American

---

* Comparable White House pandering did not attract public attention and thus Panamanian anger. In September, for example, Zbigniew Brzezinski, Carter's national security adviser, was asked at a briefing what the United States would do if Panama announced in 2000 that it was closing the Canal for repairs. He replied, "In that case, according to the provisions of the Neutrality Treaty, we will move in and close down the Panamanian government for repairs." That remark stayed private until his memoirs were published in 1983.

newspapers largely ignored those statements until Senate hearings began on September 26 and senators complained about them.

Human Events quoted Escobar at length in three issues. On September 3, it quoted him as having said on August 12 that Panama would take "a course of violence" if the Senate rejected the treaties. A week later, it said he had given the "green light" to violence intended to force the United States to give up its bases before the December 31, 1999, transfer date. Human Events reported he made this clear at another point in the August 12 speech when he said he agreed with "theories" that "we can get more, much more, through confrontation." He continued: "When one wants confrontation, one puts his knapsack on his back, his bomb at the waist and goes to stage confrontations."

Finally, on September 17 it quoted Escobar as saying at an August 24 press conference that the neutrality treaty did not give the United States the right to decide "when neutrality is violated" and to act on that judgment, nor any "rights to intervene in Panama." That statement may have reflected no more than the intense Panamanian sensitivity to the word "intervene." But it sounded to Human Events like an assertion that the United States' " 'right' to guarantee the canal's neutrality means nothing at all." A separate story, also based on that press conference, said Escobar "recently told newsmen in Panama that U.S. warships would not have the right to pass through the canal during wartime on a preferential basis." He contended that the United States had sought such a right in treaty negotiations to pacify the Pentagon, but that the treaty's language of "expeditious passage" did not mean U.S. ships could go to the head of the line. He did not explain what it did mean, but said the incorrect United States version was offered because "They have to sell their merchandise."

Other organizations employed traditional political approaches, too. One of the New Right organizations, the Conservative Caucus, was different from its allies because it did more than raise and spend money. It had chapters and members. It organized public meetings around the country to spur opposition. Its national chairman, Governor Meldrim Thomson of New Hampshire, went before the American Legion convention on August 24 to tell the veterans that the Canal treaties posed a critical question about the nation's future: "Will America continue her flight from greatness or will we, in the spirit of our Founding Fathers, draw the line of reckoning at the Big Ditch and there stand firm against the rising tide of communism in the Caribbean?" The caucus held its own protest rally in Washington on the evening of the signing ceremony, with members carrying umbrellas to mock Carter as the equivalent of Britain's pre–World War II prime minister, Neville Chamberlain. At that September 7 rally, held near the site of the signing ceremony at the Pan American Union and timed to coincide with the signing, Phillips told about 150 followers, "President Carter is a human rights hypocrite for collaborating with the present regime in Panama." But when Phillips led his group toward Lafayette Park across from the White House, they discovered the area was already occupied by a much larger, leftist demonstration protesting United States "imperialism" and Carter's dining with dictators.

The Conservative Caucus held rallies in many states in October, though its newsletter, while boasting of 300,000 members, printed a headline that read, "Hundreds Attend Rallies around the Nation." It also sent nearly 500 copies of radio and television ads, with excerpts of Reagan's September 8 Senate testimony, to stations around the country. But it did not buy broadcast time, instead asking stations to run the ads as a "public service." It never claimed they were widely aired. By the time the Senate had approved the treaties, the caucus said it had held fifty-three statewide training sessions on how to fight ratification at the congressional district level.

The John Birch Society, widely labeled extremist in its heyday in the 1960s because its founder, Robert Welch, labeled President Eisenhower a communist, had lost influence and become a pariah to the rest of the Right by the seventies, thanks largely to the efforts of William F. Buckley Jr. But it was still around and involved, stressing a communist threat to the Canal, even conducting a summer camp in Nevada to recruit young members and educate them against "the Communist way," which included the Canal treaties. Its *Review of the News* stated, "As Bunker and Linowitz reached the final stages of their deal with the repressive Marxist dictatorship of General Omar Torrijos, an agreement calling for U.S. abandonment of the Panama Canal and Canal Zone, high-level agents of the Soviet Union had already moved into Panama in expectation of filling the vacuum." It sold bumper stickers saying, "Mr. President: A Panama Sellout Might Lead to Impeachment!" at two for a dollar. And it collected signatures on petitions. At the North Carolina State Fair the society collected 240 petitions with a total of 1,189 signatures, calling on Senator Robert Morgan to "take appropriate measures to retain U.S. sovereignty over the Panama Canal."

Other groups were active, too. Young Americans for Freedom (YAF), founded by Buckley in 1960, sold buttons at its convention (where Reagan

Howard Phillips addresses a Save Our Canal rally in Atlanta, March 1978.
(Conservative Caucus)

announced his opposition to the treaties) referring to Carter's hometown in
Georgia and urging, "Give 'Em Plains, Not Our Canal" and collected 35,000
signatures on petitions against the treaties. And together with the College
Young Republicans (and with $383 from the American Conservative Union),
YAF hired an airplane to circle the University of Tennessee's football stadium
on November 5. It was Homecoming Day, and 82,573 fans were gathered to
watch Tennessee beat Memphis State, 27 to 14. They also saw the plane and
its banner, which read, "KEEP OUR CANAL—WRITE SEN BAKER—ACU." They also
passed out 2,000 postcards at the game for people to send to Baker, urging
him to vote against the treaties.

Under Crane's leadership, the ACU played the biggest visible part in the
Right's anti-Canal effort. It had begun focusing on Baker earlier, with an ad
in the *Nashville Tennessean* proclaiming, "If you are concerned about the giveaway of the Panama Canal (and you should be), then don't delay making your

opinion known to Senator Howard Baker." In the next three days, Baker received 3,600 letters, almost all opposing the treaty. The ACU's Florida members heard from Senator Helms, who told them on September 11 that Baker "is squirming like a worm on a hot brick." Crane told the same meeting, "Howard has been kind of teetering on the brink. We want to make sure that Howard gets religion."

The ACU produced the single biggest innovation of the treaty fight—the infomercial. Annoying but effective paid television programs touting products—diets, skin creams, exercise equipment, hair restorers, and so forth—did not come into vogue until 1984, when the Federal Communications Commission ended limits on how much commercial time a station could show. Political campaign infomercials that seemed like public affairs discussions—as distinguished from speeches, or "telethons" that resembled variety shows with appeals for money—did not start appearing until the 1990s, when Ross Perot used them.

The organization began airing a half-hour television program on October 29. The program opened with Crane sitting on the edge of a desk, saying, "This may be the most important TV program you have ever watched." He warned that Carter and the Senate "are preparing to ignore your expressed wishes" by giving "away the American Canal at the Isthmus of Panama." The program showed film and animation of the Canal in operation as Crane described it as an "engineering marvel" and told of the lives lost in building it. Crane introduced the other speakers, and after each of them he urged the audience to write their senators and to pledge at least ten dollars to the ACU for its fight to save the Canal.

Next, Jesse Helms accused the administration of trying to blackmail Americans by warning of the threat of sabotage. He denounced the State Department, asking, "How many times have we seen these people waver and buckle, and apologize to those who would destroy freedom in the world?" Then the retired Canal Zone judge, Guthrie Crowe, told the audience, "The United States owns the Canal and the 647 square mile Canal Zone as much as it owns Louisiana, Manhattan, Alaska or Texas." He contended the 1903 treaty meant "absolute U.S. Sovereignty" and "forever." Senator Jake Garn of Utah warned that once sovereignty was conceded, Panama was likely to kick the United States out regardless of the provisions of the treaties.

Then Major General J. Milnor Roberts, executive director of the Reserve Officers Association, warned against the neutrality treaty, saying it would

Representative Philip Crane, chairman of the American Conservative Union, arguing against the treaties on the ACU's television infomercial (American Conservative Union/Center for Print and Broadcast Media)

"guarantee peaceful passage for all ships—including ships of any enemy and its allies in time of war. This means that Communist troops and supplies could be shipped right under our nose in order to kill American troops." Phelps Jones, director of National Security and Foreign Affairs for the Veterans of Foreign Wars, agreed, warning that communists supported the treaties so they could gain "influence, if not full control of this vital international waterway." As Torrijos's face filled the screen, Paul Laxalt said that "privately, many Latin-American leaders fear turning over the Canal—and their own shipping security—to anyone with strong ties to Fidel Castro." Thurmond warned that giving up the Canal would mean higher tolls and, consequently, higher prices for American consumers. Crane closed by quoting David McCullough, author of *A Path between the Seas*, as if he opposed the treaties, although McCullough had testified in favor of them.

The program was shown 209 times, with a total audience estimated at 9 million. Aside from the letters to senators, the ACU itself heard from 58,000 people. Ninety percent of those names were new to the organization and were added to its mailing list. The program also netted the organization $245,000 after paying production costs and buying air time.

The Right's primary weapon was the mail. Although George McGovern's 1972 campaign had shown the power of direct mail in politics, this was a huge campaign on a particular political issue, not a candidate. The Right did not defeat the treaties, but it got a message out. The Conservative Caucus sent out 3 million pieces of mail. The National Conservative Political Action Committee (NCPAC) sent out about 500,000. Two lesser-known organizations, the American Security Council and the Council on Inter-American Security, each sent out 2 million letters. So did the American Conservative Union. They resonated more than some bigger campaigns (like a mailing of 20 million letters attacking pornography that Viguerie put out a few years earlier) because this time there was to be a vote on particular measure, and soon. Recipients, Viguerie said in 2007, "could understand clearly how they could help make a difference."

One of the most imaginative ideas came from Phillips (mailed out by Viguerie), a mailing of two pennies and a form letter to members, urging them to send a penny to each of their senators to reenact the slogan used against revolutionary France and again when the Barbary Pirates harassed U.S. shipping: "Millions for Defense, Not One Cent for Tribute!" The Phillips letter also made a desperate appeal for money, saying, "We are almost overdrawn at our bank."

That was a typical approach—a plea for funds combined with an appeal to write to senators. The American Conservative Union sent members requests for money accompanied by postcards addressed to Baker, demanding that he vote no and "inform me of your view." By January 1978, Baker's office had received 37,000 postcards and letters. The John Birch Society had its members send lawmakers copies of the *Birch Log*, another of its publications, warning of "the red government of Panama" and denouncing Ambassador Bunker as "one of the losers who arranged our defeat in Vietnam." A NCPAC mailing marked "urgent" asked recipients to "send a $5 or $10 contribution today to help defeat liberal senators who want to give our Panama Canal away." It asked, "What's next on the liberals' agenda? Do we have to give Alaska back to Russia and pay them at the same time?"

Another Phillips mailing sent out draft letters intended for several senators who voted for the neutrality treaty in March 1978—Bob Packwood of Oregon, Dennis DeConcini of Arizona, Edward W. Brooke of Massachusetts, Paul Hatfield of Montana, Sam Nunn of Georgia, John Heinz of Pennsylvania, and Dick Clark of Iowa. It warned, "So long as I live, I will remember the politicians who voted to surrender American interests in Panama to a pro-Castro dictator. Whenever you may again be a candidate for office, I will do all I can to defeat you." But it gave them a chance for redemption:

> If you will vote against the Panama Canal surrender on Round Two, the vote on the main treaty, and if the treaty is thereby defeated, I will take your name off my Personal Dishonor Roll and wipe the slate clean. Frankly, Senator, I care more about my country than I do about you or your political career. I will hold no grudge for your first vote, if you play a pivotal role now in letting America keep our canal.

Some of those on the mailing lists dutifully forwarded the postcards or letters the conservative groups had sent them. Others argued the case against the treaties themselves, in varying proportions of emotion and reason. Many senatorial correspondents were simply abusive, with the words "treason" and "traitor" common. No one calculated the overall postal load at Capitol Hill, but one senator, John Culver of Iowa, received 4,985 letters and postcards in a single week in February 1978, three months after he had announced his support of the treaties.

William Rusher, publisher of *National Review*, wrote a few years later that

> the largest net benefit to any of the warring parties, as a result of the whole affair, was undoubtedly the massive accretion of new names acquired by conservative mailing-list entrepreneurs like Richard Viguerie. Viguerie himself estimates that the campaign to petition the Senate not to ratify the treaties yielded the names and addresses of some half million additional voters who could later be approached on behalf of related conservative causes (e.g., Reagan's 1980 presidential campaign). Of such defeats are brighter tomorrows born.

But there was more to it than that. Yes, the names were buttons for Viguerie or someone else to push in a future direct-mail campaign—although in fact Canal donors did not turn out to be particularly generous on other causes. More immediately, though, they were also Americans ready to involve themselves in politics then and there and become active in the 1978 and 1980 elections.

Their names had not been unearthed as a result of highly selective data mining of the sort the Republican National Committee used in 2004—finding potential votes among stay-at-home mothers in West Virginia or subscribers to car magazines in Ohio. Viguerie said he relied mostly on people who had already given money to one of his other causes. The mailings themselves energized people drawn from those various interest groups, such as foes of gun control or supporters of George Wallace. While people in one of those camps might not have been willing to get active on behalf of another, the mailings over the Canal brought the conservative grass roots together, raised enough money to pay for more mailings, and built the movement.

10

For all their unity and mastery of techniques, the treaty's opponents did not have one weapon they hoped for and the Carter administration feared: the energetic leadership of Ronald Reagan. Reagan's own words had given them reason to expect that sort of role. Before his August 1977 meeting with Ambassadors Sol Linowitz and Ellsworth Bunker, Reagan had told CBS News on August 16, "If nothing is contained in those specifics of the treaty to alter my feeling about giving away the canal, and it is very unlikely that there is, I am going to do everything I can to persuade people that they should make their feelings known to their congressmen and senators about not ratifying the treaty." He used the "do everything I can" line again a week later in an interview with the *New York Times*. He made a similar promise later, in a November 5 fund-raising letter for his political action committee, Citizens for the Republic, when he said, "Without equivocation, I am going to do everything I can to win this fight and keep the canal."

But Reagan, who had made keeping the Canal a central political issue in 1976, was only a supporting player when the issue was decided. He still opposed the treaties, and he said so, but he avoided the most dramatic and public events staged by the opposition. And perhaps even more important, when he did speak, he avoided the blunt, emotional language of 1976. He did not talk about a "tin-horn dictator." And "rights of sovereignty" could not stir emotions the way "tell the general we bought it, we paid for it, we built it and we intend to keep it" could.

The shift in tone was occasionally noted, especially among conservatives who thought Reagan was not doing enough. But at the time it went unexplained. Pete Hannaford, the longtime Reagan aide who was there for his August 25 meeting with Ambassadors Linowitz and Bunker in New York, said in a 2006 interview that there was a simple reason for Reagan's restraint. After the diplomats left, Hannaford said in 2006, Reagan asked, "What if they are right?" That question, Hannaford said, "led to the decision for Reagan not to be in the forefront of the issue." He explained, "Both Reagans liked Linowitz a lot. It's not that he changed their minds but they took him seriously."

Human Events may have caught a whiff of that reserve even when it reported Reagan's enlisting in the opposition. "With Reagan now in the thick of the battle," it wrote, opponents will be in a strong position—"assuming he stays there."

The Denver appearance on January 20, 1978, was the only time between the signing of the treaties and their ratification that Reagan joined the organized opposition before the public. He skipped the signing day rally at the Capitol. He could not find time to tape an appearance on the single most widely seen opposition effort, the American Conservative Union's television program. He did make three other appearances, but at settings where cheers and applause would not have been appropriate.

He did not testify before either the Senate Foreign Relations Committee or the Armed Services Committee, which formally considered the pacts. At each he would have faced hostile questioning from supporters of the treaties. Instead, on September 8, 1977, the day after the pacts were signed by Carter and Torrijos, he appeared before Senator James Allen, a conservative Alabama Democrat, and his Judiciary Subcommittee on the Separation of Powers, where no one supported the treaties. All four senators present (including Jesse Helms, who was not a member of the subcommittee) praised Reagan and asked softball questions.

Reagan warned the subcommittee that Panama could order the United States to leave as soon as the treaties were approved because of its newly clarified sovereign power. He contended that since the Canal had never been sabotaged in World War II, it was not vulnerable now. He predicted, "There is a very grave danger that the world will not see this as a magnanimous gesture. It will see it—and with some justification—as, once again, the United States faced with the possibility of confrontation, backing away." Frank Moore, Carter's chief congressional lobbyist, shrewdly caught the tone when he reported to his boss that Reagan "was the star attraction before the Allen Subcommittee on Separation of Powers. Reagan attacked the treaty but not with the vigor of his '76 effort, which is more evidence that the early attention to Reagan may have paid off."

That same afternoon Reagan went to the National Press Club to discuss foreign policy more generally, offering the Canal treaties as representative of the weakness he said President Carter displayed. "What guarantee do we have that Panama will even honor the treaty?" he asked. "After all, the Panamanians know as well as the rest of the world that it was under the guise of détente that we let the Soviet Union get away with the biggest military buildup in history, and it was under the guise of the Paris Peace Accords that we let the North Vietnamese get away with literal murder. Why, then, should a Panamanian regime feel any more bound by its promises to us?"

He did face questioning, firm but friendly, four months later. On January 13, 1978, he debated the issue on public television with William F. Buckley Jr. Visiting Panama in October 1976, Buckley had gauged Panamanian resentment and decided that Torrijos could be trusted. He decided to support a turnover of the Canal. In the debate, Reagan asserted, "The world would see it as, once again, Uncle Sam put his tail between his legs and crept away rather than face trouble." Buckley said, "We need the Panama Canal with a people who are residents of the Panama Canal, who understand they are joined with us in a common enterprise" and see that "we are big enough to grant little people what we ourselves fought for 200 years ago." The two friends were plainly enjoying themselves. At one point Reagan wondered why his arguments had not made Buckley see the light and cross the room to his side. "The force of my illumination would blind you," Buckley cheerfully replied. The illumination was dimmed by the scheduling; on most public television stations the debate ran opposite the Super Bowl.

The good humor lasted long after that evening in Columbia, South Carolina. Buckley recalled that the next time he went to dinner at Reagan's house in Pacific Palisades, a few months later, his host had decorated the driveway with three cardboard signs with messages written in crayon, recalling his blunter language of 1976: "WE BUILT IT!" Then, "WE PAID FOR IT!" and, on the front door, "AND IT'S OURS!" But this time he meant his house.

Reagan also accepted an offer from CBS to speak on national television in response to Carter's fireside chat of February 1. On February 7, Reagan explained that giving up the Canal might lead to the loss "of our own freedom."

He said Carter's claim that he was following three past presidents was false because Carter had gone further and abandoned "rights of sovereignty," which his predecessors had not. (In fact, both the 1967 treaty under Johnson, and the Kissinger-Tack principles, approved by Nixon and Ford, clearly involved giving up the Canal and any U.S. right to act as a sovereign power in the Zone.)

Otherwise, Reagan's opposition was conveyed mainly in his syndicated radio broadcasts and newspaper columns, although on one occasion he called an uncommitted senator, Sam Nunn of Georgia, to try to talk him into opposing the treaties. His five-minute daily commentaries had a good number of broadcast outlets, and an audience estimated at 20 million listeners a week, but they never stirred national notice.

In those broadcasts, he criticized the treaties from time to time. Once he claimed that the United States had no role in the revolution that created Panama and he later suggested, "You know, giving up the canal itself might be a better deal if we could throw in the State Department." He said treaty support by the Joint Chiefs of Staff should be disregarded because they "are bound by the military code to support the policy of the Commander-in-Chief, the President," and that more attention should be paid to retired officers, who were not so constrained and could speak sharply in opposition.

His King Features Syndicate columns, like his broadcasts, frequently quoted opinions he agreed with. The most dramatic was a March 14, 1978, column citing General Daniel Graham, the former head of the Defense Intelligence Agency. Using language that he would not use on his own, Reagan quoted Graham as saying, "Torrijos and his Guardia Nacional cohorts constitute a mob of racketeers involved in the drug trade, prostitution, gambling and shakedowns that can only be compared to the Mafia." On January 17, he warned, "Given the volatility of Panamanian politics through the years and the designs that Fidel Castro & Friends have on the area, who is to say that in six months, a year, two years, after the treaties were ratified, we would not be told one day to pack up and 'git'; that the canal was being nationalized."

A careful reading of those transcripts and columns suggests that Reagan, while abiding by a political decision not to be the leader of the treaty opposition, and concerned that Linowitz and Bunker might be right about the dangers of rejection, chafed at the role he had chosen. He seemed uncomfortable with staying largely on the sidelines when a treaty he feared would lead other countries to take advantage of the United States went forward.

An all-out Reagan effort might have defeated the treaties. But his friend Buckley thought that would have cost him the presidency. Buckley wrote in 1983, "I think, ironically, that Reagan would not have been nominated if he had favored the Panama Canal Treaty, and that he wouldn't have been elected if it hadn't passed. He'd have lost the conservatives if he had backed the treaty, and lost the election if we'd subsequently faced, in Panama, insurrection, as in my opinion we would have."

"WHY NOW? AND WHY ME?"

HOWARD BAKER AND THE TREATIES

Howard Baker's initial reaction when President Carter called him in August 1977 to say that the Panama Canal treaties were almost complete was a mixture of surprise and annoyance. Even though Ambassadors Sol Linowitz and Ellsworth Bunker had briefed him in June, the issue had languished for years, and so he was not prepared for the call from the White House, asking for his support. Baker recalled in a 2005 interview, "I wish he hadn't asked. It was an unwelcome—in my own mind—an unwelcome challenge." At the time, he thought, "This had been kicking around for years, and why now? And why me?"

Baker had been encouraging to Linowitz and Bunker, but he did not look forward to a Senate fight over the issue that had divided his party in 1976. But, he said in 2005, "Here the President of the United States was addressing me as leader of the Republicans in the Senate. That's why I had to take it seriously." He would not give Carter the promise of support the president sought. So Carter asked him if that meant he would oppose the treaties. Baker said he did not mean that either, but that he meant to study the issue carefully and thoroughly. (Carter's note on the conversation was more upbeat; he wrote that Baker "favors Treaty; needs details.") Three weeks later, Baker told a Kiwanis Club luncheon in Maryville, Tennessee, that he had told the president, "I had decided not to decide what my view on those treaties would be for the time being." He said he first wanted the Foreign Relations Committee to examine the treaties, taking "a methodical, logical, non-emotional approach to a highly volatile, explosive issue."

Howard Henry Baker Jr. took that call from Carter at his home in Huntsville, the seat of Scott County, Tennessee, nestled close to the Kentucky state line. His family had deep roots in the area. His father, an attorney, had been a congressman and was succeeded at death by the younger Baker's stepmother. Two of his great-grandfathers had served as majors in the Union army in the Civil War when much of East Tennessee rejected the state's decision to secede. After the war, the region stayed with the Republican Party, while the rest of the state was solidly Democratic.

As a teenager, Baker developed a lifelong hobby of photography, and in later years he was often seen on public occasions with a camera dangling from his neck. He left Huntsville for military school, and when he graduated at age eighteen in 1943, he entered the Navy's V-12 officer training program. After the war he studied law at the University of Tennessee in Knoxville, fifty-five miles southeast of Huntsville. On graduation, he joined his father's law office as a junior partner. He developed a strong reputation as a defense attorney; none of his sixty-three clients in murder cases was ever sentenced to death. He also ran his father's winning campaign for the House in 1950, and the next year married Joy Dirksen, the daughter of Everett Dirksen, the Republican senator from Illinois.

His father died in 1964, but Baker did not seek his seat in the House. Instead he ran for the Senate that year. The Republican Party had been growing stronger in Tennessee, especially in presidential years. But in 1964 Barry Goldwater's insistence that the Tennessee Valley Authority should be sold to private industry was too much of a burden for a fellow Republican to overcome. Baker lost to Congressman Ross Bass in a race to fill the last two years of Estes Kefauver's term, open after Kefauver's death in 1963. But in 1966, after the Democrats split between Bass and former governor Frank Clement and narrowly chose Clement, Baker ran a strong campaign for the full term, openly appealed for black votes, and won a landslide victory, the first Republican ever elected to the Senate by the voters of Tennessee.

When Baker arrived in the Senate in 1967, Dirksen was the Republican leader. They clashed that spring over Dirksen's effort to undo Supreme Court rulings that legislative and congressional districts had to be nearly equal in size. The first of those cases had arisen in Tennessee, and Baker strongly supported them as necessary for the Republican Party's growth. Baker said in a 1996 interview that he had "gone from adulation to opposition in one fell swoop," as he joined with Senator Edward M. Kennedy of Massachusetts in working through the summer to defeat Dirksen and other old-guard senators. That effort brought him important attention in Washington; David Broder of the *Washington Post* wrote, "Defeating bad legislation, as Kennedy and Baker have done, is every bit as difficult as passing a good bill, but not nearly so long remembered."

But what brought Baker to national attention was neither that effort nor serious work on environmental legislation and revenue sharing—unrestricted federal aid to states and localities. It was the Senate Watergate hearings, a television spectacle that riveted the country in 1973. Senator Sam Ervin of North Carolina chaired the special committee doing the investigation and worked well with Baker, who was the committee's Republican leader. Ervin gave Baker the power to issue subpoenas, a rare privilege for the minority on any Senate committee. Baker had believed Nixon when he said he had not been involved in the break-in or the cover-up, but he grew skeptical as time passed. Ervin's folksiness made him a national icon, but Baker's question, "What did the President know and when did he know it?"—first asked of former White House counsel John W. Dean III on June 28—crystallized the issue before the committee, the special prosecutor, and the House Judiciary Committee's impeachment proceedings over the next fourteen months.

Baker thought about running for president in 1976 if Ford did not. Then he hoped for the vice presidential nomination Ford gave to Bob Dole. He had also run unsuccessfully to succeed Dirksen as Republican leader after Dirksen died in 1969. Hugh Scott of Pennsylvania defeated him, and did so again in 1971. But when Scott retired after 1976, Baker finally won. The 19 to 18 margin over Robert Griffin of Michigan brought Baker the position that in a few months would provide him, like it or not, a pivotal role on the Canal issue.

Dozens of senators see themselves as potential presidents, but Baker was also seen that way by much of the Washington press corps. He was viewed generally as a conservative, though some conservatives had their doubts. His 1976 voting record was measured at 57 percent right by the American Conservative Union. That record, along with Watergate and his border state background, made him the potential opponent the Carter White House feared most.

Senator Baker's interest in running for president put him in a nearly unique position politically as he faced the Canal treaties. His colleagues might worry about how their votes would affect their chances of reelection to the Senate. But he also had to consider how they would affect his chances of winning the Republican presidential nomination. The only other Republican senator thinking of running in 1980 was Bob Dole; early on, the Kansan made it clear that "looking down the road" to the 1980 Republican contest, as he put it to the *New York Times*'s Joseph Lelyveld, dictated his stance, even though he did not feel intensely about the issue. "Anyone who thinks he's going to take this issue away from Ronald Reagan is kidding himself," Dole said. "Reagan found it, he built it, and he's going to keep it. But one thing he doesn't have is a vote in the Senate. If we're going to make a role for ourself, it'll be on the floor of the Senate."

While Baker was telling reporters and constituents of his decision not to decide until he knew all he could about the treaties, he solicited the views of his staff on what they thought the consequences of his decision would be. Ron McMahan, his longtime press secretary, told him he would lose some votes in Tennessee but could still win reelection in 1978 by a "safe margin" if he voted for the treaty, but that choice would diminish chances of either nomination or election as president. Therefore, McMahan wrote, "The prospects are that Baker will have to vote against the treaty." Rob Mosbacher, a legislative assistant, wrote that, in political terms, "There is really only one question to be answered; Could you win the nomination after supporting ratification of the treaty, if you were to run?" He said that even though supporting the treaty would not help win it, Baker should do so anyway. Howard Liebengood, Baker's top legislative aide, wrote, "The issue is one of confrontation between statesmanship and politics, and of a magnitude that lends a chilling quality to the 'Would you rather be right than President?' cliché."

Jim Cannon, a former aide to Vice President Rockefeller and President Ford whom Baker hired in the minority leader's office to pave the way for a presidential run, simply told him that if he voted for the treaties, the Republican Party would not nominate him for president. He and Baker both recalled Baker's snapping, "So be it." In a 2005 interview with the author, Baker recalled, apologetically, "It sounds too grand by half, but in effect what I said was, look, you know, if I'm going to be serious about this thing, I can't decide it on the basis of political components. It's an important issue and I will think about it."

When the Foreign Relations Committee began its hearings on September 26, Baker recalled his decision not to decide. But he questioned administration witnesses sharply over Escobar's interpretations of the treaties' language about the right of the United States to take action to keep the Canal open and neutral and to get its ships to the head of the line for passage through the Canal in emergencies. He asked Linowitz if he could get Panama to officially repudiate Escobar's statements. Linowitz replied, "We will try," and Baker responded, "Unless we can have a clear understanding that these statements are not the interpretation placed on these treaties by the Panamanians the chances for advice and consent are greatly diminished."

The concern over Escobar's language was widespread in the Senate, even among some whose support for the treaties was not much in question. So, on October 11, Carter invited thirteen senators to the White House to discuss the situation. Baker later told reporters that the discussions were "frank and candid" and that Carter knew "that the treaties are in trouble." He also said that it appeared Carter was trying to get Torrijos to agree to clarifying language. That was what Carter had in mind, and on October 14 Torrijos stopped in Washington on his way home from a European trip. After several hours of negotiation, both between Carter and Torrijos and among aides, a "statement of understanding" was issued at the White House. It nailed down the "expeditious passage" language, saying that meant American warships could "go to the head of the line of vessels in order to transit the canal rapidly." And it said that each nation had the right "to act against any aggression or threat directed against the Canal or the peaceful transit of vessels through the Canal." But, to reassure Panama a few days before that country's October 23 plebiscite on the pacts, it said that power did not create "a right of intervention of the United States in the internal affairs of Panama."

The statement was welcomed by Baker and Byrd, although Baker had warned in advance that more than a joint statement might be needed. And while both Carter and Torrijos acknowledged the agreement, it was not signed by either of them. Linowitz told the senators it was unsigned because it added nothing. The more important reason was that Torrijos had been reluctant to sign it before his country's referendum on the treaties.

After the September 26 session, Baker hardly ever attended the Foreign Relations Committee hearings, relying on Cran Montgomery, his foreign policy aide, to stay and keep him up to date on what was going on. But he invented another way of informing himself on the issue. He hired two consultants, one on each side, to debate the treaties as he presided, like a judge in a moot court competition, reading briefs and then challenging arguments. The pro-treaty voice was William D. Rogers, a Democrat who had been assistant secretary of state for Latin America and then undersecretary under

Ford and Kissinger. Rogers had visited Torrijos along with Bill Clements and General George Brown in 1975 when they promised to make a deal after the 1976 election. The anti-treaty expert was Roger W. Fontaine, director of Latin American studies at Georgetown University's Center for Strategic and International Studies. Fontaine had come to the attention of Baker's staff with an August op-ed piece in the *Wall Street Journal*. He argued that the rationales for the treaties were false because sabotage would not be in Panama's interest, that a full-blown insurgency was not in prospect, and that world opinion was unlikely to see the United States as benevolent. "This treaty might just as well reinforce the notion that America is acting, not from generosity, but from weakness," he wrote.

Fontaine admired the way Baker sought information. In a 1995 interview, he said of Baker: "He certainly was never satisfied with a vague response or generalities; he wanted to know precisely what the problem was, what the issue was, what do the Panamanians say, what the Panamanian landscape was, what's Torrijos like, that sort of thing. And it could cover almost anything, not just the technical aspects of the treaties but the whole situation." Rogers saw Baker's approach the same way, explaining in a 1993 interview, "He wanted to understand in all their complexity each one of the issues involved in the Panama Canal treaties, and there were a very large number. They ranged all the way from financial relationships; the capacity of the Panamanians to undertake to manage the canal after the year 2000; lands and buildings that were going to be turned over by the United States when it evacuated the Canal Zone; jurisdictional, technical, legal issues of international law."

Baker also took one very political step, commissioning a poll of Tennessee voters. That survey, conducted from December 10 to 18, showed that 45 percent of Tennesseans opposed the treaty and 23 percent favored it. Another 32 percent had no opinion, which led the pollster, Charlie Roll, to say the Canal was "somewhat less than a burning issue on a universal basis." But the survey also showed—as did some national polls at the time—that the addition of such "guarantees" as U.S. ships going to the head of the line waiting to enter the Canal and U.S. defense of the Canal could turn initial opposition into support, by a 58 to 34 percent margin among Tennesseans. Cannon analyzed the findings in a New Year's Day, 1978, memo, saying that the "careful political course" would be to oppose the treaties. He warned that "conservatives would be resentful and have long memories," and might endanger his position as leader if he could carry only a few Republicans with him to support ratification. On the other hand, Cannon wrote, "For you to lead the fight for 'guarantees' will tend to increase perception of Baker as a leader with courage, knowledge about foreign policy and defense, and the kind of competence now lacking in the White House."

Baker expressed annoyance with the administration's constant solicitude toward Panama's feelings and its efforts to forestall any reservations or amendments. "I really get a little impatient with these statements that I hear from time to time that the Panamanians won't stand for any change in the treaty," he told the *Christian Science Monitor* in late October. "Why are we so worried about the Panamanians? Nobody's worried about our attitude."

In December, Baker tasked Rogers and Fontaine to show how the treaties could be improved enough to make them acceptable. The key was to give the October 14 Carter-Torrijos statement a more formal status. Rogers thought a statement of understanding would do; Fontaine said an amendment would be required. Baker's aides, Cran Montgomery and Howard Liebengood, agreed with Fontaine. They said a formal amendment would carry more weight politically, taking the language of the statement of understanding on defending the Canal and U.S. warships going to the head of the line in emergencies.

There was one more thing to do before taking a position. Baker had decided early on that he had to go to Panama to see the situation and the players for himself, and, most of all, to see if Torrijos would be able to live with the changes Baker considered essential if the treaties were to be approved.

12

For several months after the treaties were agreed on, senators traveled to Panama to marvel at the Canal, talk to Americans and Panamanians, and, in varying degrees, learn about the issue or reinforce their existing opinions. About half the members of the Senate made the trip from August 1977 through January 1978. At one point the government-controlled newspaper *Critica*'s political columnist wrote that his countrymen were feeling like inhabitants of a zoo.

The first posttreaty trip was taken by Senators Strom Thurmond of South Carolina, Jesse Helms of North Carolina, and Orrin Hatch of Utah. Before leaving on August 18, Thurmond told reporters that the more he talked to State Department officials about the treaties, "the more I am convinced that the United States must retain sovereignty over the canal." After a twenty-hour visit that included talks with American diplomats and Canal Zone workers, but no meeting with Panama's president, Omar Torrijos, whom most senators wanted to size up, Thurmond held a news conference to report his findings. He stated, "It would be a mistake for the United States to ratify those treaties." Helms said a few weeks later that his visit had shown him that Panamanians were not concerned about who ran the Canal: "The Panamanian citizens probably couldn't care as much about this thing as our citizens do."

Just after their return, Thurmond and Helms appeared on the August 21 broadcast of NBC's *Meet the Press*. Helms told the NBC audience the threat of sabotage was being encouraged "by our own State Department." Moreover, he said, because there had been no sabotage in World War II, "I think this is a red herring." Both dismissed the arguments of the Joint Chiefs of Staff. Thurmond commented, "Any military man today, if he expresses himself, that is not in accord with the policy of the administration, will have his career ruined. He might as well retire."

Although they were hardly the only naysayers among the traveling senators—Barry Goldwater was another—it was more typical for senators to come away more supportive of the pacts than when they arrived, and often impressed with Torrijos. The first major trip of that sort was led by Senator Robert C. Byrd, who had none of the singular political problems that faced Howard Baker. He was not running for president. West Virginia's Republicans had not even run a candidate against him in 1976. He had joined one of Thurmond's earlier resolutions opposing transfer. But as majority leader he could reasonably be expected to support the president from his own party.

Byrd was an intensely self-educated poor boy from mining country who completed an American University law degree while studying nights even though he had never earned an undergraduate diploma. And as a newly elected majority leader with a record as a parliamentarian rather than a lawmaker, he did not want to lose if he decided to back the treaties. As he wrote in his autobiography, Senate adoption of the treaties with his support would mean "that I had surmounted my 'technician' image as a leader who merely 'made the Senate trains run on time,' a Washington cliché that rankled me most."

His preparation included talks with Carter and with Zbigniew Brzezinski, the president's national security adviser. On November 7, just before his trip, Byrd lunched with Brzezinski. The next day, Brzezinski wrote him to address the concerns Byrd had raised. He told him that if the Madden or Gatun dam was destroyed, the Canal would be idled for at least two years, adding, "The 51 mile length of the Canal, the two dams, the six locks, the Gaillard Cut, and the nineteenth century hydraulic technology which opens and closes the locks—all make the Canal exceedingly vulnerable. If there were a hostile environment, it would be very costly in terms of manpower to protect the Canal against sabotage, and there is no guarantee that the Canal could be kept open." Brzezinski also sought to assure Byrd that Panama had no relations with the Soviet Union, and that while it had diplomatic relations with Cuba, so did eleven other Latin countries, and those ties were of no concern.

Byrd led six other Democratic senators as a delegation that arrived on November 9. Only one of them, Spark Matsunaga of Hawaii, had already declared in favor of the treaties. Byrd seemed to be looking for a way to do so. Before leaving, he said he had seen "some shifting of opinion" in the Senate in favor of them. He spoke at an embassy dinner the night the delegation arrived, telling Panamanian officials, businessmen, and educators that "any Senator voting for these treaties will pay a high political price. He will gain absolutely nothing by doing so. Therefore, you have to be tolerant and patient in bringing people around to understanding these problems and to taking this difficult step."

The delegation spent the next day with Torrijos, flying to an Indian community in the San Blas Islands where local leaders chewed the dictator out over their problems—a scene senators could easily relate to—and then to Los Santos, a cattle-ranching provincial capital. In both places, Torrijos walked among the people without bodyguards, softening his dictator's image.

The group questioned Torrijos on two plane rides and then for three hours at his Pacific seaside villa, Farallon. Ambassador Jorden wrote, "They grilled the general unmercifully," bluntly, and with "occasional rudeness." Torrijos had been told several times by the White House that the Byrd group was important, and he held his temper. Torrijos's account of the visit, transmitted to several Latin American presidents and to Carter, includes such exchanges as Howard Metzenbaum of Ohio commenting, "I must tell you in all frankness that neither I nor my constituents like dictatorships," and Torrijos replying, "I don't either." Metzenbaum also pressed him about the risk that after ratification, Soviet or Cuban influence would grow and those countries might take over the Canal. Torrijos replied that the risk of Soviet or Cuban influence was negligible—unless the treaties were rejected. In that case, he said, "I could not assure how long I could keep control of the forces from the inside and the outside."

Other senators, such as Paul Sarbanes of Maryland, pressed Torrijos over human rights issues such as exiling political opponents and summary proceedings without defense attorneys. The New Right opposition had been making an issue of these conditions in hopes of dislodging a liberal senator or two into the ranks of the opposition. Torrijos explained to Sarbanes those laws were no longer necessary and were being repealed. Metzenbaum then told an ABC News television crew the talks had been "somewhat reassuring." After a second meeting with Torrijos on November 12, Metzenbaum announced he would support the treaties.

Senator Robert Byrd and General Omar Torrijos meet Cuna Indians and discuss the Canal treaties, November 11, 1977. Senator Donald Riegle is in the foreground. (AP)

On November 11, the senators flew in helicopters over the Canal and then enjoyed a festive state dinner hosted by Panama's president, Demetrio ("Jimmy") Lakas, a Texas A&M graduate. Byrd, a first-rate country fiddle player, was persuaded to borrow a violin from the orchestra and played "Turkey in the Straw" and several more numbers. Then Lakas and Byrd swapped neckties, and Ambassador Jorden concluded the majority leader would back the treaties.

Whatever Jorden thought, Byrd still did not commit himself. But after Torrijos told a news conference after the last meeting that he would abolish the martial law provisions, Byrd said, "It was a positive step. I don't see that it can help but improve the atmosphere for ratification." And three weeks later, while not saying what he would do, he signaled support by predicting that the Senate would approve the treaties.

But even with Byrd's support now very likely, more was needed. As Byrd had told some State Department officials before the treaty was finalized,

"You're not going to get a treaty without me, and you're not going to get a treaty without Senator Baker. If you have both of us, you *might* get a treaty."

Baker had not taken a stand. Some journalists were scoffing at Baker's public posture. Cartoonists pictured him straddling the Canal. I recall quipping, but never writing, that he was getting his forefinger chapped from holding it to the wind—a line that John Lofton picked up and used in *Human Events*. Mary McGrory of the *Washington Star* described "poor, agonizing Baker" as "the Republican Hamlet of the ratification process."

However fair or unfair that was, Baker meant to go to Panama before taking a position. He had sent two aides, Howard Liebengood, his legislative assistant, and Bill Hildenbrand, secretary of the Republican minority, along with Byrd and the other Democrats. He got a thorough report on what they saw and heard. But he wanted to take the measure of Torrijos himself. So, after the Tennessee poll was in and the consultants had made their suggestions about where and how the treaties needed clarification, Baker flew to Panama on January 3, 1978.

He was accompanied by his pro- and anti-treaty consultants, William Rogers and Roger Fontaine, and a pair of Republican senators, the pro-treaty John Chafee of Rhode Island and the anti-treaty Jake Garn of Utah. Baker also brought several aides—Jim Cannon, his chief of staff; Ron McMahan, his press secretary; Cran Montgomery, his foreign policy adviser; and Howard Liebengood, his chief legislative assistant—and a few reporters. On the day he arrived, Baker met with Ambassador Jorden and embassy officials, asking for a sense of Torrijos. Jorden told him that Torrijos had become "testy and frustrated" at some questions senators had asked him. The senator told Jorden he believed "there is a real possibility that we can find some sort of common ground to agree on—but before we do that, we need to know how far Torrijos will go, will he be offended?" Jorden replied, "He appreciates candor; he will at least listen to the price."

As he had with Byrd's group, Torrijos took the Republicans among the people to show them he was accessible and responsive—not a brutal dictator. On a visit to the Atlantic Coast city of Colon on January 4, people complained to him about the $15 fee for registering their children in high school. Torrijos promptly ordered his education minister, part of the entourage, to eliminate it. When the minister said that would ruin his budget, Torrijos ordered it eliminated for students whose parents were unemployed and cut to $7.50 for others.

Baker grew impatient with the showmanship and cut short the tour (skipping a model farm) because he wanted to start talking. Torrijos agreed, and the party flew off in helicopters to Farallon. While reporters and staff waited outside, Baker talked to Torrijos in generalities. Then Torrijos took him upstairs without an interpreter, which Baker found odd, since he believed Torrijos spoke no English. In the 2005 interview, Baker recalled, "We mumbled around for a little while, both of us struggling with any semblance of language. And then finally, he said in understandable English, 'What does it take?' He said those words." Then Torrijos sent for an interpreter. Baker explained that the treaties would be defeated in the Senate as then written. But with certain amendments, he thought they could pass. He said he could support them if Torrijos could accept amendments on the right to defend the Canal and for U.S. ships to go to the head of the line in emergencies. Baker also raised the idea of the forty-year turnover period that Linowitz and Bunker had abandoned; that would mean that no sitting senator would expect to still be in office when the actual transfer occurred. Torrijos rejected the idea. Baker said Torrijos indicated agreement, or at least acceptance, of the concept of incorporating the October 14 statement's promises into the treaty. Baker pressed Torrijos repeatedly for a commitment that if those changes were adopted, Panama would agree to an altered treaty. Finally Torrijos told him he would be flexible, and Baker said that then he would try to get amendments passed.

They came out for a press conference that turned sticky. Baker had told American reporters the night before what he intended to tell Torrijos, and the first question was put to the general, asking if Baker had told him the treaties could not pass as they were. Taken by surprise, he said, "No, we did not go into that." Pursued on what Baker had told him, Torrijos conceded, "Well, he has his reservations," and stalked off. Baker then insisted he had told Torrijos that "the treaties, as they are presently written without amendment or change, have no chance of passing the Senate." But he also told reporters that with appropriate changes, he could support the pacts, his first public declaration on the issue.

The following day, January 5, Torrijos conferred with advisers about what Baker had told him, and *Critica* observed that the visiting senators had "reasonable objections." Meanwhile, the senators were confronted by the dark side of the government of Panama. Lieutenant Colonel Manuel Antonio Noriega, head of the National Guard's intelligence section, conducted a briefing on the

Canal's vulnerabilities and explained how U.S. forces alone could not protect the Canal. Montgomery, Fontaine, and Jorden all said the senators viewed it as a threat. In a 1992 interview Montgomery recounted that Baker's neck grew red as he listened to what seemed to mean the following: "If these treaties are not approved, this is what we can do to it and this is what we will do to it." When the presentation was finished, Noriega, who had saved Torrijos from an attempted coup against him in 1968, came up to Baker and said Torrijos had asked him to make the presentation. Baker snapped, "Tell the general I got the message."

The senators met Torrijos again on January 6, their last day in Panama. Again the conversation was "candid and friendly," Ambassador Jorden reported to the State Department. At a final press conference, Baker told reporters General Torrijos was

> a man dedicated to the future of the people of Panama, firm in matters of principle, but flexible in his appreciation of political realities. In that same spirit of directness which marked all our conversations, I again told Gen. Torrijos today that in my view the treaties cannot pass the Senate as they are. I told him that the people of the United States are deeply divided over the treaties. But I emphasized that with necessary additional guarantees, I believe the Panama Canal treaties could receive more than the necessary two-thirds majority in the Senate. My hope is that the Senate, in the constitutional process of debating and acting on these treaties, will so improve the present documents that the Panama Canal treaties will no longer be divisive in the States, and yet not repugnant to the people of Panama.

Baker had got ahead of himself. He had planned to announce his decision on television in Tennessee. But he could not leave the question hanging and spoke out at that last press conference. Then he did the next best thing to statewide television. He got on the phone with the *Tennessean*, saying, "I think a package of reservations, amendments and guarantees can be put together so I can support the treaty."

Still, he was out in front of Byrd. Baker traveled on to Mexico, Colombia, and Brazil, and it was Thursday, January 12, before he and Byrd caught up by telephone. The next day Byrd told a press conference that he would support the treaties and work hard to get them approved. "This is not a passive endorsement," he said. Byrd said he and Baker agreed to "attempt to arrive at an understanding as to the language that would enhance support for the treaty, not only in the Senate but among the American people." The task was hardly over, he said: "I don't think the treaties will be easily passed. It will be a difficult battle, hotly debated."

Byrd and Baker not only developed language to put the gist of the Carter-Torrijos statement into the treaty but also developed a strategy to enable every senator to claim credit for the changes; they prevailed on the Foreign Relations Committee not to add their amendments before sending the treaties to the Senate floor, but merely to recommend that the Senate attach them. That way, every senator who wanted to could cosponsor the amendments.

Byrd arranged to be the committee's last witness on the treaties. On January 26, 1978, he testified that he shared most Americans' pride that "the creation of a water passage across Panama was one of the supreme human achievements of all time, the culmination of a heroic dream of 400 years and of more than 20 years of phenomenal effort and sacrifice." But he also said the Senate should "try to understand the pride and the aspirations of the Panamanians. It is their nation—their nation, not ours, not my State of West Virginia—that is bisected by a strip of land and water controlled by a foreign power." The Canal was obviously vulnerable to "sabotage, to terrorist activity, to guerilla action," he said, and therefore it was in the best interest of the United States to give Panama "a greater stake in the canal and thus a stronger interest in its efficient and unimpeded operation." But he also acknowledged that there was "no political mileage" for any senator in voting for these treaties.

Baker responded, recalling his warning to Torrijos that the treaties could not pass without changes, and Torrijos's willingness to see changes made. He said he and Byrd had generally agreed on the changes that needed to be made and on how the committee and the Senate should proceed. He predicted a difficult fight, stating, "The battle is not over. I think we can win it, but it is not over yet." Still, he said that approval "is in the best interests of my country, and that it is in the best interests of my party and of the Senate."

13

The treaty-making process is one of the stranger, less understood processes of the American government. Treaties are negotiated, sometimes for years, with other countries. The president and foreign chiefs of state sign them. In most other nations, that effectively ends the process, and the treaty takes effect, although Panama's constitution required a popular referendum because the Canal was at issue, and confirming referenda are sometimes obligatory elsewhere.

But in the United States the Senate has to agree, by a two-thirds vote, before a treaty can be ratified and take effect. Sometimes a president does not even bother to ask for unlikely Senate approval, as Johnson did not with the 1967 Canal treaty or President Clinton did not with the Kyoto Protocol on Climate Change of 1998.

When Carter asked the Senate to support the two treaties, one to turn over the Canal to Panama in 1999 and the other (which the Senate considered first) to guarantee the Canal's neutrality and accessibility, technically speaking he was not asking the Senate for "ratification." That word appears nowhere in the Constitution. The Senate votes on a resolution that begins, "The Senate advises and consents to the ratification of the Treaty . . . " If it consents, the president exchanges documents with the other parties, and the treaty is in fact ratified. A president can change his mind and decide not to put the treaty in force by withholding the actual ratification documents. President William Howard Taft did that in 1912 after the

Senate gutted two treaties providing for arbitration of international disputes, pacts that were popularly known as the "peace treaties."

As Taft found out, the process in the Senate is not as simple as an up-or-down vote. The Senate can amend the treaty itself, or it can seek to alter it in less obtrusive ways by attaching conditions or reservations to the resolution approving ratification. And those alterations do not require a two-thirds vote; a simple majority is enough. If the Senate does change the treaty in any of these ways, the other country has to decide if it accepts the altered pact. Senate opponents of the Panama Canal treaties sometimes sought to change them in ways they knew Panama would reject.

★ In order to win Senate approval, Carter had hoped in August to "sell the American people on the fact that the terms of the treaty are beneficial." He never did. That made the push for ratification intensely difficult. As Byrd had explained in Panama, and as the administration recognized, senators would have to vote against their electoral self-interest if the public remained hostile to the treaties.

The American people had ample opportunity to make their opinions clear. By the midseventies, traditional polling organizations such as Gallup, Harris, Roper, and the Opinion Research Corporation had been joined in the polling field by the three television networks, which collaborated with such news organizations as the Associated Press and the *New York Times*. As a result, the Panama Canal issue was one on which the public was polled at least twenty-five times—and that does not count polling done for the administration or political parties—between 1975 and 1978.

Different question wordings produced different results, and both Gallup and Harris sometimes included the guarantees promised by the Baker-Byrd amendments in descriptions of the treaties they were asking about. That approach produced the most favorable responses. For example, in January 1978, Gallup asked: "The treaties would give Panama full control over the Panama Canal and the Canal Zone by the year 2000, but the United States would retain the right to defend the canal against a third nation. Do you favor or oppose these treaties between the U.S. and Panama?" Forty-five percent of respondents favored and 42 percent opposed, a virtual tie considering the margin of sampling error, but still cause for confidence if compared with earlier polls that asked, as the *New York Times* and CBS News did in October: "As you know, the Senate now has to debate the treaties that President Carter signed granting control of the Panama Canal to the Republic of Panama in the year 2000. Do you approve or disapprove of those treaties?" That question found 29 percent in favor and 49 percent opposed.

Pat Caddell, Carter's pollster, asserted in a memorandum for the administration in early February that the polls showed "the proponents seem to be gaining momentum." His own question, which asserted that the United States could defend the Canal and that Panama would keep it open, had seen approval support grow from 25 percent in August to 30 percent in October, to 35 percent in January, and to 37 percent in February. But even that loaded question still found a plurality of 46 percent opposed.

The polls did show that a majority of the public said they would favor the treaties if they were amended to guarantee the right to defend the Canal and send U.S. ships through first. As early as October, the *Times*/CBS News pollsters followed up by asking people who disapproved or had no opinion of the pacts if they would support them if they "felt the treaties provided that the United States could always send in troops to keep the canal open to ships of all nations." With that proviso, 63 percent approved and 24 percent disapproved. Other questions by other pollsters conveyed the same message. But the public, never fully engaged on foreign policy issues short of war, was not following Senate action amendment by amendment. It was never convinced that the treaties, even as amended, did protect American interests. Proof came when Harris asked, in June 1978, "All in all, do you favor or oppose the treaties on the Panama Canal passed by the U.S. Senate?" Thirty-five percent of respondents favored, 49 percent opposed, and 16 percent were not sure. Roper found 30 percent in favor and 52 percent opposed in June. NBC found 34 percent approval and 56 percent disapproval in September.

Caddell's argument that support actually increased is not borne out in polls taken by others. The *Times* and CBS kept asking the same question. In January, at about the same time as Gallup, they found approval unchanged at 29 percent and disapproval at 51 percent. And before the second treaty was voted on in April, they updated the question to reflect the approval of the neutrality treaty and asked if people approved or disapproved of the treaties. Thirty percent approved and 53 percent disapproved. As Bernard Roshco, the State Department's senior public opinion analyst, concluded in *Public Opinion Quarterly* after the fight was over, "The trend that was confirmed most strongly could have been graphed with a straight horizontal line."

The unchanging attitudes were not the result of any lack of effort by the Carter administration. By the end of February 1978, the State Department had sent its people out for 476 public appearances around the country. Pastor patiently explained to senators who would listen how easy it would be for unhappy Panamanians to blow up the Canal. Carter himself spoke by telephone hookups to six "town meetings" around the country and traveled to New Hampshire to boost the treaties, and then gave a long-promised nationally televised speech on February 1. He contended that President Theodore Roosevelt, if alive in 1978, would endorse the treaties and "join us in our pride for being a great and generous people with a national strength and wisdom to do what is right for us and fair for others."

But even though the administration would tell reporters that its polling data showed a sharp drop in opposition to the treaties, Hamilton Jordan concluded some time in the fall that a dramatic turnaround in public opinion was not going to happen. He said in a 2006 interview, "I had a snaky feeling. A third of the people were for it and we needed two-thirds of the Senate. Damn tough. We realized at some point pretty early on in the process, I realized, we weren't going to turn their voters in Tennessee and Texas and Georgia around."

Instead the focus turned to creating a comfort zone for senators, persuading leading citizens like editors or leading businessmen or campaign donors of the merit of the treaties. Those White House briefings that began in August continued throughout the winter, with Carter, a treaty negotiator, and a member of the Joint Chiefs of Staff at the lectern and the First Lady on hand, too. The briefings were persuasive; as Herman C. Selya, a Rhode Island businessman, wrote in a typical thank-you note, "As a deep-rooted Republican, I can only thank you for the courtesy that you and Rosalynn showed me at our home on Monday, November 7th. The briefing was factual, accurate and enjoyable and I appreciate how nicely we were all treated and I consider it a great honor to have been invited to the Whitehouse. Of course, I am now a believer in your Panama Canal Treaty and will work for it." Another guest, Lieutenant Governor Lowell Thomas of Alaska, reported to his state's radio stations: "The briefing was most impressive; the reasoning for the treaties quite persuasive. And the President indeed is a convincing salesman."

"We went to the elites," Jordan said, after concluding that "we can't change public opinion, but we can build a firewall" to protect senators from its wrath.

★ Of all the outsiders who enlisted to help the administration make its case, none was more important than John Wayne. The movie actor, a friend of Reagan's since their days of fighting Communist influence in Hollywood and a very conservative Republican himself, had friends and business connections in Panama dating back to the 1930s.

After the treaties were agreed on, Wayne sent Torrijos a friendly message. Torrijos showed it to Ambassador Jorden, who told him Wayne was an American folk hero whose support would mean a lot. Torrijos replied and asked Wayne to "help your fellow countrymen" understand the great future the treaties promised both countries. At Torrijos's urging, Arturo McGowan, another friend of Wayne's, called and arranged to come to California to tell him about the treaties. McGowan's visit nailed down Wayne's backing.

But the hero of Westerns and war movies wanted to do more than just announce support; he wanted to get in the fight. Wayne did not want to come to the White House for a briefing; he wrote Carter that he feared that would look as though "I was wearing somebody else's collar." So McGowan got in touch with Pastor for help, and Pastor wrote drafts of letters and articles for Wayne, who added blunt words of his own. In an October statement he mailed to all senators, and to anyone who wrote him, Wayne defended Torrijos against the charge that he was Communist or a Marxist. He wrote, "Quite obviously, there are some Communists in general Torrijos' administration as there have been and probably still are in ours." But he insisted, "General Torrijos has never followed the Marxist line" and when he said in Cuba that its system "was not necessarily the right medicine for Panama," he was being as direct "as a visitor could be."

In an op-ed article, Wayne sanitized that statement a bit, removing the references to Communists in both governments and a comparison of the United States' controversial ambassador to the United Nations, Andrew Young, to Escobar. But he kept the declaration that "common decency to the dignity of Panama demanded a re-evaluation of our treaty" of 1903, and then he argued that the treaties would protect U.S. interests. The *Washington Post* published the article with a picture of Wayne in his Academy Award–winning role of Rooster Cogburn, with eyepatch and rifle, under the headline "Treaty Support from—Yes—John Wayne." The *Los Angeles Times* used the headline "Listen, Pardner, Let's Back That Treaty." Wayne tried to persuade his friend Reagan to change his mind about the treaties, but when he saw Reagan's fund-raising letter, he exploded. "Dear Ronnie," he wrote Reagan, "I'll show you point by God damn point in the treaty where you are misinforming people. This is not my point of view against your point of view. These are facts." He said he was unhappy to see that Reagan was "merely making statements for political expediency" instead of taking a leadership role. "You have lost a great and unique 'appointment with history,'" Wayne wrote.

John Lofton Jr., editor of the ACU's *Battle Line*, denounced Wayne, writing, "Since you're a straight-from-the-shoulder kind of guy, I'll mince no words: you've been had. By whom, I don't know, but you've definitely been sold a bill of goods." He added, "Duke, you haven't done your homework." The combative Wayne responded again, with an op-ed piece in the *Chicago Tribune*, scoffing at Lofton's arguments about sovereignty, military bases, and costs.

Wayne never testified in Washington, but when Torrijos was entertaining several members of the Foreign Relations Committee at lunch in January in Panama, Wayne walked in and spoke to them. He said the treaties were "the right thing to do" even though his stand had stimulated the first hate mail he had ever received. He also circulated his letters to all members of the Senate, and many treaty backers found him a valued ally. Frank Church, the Idaho Democrat who was floor manager for the treaties but feared Idaho voters' opposition, put Wayne's photograph together with him on the cover of his March newsletter. Paul Hatfield, a Montana Democrat, unsuccessfully sought a local appearance by Wayne to help him with constituents if he voted for the treaties. (Alan Cranston, the Senate Democratic whip, did provide lesser political comfort for Hatfield. Cranston got Representative Max Baucus, the Democratic congressman who would be his opponent in a primary for the Senate nomination that year, to announce that he supported the treaties, taking some political heat off Hatfield.) As to Wayne, there was no measurement of his impact on the public, except for a cartoon in the *Chicago Tribune*, which had a pollster reporting his latest findings on the Canal issue as 22 percent "no," 17 percent "yes," and 61 percent "whatever side it was John Wayne said he was on."

★ Besides arguing the merits of the treaties and warning senators that a defeat would weaken Carter and the presidency itself, the administration had three more kinds of incentives to offer senators to make it easier to vote for ratification. The easiest was attention. Senator Richard Stone, a Florida Democrat, got an opportunity to show off when he persuaded the White House to have Carter send him a letter effectively reasserting the Monroe Doctrine

"As for the Panama Canal Treaty 22 per cent said 'no,' 17 per cent said 'yes,' and 61 per cent said 'whatever side it was John Wayne said he was on'!"

Wayne Stayskal cartoon on the influence of John Wayne, December 30, 1977 (Reprinted with permission of the *Chicago Tribune*; copyright Chicago Tribune; all rights reserved)

by pledging "to oppose any efforts, direct or indirect, by the Soviet Union to establish military bases" in Latin America and to "maintain our bases in the Caribbean necessary to the defense of the Panama Canal and the security of the United States." The *Miami Herald*'s columnist Tom Fiedler ridiculed the importance of the declaration substantively but said, "It is apparent that by getting the White House to respond to his conditions, Stone provided himself with an excuse for his rather dramatic flip-flop on the issue over the past year."

Senator S. I. Hayakawa, who came to national attention in 1968 when as acting president of San Francisco State College he used police to break up Black Student Union demonstrations, had uttered one of the most quoted comments on the Canal during his 1976 Senate campaign. He said, "We stole it fair and square." Even so, he voted for the neutrality treaty in March. But he was making trouble over the handover treaty and wrote Carter to say that the biggest problem the treaties had was an overall image of weakness in U.S.

foreign policy. He told Vice President Walter Mondale that if he could talk to Carter regularly about foreign policy, he would be reassured and could vote for the treaty. Carter played along, even reading a semantics book Hayakawa gave him and praising it by telephone the next day. He promised the senator the frequent meetings he sought. In fact, they never met again.

Then there were deals, giving a senator something more concrete than a statement about the Monroe Doctrine in exchange for a vote. It is impossible to know how many such deals took place. The Carter Library provides almost no hints of them in its otherwise voluminous files on the Canal treaties, probably in deference to Carter's hostility to the idea of deal making. As Bob Beckel, the chief White House lobbyist on the treaties, said in a 2005 interview, "Carter would not engage in any dealing. We had to go through Mondale to get things done. I'm not sure Carter knew how much we were putting in." Mondale's papers at the Minnesota State Historical Society have nothing on the issue, although in a 2006 interview Mondale recalled telling Howard Baker that after the Canal fight, the administration had no dams or bridges left to give.

But the White House position was not as inflexible as Carter said he wanted. Frank Moore, the top White House lobbyist with Congress, put it this way in a memo to Carter: "No overt offers to trade for a vote on Panama should be made. The press is on the lookout for these 'deals' and have made several inquiries to undecided Senators asking if we have offered favors in return for votes." But he continued, "This is not to say that the Administration cannot do things to improve a Senator's general political security in his State. A Senator who is more politically secure will be more able to vote his conscience on the Treaties." And even Carter acknowledged in his memoirs that he approved a desalinization plant in Oklahoma because it might help win support of Republican Senator Henry Bellmon.

And the files do show senators asking for things. Spark Matsunaga, a Hawaii Democrat, quickly promised support, then asked to have sugar legislation tweaked to help his state. Hayakawa asked in December for a retreat on administration support for expanding the Redwoods National Park. He was rejected, but the administration promised him economic help for logging communities. Beckel recalled senators asking for help on matters such as naval shipbuilding contracts or Amtrak routes. Moore characterized the results this way in a 1984 interview with George Moffett: "By the end they were coming in with lists of demands, four or five senators. We had to put an informal task force on it. It was mostly appointments, weather stations, small projects, loose ends mostly but it kept us busy. As soon as one list was done they'd come back with another."

But there were two cases where much of the press was convinced there was a bargain for a vote. One involved copper purchases sought by Senator Dennis DeConcini, an Arizona Democrat. The other, also reported first by Martin Tolchin in the *New York Times*, dealt with farm legislation sought by Herman E. Talmadge of Georgia, chairman of the Agriculture Committee. Tolchin's story led Senator Bob Packwood, an Oregon Republican, and the *Wall Street Journal* editorial page to accuse the White House of playing the television game show *Let's Make a Deal*. Jesse Helms observed, "I don't want to appear crass, but our side can't buy any copper. Our side can't appoint any judges. Our side can't promise a senator he won't have an opponent."

On the farm bill, Tolchin wrote, "The White House quietly changed its position today on the $2.3 billion emergency farm bill to conform to the wishes of a Senator whose vote it is wooing on the Panama Canal treaties." The story never said there was an acknowledged quid pro quo, but it implied it. *U.S. News and World Report* came even closer, saying, "The President abruptly dropped his opposition to a bill providing an extra 2.3 billion dollars to farmers who retire crop land from production—a pet proposal of a fellow Georgian, Herman Talmadge, who then came out for the treaty."

It seems likely that if the Canal figured in the decision at all, it was in the sense of a thank-you, a way to enhance Talmadge's standing. Talmadge denied there was any "trade-off," saying on his weekly radio broadcast, "That's utterly and completely false. I haven't talked with the President about the Panama Canal treaties since January. The Administration has no position insofar as I know about the farm bill. When they testified before us they had no position. I don't know whether they favor it or oppose it or whether the bill will be vetoed. I have been promised nothing. I have received nothing. And I expect nothing." But despite Talmadge's claimed ignorance of the administration's views, Howard Hjort of the Department of Agriculture had sat next to him at a committee meeting and said the administration had withdrawn its opposition to the chairman's bill. Whatever else may have been in his mind, Moore had told Carter that while the Talmadge bill was still unacceptably expensive, it was "less objectionable" than a competing measure, so "we should not oppose it as strongly as the Dole proposal." Finally, although Talmadge did not announce his position publicly until March 14 (the day after Hjort's announcement), Carter's tally of where senators stood noted that in February his home state senator had told him, "Can hold nose & vote for it."

The copper move was directly tied to a senator's vote. The American copper industry was in a slump because of competition from Africa and South America. Mining companies were pressing the government to prop up prices by buying copper for the nation's strategic materials reserve. Arizona was the biggest domestic producer of copper, and DeConcini, an Arizona Democrat just elected in 1976, took up the cause, pressing for a government purchase five times as large as the 250,000 tons the industry was seeking.

DeConcini was in a difficult position on the Canal treaties, which his Arizona constituents strongly opposed. If his fellow Arizona senator, veteran Barry Goldwater, had supported them as once seemed possible, that might have provided the freshman some political cover. But Goldwater did not. So DeConcini repeatedly mentioned the copper issue when administration lobbyists brought up the Canal. In a rare bit of irony for a Carter administration memo, they advised the president:

> You should know that DeConcini has said he realizes you are dealing with copper stockpiling now. He knows you will make that decision without regard to his vote on Panama. He does not want you to think he is connecting the two issues in any way. He was very sincere about this, even though he desparately [sic] needs the political benefits that would flow from a favorable decision. He is a fine man and an excellent Senator.

Carter, joining the irony, underlined the last sentence.

The week before the vote on the first treaty, DeConcini recalled soon after, the administration told him it was ready to buy copper. "Up pop some people from the vice president's office," he told Donnie Radcliffe of the *Washington Post*. "I said 'Does this have anything to do with the Panama Canal?' and they said absolutely not. They were talking about 225,000 tons and I said it wasn't going to work—too little too late—but I didn't want to say 'forget it'."

But $250 million worth of copper was not the administration's biggest problem with DeConcini. The strategy of Baker and Byrd in crafting leadership amendments—that dozens of senators could cosponsor and claim they had made the treaties palatable—inevitably invited other senators to submit changes of their own. Some were designed to make the treaties unacceptable to Panama. The first of those was proposed by Senator James Allen, a conservative Alabama Democrat, to allow the president to keep U.S. troops in

Panama after 1999 if he "deems it necessary for the protection of the Canal." Byrd called it a "killer amendment" and beat it back, as the leadership did on seventy-seven amendments in all.

Many seemed like eyewash, only a bit more serious than the Stone reassurance. Sam Nunn, a freshman Democrat from Georgia up for reelection in 1978, announced his support after the administration and the Senate agreed to his proposal announcing that nothing in the neutrality treaty should preclude the United States and Panama from agreeing to station American troops in Panama after 1999. Of course, nothing had ever prevented such an agreement. Nunn defended it in a 2007 interview, saying that while it had obvious political advantage, it would also greatly simplify making any new agreements about troops. The reservation may have helped the administration more than it knew; Nunn said in 2007 that Talmadge, the senior senator from Georgia, and Russell Long of Louisiana had told him they would vote however he did.

In Mondale's office off the Senate floor, State Department officials worked with Moore and Beckel on many of the proposed changes, often writing acceptable language even while maintaining an official position of opposition so the senators involved could claim to have overcome the administration. But they could not handle DeConcini, who said the treaties were not clear about whether the United States could intervene if some internal problem in Panama closed or hindered the Canal's operation. He demanded a change—in this case a reservation to the resolution of ratification—to spell that out. Ambassador Jorden warned that the change was unacceptable to Panama, but the administration gave in to DeConcini just before the first treaty was approved on March 16. Deputy Secretary of State Warren Christopher told George Moffett in 1983 that he had no real choice because agreement was the price of the votes of not only DeConcini but also two other Democrats, Kaneaster Hodges of Arkansas and Paul Hatfield of Montana. (Hodges told George Moffett that Christopher was mistaken; he said he would have voted for the treaty even without the DeConcini measure.) The final wording said that "if the canal is closed, or its operations interfered with," the United States could take actions it thought necessary, "including the use of military force in Panama to reopen the canal or restore the operations of the canal." After that wording was agreed on, DeConcini said he still wanted an even bigger copper purchase before he would promise his vote. Beckel pretended to call the Pentagon and get it done.

President Carter and Senator Dennis DeConcini meeting on the Canal treaties, March 15, 1978 (Jimmy Carter Library)

There were all sorts of frantic last-minute maneuverings. Some senators, like DeConcini and Edward Zorinsky, a Nebraska Democrat, seemed to relish the limelight. Others, like Bellmon, shunned it. Vice President Mondale and Hamilton Jordan, accompanied by Lee Kling, a key Democratic fund-raiser, Robert Strauss, former party chairman and Carter's trade negotiator, and Russell Long, chairman of the Senate Finance Committee, arrived at Kentuck-ian Wendell Ford's office the day before the vote at 7:15 A.M. They failed to win him over, even though Ford told an aide they called him a "traitor and a skunk at the garden party" and threatened him with a primary opponent. Edward Brooke, a Massachusetts Republican, told colleagues a crude offer, which he would not describe, from the White House almost persuaded him to vote no. But a last-minute phone call from Carter to Howard Cannon did produce an unexpected aye vote, enabling Byrd to let his fellow West Virginia Democrat, Jennings Randolph, who was worrying about that fall's election and waited until the end of the roll call to vote, off the hook. The vote was 68 to 32, and the first treaty was approved on March 16, 1978. Fifty-two Democrats and 16 Republicans (at least 5 because of Baker's influence) voted aye; 10 Democrats and 22 Republican voted nay.

On the face of it, approval of the second treaty, the one actually turning the Canal over to Panama, should have been easier. Although opponents mounted new radio and newspaper ad campaigns against a few supporters they hoped to turn around, in the Senate switching seemed unlikely. Robert Griffin, a Michigan Republican and a leading foe of the treaties, said, "A Senator can't afford to flip after his first vote."

But while White House aides celebrated, the Panamanians were furious, not only at the DeConcini reservation itself but at his speech explaining it. He had told the Senate his change was necessary because foreign attacks were not the only danger. "Internal Panamanian activities might also be a threat to the waterway, should we give it up. Labor unrest and strikes, the actions of an unfriendly government, political riots or upheavals—each of these alone might cause a closure of the canal." And he said the United States had to be able to intervene without Panama's consent, because if the closure had been caused by Panamanian action, such consent would not be given.

Some of Torrijos's associates managed to talk the Panamanian leader out of rejecting the neutrality treaty then and there. Instead he announced that Panama would wait to see the whole package before deciding what to do. But Torrijos told Carter something had to be done about the DeConcini reservation because Panama could not accept it. After a few days, he complained to the United Nations about it, which angered some senators but persuaded others that something had to be done. While the administration worried about losing DeConcini and others if his language was watered down, several liberal Democrats threatened to vote nay if it was not. George McGovern, the South Dakota Democrat who won his party's 1972 presidential nomination demanding an end to the Vietnam War and then lost in a landslide to Nixon, said: "I can't support these treaties in their present form. As I say, I think the Senate has insulted the independence of the people of Panama. We have undercut our own standing in the hemisphere. We have revived the diplomacy of the big stick, and none of this serves the interest of the American people." McGovern's threat to vote nay was joined at a news conference by

Floyd Haskell of Colorado, Howard Metzenbaum of Ohio, and Daniel Patrick Moynihan of New York.

DeConcini, who was threatened with an effort in Arizona to recall him from the Senate because he had voted for the first treaty, blithely announced that he intended to attach an even stronger intervention provision to the second treaty. Meanwhile, Panama's ambassador in Washington, Gabriel Lewis, was trying to persuade the administration to act decisively to undo the first DeConcini measure. When the administration seemed reluctant, he started pressing friendly senators like Church and Sarbanes, which in turn annoyed the administration. But his approach worked. On Thursday, April 13, Byrd announced that the Senate leadership was taking charge of the problem, drafting a reservation to the second treaty reaffirming the principle of nonintervention. Without a change, he said, approval of the second treaty would be a hollow victory: "Just to get 67 votes for a treaty, and then to have it rejected, and have the United States roundly criticized by all the Latin American countries, and the world, would harm the United States and the Senate," Byrd told the *New York Times*.

Byrd, Church, Sarbanes, Christopher, Ambassador Lewis, and William Rogers (now serving as an adviser to the government of Panama) met at the Capitol on Sunday morning, April 16. This was a unique diplomatic-legislative exercise. They negotiated wording, as seriously as Linowitz and Bunker had done months earlier. They compromised, taking some of each other's preferred words and in the end agreed on language promising that any U.S. action to keep the Canal functioning "shall be only for the purpose of assuring that the Canal remain open, neutral, secure and accessible, and shall not have as its purpose or be interpreted as a right of intervention in the internal affairs of the Republic of Panama or interference with its political independence or sovereign integrity." It promised nonintervention and conspicuously omitted the painful phrase "use of military force in Panama"; it salved the sting to Panama of the original DeConcini language.

Torrijos accepted the language that night, calling it a "dignified solution to a difficult problem." That enabled Byrd, Church, and Sarbanes to persuade liberals like McGovern and Edward Kennedy to go along the next day.

That still left DeConcini, who had enjoyed his star turn, although some editorial pages mocked him. He wanted to put the phrase "use of military force in Panama" back into the new wording. But Byrd, in his twentieth year in the Senate and on the verge of a foreign policy achievement that no one who knew him growing up in the coal towns of West Virginia could have imagined, was the majority leader. He talked to the freshman senator for forty-five minutes, but then told him: "It has to be like this, Dennis. I will not accept any changes."

Byrd allowed DeConcini to announce the new language as his proposal. The next day, April 18, the Senate adopted it overwhelmingly and then voted to give up the Canal and the Canal Zone. That vote was 68 to 32, identical to the vote on the neutrality treaty in March. No senator had switched, in either direction.

★ The decision to give up this great monument of the American Century was historic. Not only did it mark a singularly courageous moment in American politics. It also probably preserved the Canal itself. For if the second treaty had been defeated or left without a palliative to DeConcini, as Torrijos told his fellow citizens that night, he would have ordered the National Guard to attack the Canal out of frustration. U.S. forces were ready, but if they had thwarted an attack that night, others would have followed, and the Canal would quickly have become too risky a route for shippers to use.

At another level, approval of the treaties showed Carter's administration at its most effective, achieving what Charles O. Jones called "one of his most impressive victories on Capitol Hill." The president's own investment of time in briefings, and the related efforts of his staff and the State Department, created what Robert Strong in *Presidential Studies Quarterly* called "a climate in which a vote for the treaties would not be an act of political suicide" for many supporters. Strong also argued that Carter won on the Canal where Woodrow Wilson—whom Carter admired for his moral approach to foreign policy— lost on the League of Nations by being willing to make some compromises with the Senate.*

On a less profound level, the Senate debate on the Panama Canal treaties was itself historic. It lasted from February 8 until April 18—ten weeks—with time out for two recesses and an occasional urgent piece of legislation. It took

---

* This may be too severe a judgment of Wilson. He did compromise early before rigidly rejecting reservations later, after he was paralyzed by a stroke. Moreover, it is unclear that any compromise would have satisfied Henry Cabot Lodge and won a two-thirds majority in the Senate. Lodge was not only Wilson's implacable enemy but also the Senate majority leader.

the Senate longer than any treaty except the Treaty of Versailles. It was broadcast on National Public Radio—the first time Senate floor activity had been broadcast. Moreover, unlike what passes for debate on C-SPAN today, which is really no more than serial monologues interrupted by quorum calls, senators actually listened to each other and argued.

Though millions of listeners heard more than they cared to about parliamentary procedures, the debate sometimes soared. Byrd invoked Brutus before the battle of Phillipi, "There is a tide in the affairs of men which taken at the flood leads on to fortune," or hailed treaty supporters but warned that, politically, "your badges of courage may be the dents in your armor." Laxalt argued that giving up the Canal would demonstrate weakness and prompt other challenges by showing that "the big boy backed down." Baker disagreed, saying, "It is a measure of our strength, not weakness, that the United States can deal fairly, at arm's length, and in the spirit of true partnership with a smaller, less powerful nation." Garn for the opponents and Church and Sarbanes for the supporters of the treaty often spoke eloquently and to the point.

But those shining moments were not the norm; repetition was. All the serious arguments could have been made in a week or two—or maybe three if every senator wanted to be heard.

The real significance of the ten weeks was not the time it gave senators to think, debate, and persuade and to polish the treaties. The significance of those ten weeks was the time it gave for the New Right to press its case, to rally millions of Americans to object, and to create a new weapon to use against liberal and moderate senators, Democrat and Republican. "We've raised money and rallied our troops for the battles ahead," said Viguerie.

14

When the Senate approved the handover treaty, the Right's
agenda turned to proving that its threats about voters were
more than just talk. The Right had already mounted one trial
run at punishing a supporter of the treaties, Representative
John B. Anderson of Illinois. But Anderson survived the March
21 Republican primary, and it was not much of a test. After all,
as a member of the House, he had only spoken, not voted, in
favor of giving away the Canal. One senator, Tom McIntyre
of New Hampshire, already had an opponent who was making the race because he thought the Canal should be kept as an
American possession.

★ Gordon Humphrey became a Republican around 1970 the
way a lot of people did as the old New Deal coalition disinte-
grated. He decided that the Democratic policies he believed in
growing up as a machinist's son in Connecticut simply did not
work. "I followed my heart when I was young," he said in 2005,
"and ultimately came to the conclusion that however heartfelt
liberal sentiments might be, that they did not work, in fact
were counterproductive, and sort of gradually transformed into
a conservative over time."

When Allegheny Airlines assigned him to Boston as a copi-
lot in 1975, Humphrey settled in New Hampshire because he
thought Massachusetts' politics were too liberal and its taxes
too high, and because he loved New Hampshire's hiking and
skiing. And he ran for the Senate in 1978 because it looked as
though no one else was going to fight McIntyre over the Canal.

Senator Gordon Humphrey (U.S. Senate Historical Office)

It was not his introduction to politics. He had supported Hubert Humphrey for president in 1968, and he served as a member of the Alexandria, Virginia, Democratic Committee, where nearly forty years later he was remembered by one old-timer as "good-looking, pleasant," and "not very assertive."

His next political involvement led to his Senate candidacy. In mid-1977 he enlisted into the ranks of the Conservative Caucus, whose national chairman was New Hampshire's governor, Meldrim Thomson. Howard Phillips,

Senator Tom McIntyre (U.S. Senate Historical Office)

running the organization, sought to establish active chapters in every congressional district to make conservative pressure a grassroots reality across
the nation. Humphrey started working as the organization's unpaid state
director, traveling around New Hampshire on days when he was not flying,
finding dedicated conservatives and encouraging them to get active. Phillips
thought he was a first-rate organizer.

The Canal treaties were foremost among the issues Humphrey used to gather members. The pacts angered Humphrey, and he threw himself into various opposition activities. Not long after agreement on the treaties was announced, he organized an August 21, 1977, Conservative Caucus meeting in Concord where Thomson and Phillips denounced them. Phillips said McIntyre would be a "political sitting duck" because of the treaty. On January 7, 1978, Humphrey published an article in the *Manchester Union Leader*, predicting that if the treaties were ratified, Soviet and Cuban military help would transform Panama into "The Peoples' Democratic Republic of Panama," which would seize the Canal in December 1980. A week later, he organized a "Save the Canal" rally at the state house in Concord, featuring Governor Thomson warning that communism in the Caribbean would spread if the Canal was surrendered. Another rally held in February offered bumper stickers that read, "Give Away Carter, Keep the Canal"; a photograph of the event in the *New Hampshire Sunday News* (the Sunday edition of the *Union Leader*) showed Thomson listening attentively as Humphrey spoke.

That picture symbolized how Humphrey was moving out onto one of the strangest political playing fields in the nation. Thomson and the *Union Leader* were what made it weird. Thomson was first elected governor in 1972, and in a few years he had gained a national reputation as an extremist (or a nut) who said or did any fool thing that came into his head. He proposed that the state's National Guard be armed with tactical nuclear weapons. He lowered the flag at the capitol on Good Friday. And he was running around the world, spending a lot of time in Taiwan and jetting off to South Africa to praise apartheid. His domestic travels included appearances before the John Birch Society.

William Loeb's *Union Leader* was among the two or three worst newspapers in the country, almost unrivaled for slanted coverage and uncivil language. But it was the only statewide paper, and in this campaign it would print attacks from almost anybody on McIntyre and blast him in front-page editorials as a "liar." That put McIntyre in the company of President Kennedy, "the number one Liar in the United States," and President Carter, labeled as both a liar and an "idiot." President Ford was "Jerry the Jerk," President Eisenhower was "Dopey Dwight," Senator Margaret Chase Smith of Maine was "Moscow Maggie"; when George McGovern ran for president, he was "the Communist candidate." Loeb was reclusive, living across the state line in Pride's Crossing, Massachusetts. Once when reporters traveled there to interview him in 1972, he pointed a loaded pistol at one of them.

But Loeb and Thomson had not been able to beat McIntyre before, and no one thought a race against him would be easy. Humphrey recalled in 2005, "Everyone thought McIntyre was invincible, and it looked like he wasn't going to have any serious opposition. So I pitched my hat in the ring." By "serious opposition," he meant tough conservative opposition that would focus on the Canal. One of the other Republican hopefuls, James Masiello, was against the treaties but did not make a big issue of them, and the other, Alf Jacobson, supported the pacts. Masiello, the former mayor of Keene, and Jacobson, the president of the state senate, were both better known than Humphrey, and when Humphrey announced on February 27, Thomson himself had not yet ruled out running. Indeed, when Humphrey went to Concord to meet the governor and tell him he had decided to run, Thomson suggested he try for a lesser office, then dismissed him as an "upstart" in a conversation with Jerry Carmen, the state Republican chairman. There was some truth to the label. Indeed when the thirty-seven-year-old pilot announced his candidacy on February 27, he was unknown enough so that he wore a badge on one arm saying, "Hello, my name is Gordon Humphrey."

McIntyre was sixty-three, a New Hampshire native, and a decorated infantry major in World War II, whom even Carmen acknowledged was known as a "war hero." An Irish Democrat, his personality was almost the stereotype of a Republican New Englander—frugal and taciturn. Moreover, in 1962 McIntyre was the first New Hampshire Democrat elected to the Senate since 1932. He had been reelected in 1966 and 1972, quite a feat in Republican New Hampshire. In the Senate he was liberal on domestic issues, and the author of legislation prohibiting credit card companies from charging more than fifty dollars when a card was lost or stolen and then misused. He had supported the war in Vietnam until 1969 and backed President Johnson in his battle against Eugene McCarthy in the 1968 New Hampshire presidential primary.

But McIntyre had grim forebodings about the Canal issue. He told Vice President Mondale, "I'll vote with you, but don't expect me to be here next year." And on the day of the first vote, he told his wife, Myrtle, as he left for the Senate floor, "Come on and watch me lose my seat."

In 1974 he had written constituents to say the United States had to help Panama "understand that the best guarantee of her sovereignty, security, prosperity, and nationhood lies in maintaining the historic grant of sovereignty to the U.S. in the Canal Zone." McIntyre had cosponsored Strom Thurmond's 1974 and 1975 resolutions calling the negotiations "a clear and present danger to the hemispheric security and the successful operation of the canal by the United States."

But when the treaties were signed in September 1977, the combative McIntyre announced that he would study the subject carefully but would not be stampeded:

> William Loeb, Meldrim Thomson and the Conservative Caucus have seized upon the Panama Canal as the issue to unseat Tom McIntyre. The Governor says that if I vote for ratification he will reconsider his decision not to run against me next year. He also intends to spearhead a mass march upon Washington to protest ratification. Howard Phillips, national director of the Conservative Caucus, says conservatives should make a "political sitting duck" of Tom McIntyre over the Canal treaty and that the Caucus can "make it a political impossibility for McIntyre to vote for that treaty. . . . Mr. Loeb and Mr. Thomson and the Conservative Caucus can take their threats and run them up and down the Governor's flagpole."

The Conservative Caucus kept up the pressure, declaring in December that McIntyre "is hereby publicly censured and is requested and required to respond publicly" at a February caucus meeting to explain himself. Failure to appear, the resolution said, would be evidence that he meant to vote for the treaties. Then it awarded a fifty-dollar prize to Hillary Lowell, a high school senior, for an essay on the Canal issue that declared, "America is being pushed around by a smaller less powerful nation than itself, which shouldn't be allowed to happen." Giving away the Canal, she wrote, would be "ridiculous, harmful, and stupid."

McIntyre insisted he still had questions he wanted answered before he decided how to vote. Humphrey hit at that posture as he was first being identified as a "Senate Aspirant" in the February 18 *Union Leader.* He issued a statement saying, "The people of New Hampshire have watched in disgust for five long months while Senator McIntyre has squirmed and twisted to avoid taking a stand on the Panama Canal surrender." He continued, "The people of New Hampshire are wise to him. Whichever way McIntyre finally flops, I cannot escape the conclusion that he has been searching desperately for an effective way to sell surrender to the people back home."

When Humphrey announced his candidacy nine days later, he made it clear the Canal would be his signature issue. He said it was "the most strategically important facility in the western hemisphere. Every major naval contingency plan depends heavily on the canal. And Washington is lying when it says the canal is unessential." He also said he wanted to limit how much the "piggish government" could take from individuals in income taxes, to spur energy development by eliminating the "dead hand of government," and to amend the Constitution to prohibit federal deficits. But while he was running against government, he did not spare McIntyre personally, calling him representative of the view "that the individual citizen is incompetent to take care of his own interests and that he must be watched over by paternal government."

Three days later, McIntyre announced that he would vote for the Canal treaties. He told the Senate on March 1, "After six months of hard study, I have concluded that on balance the new treaties are the surest means of keeping the canal open, neutral and accessible to our use—and are in keeping with our historical commitment to deal fairly and justly with lesser powers." He said he did not worry greatly about the sovereignty issue, quoting Bill Buckley to argue that what might have been acceptable in 1903 was no longer permissible in 1978. And he said that while the Torrijos dictatorship was not the best of diplomatic partners, "diplomacy, like politics, forces unfastidious bedfellows upon us whether we like it or not. Omar Torrijos is a diplomatic fact of life."

But the bulk of McIntyre's speech attacked the "radical right," whose threats he cited even before he said how he would vote. Acknowledging that he spoke with "anger and resentment," McIntyre said, "The campaign waged against ratification—in my state and across the nation—has impugned the loyalty and the motives of too many honorable Americans to be ignored or suffered in silence a minute longer." His litany of wounds began with Phillips's declaration the previous August that conservatives should make a "sitting duck" of him and continued through the Conservative Caucus's censure resolution. He damned the New Right as "radicals whose aim is not to compete with honor and decency, not to compromise when necessary to advance the common good, but to annihilate those they see as enemies." He said it was time for his colleagues and others of "conscience and good will to stand up and face down the bully boys of the radical New Right before the politics of intimidation does to America what it has tried to do to New Hampshire."

McIntyre lamented the passing of the days when conservatives and liberals could work together. He did not give examples, but he could have recalled how, in his first term, fiscally conservative Republicans joined with liberal Democrats to pass civil rights legislation in 1964 and 1965, and joined to ratify the Limited Nuclear Test Ban Treaty of 1963. That was, of course, the very spirit that Phillips and Viguerie loathed, and that candidates they backed would forswear.

McIntyre told the Senate, "I know the traditional conservatives of my own state. I have competed with them in the political arena. I have worked with them in behalf of our state. They are people of honor, civility and decency." But, he continued, "The New Right cannot comprehend how people of opposing viewpoints can find common ground and work together. For them, there is no common ground. And this, in my judgment, is the best indication of what they truly are—radicals whose aim is not to compete with honor and decency, not to compromise when necessary to advance the common good, but to annihilate those they see as enemies."

McIntyre hit particularly hard on Thomson for sharing a "loutish primitivism" with Loeb, ridiculing the governor's denunciation of Carter and Martin Luther King, his praise of South Africa, and his calling its prime minister "one of the great world statesmen of today." He called Thomson a "notorious armchair warrior" for telling Taiwan the United States would support an invasion of mainland China and for accusing the Joint Chiefs of pandering to Carter when they backed the treaties. On the day before the first treaty vote, Thomson said he still might run against McIntyre. He finally ruled it out on April 21, just after the second vote. An editorial in the *Concord Monitor* said that a poll showing Thomson would be beaten two to one was probably the main reason he stayed out.

Humphrey, clearly the most combative of the Republican candidates, ran hard against McIntyre all spring and summer. First he called the senator's attack on Thomson "boorish behavior" and questioned his "emotional stability." After the second treaty vote Humphrey, who could count on the *Union Leader* to carry his message across the state, said, "In voting for the treaties, Tom McIntyre has ignored the clearly stated wishes of the people of New Hampshire. Representative government has suffered a heavy blow. I urge the people to adopt the slogan 'Remember the Canal' because McIntyre is hoping voters will forget the Canal by November."

On June 1 McIntyre formally announced his candidacy for reelection, saying he hoped to "keep the focus of the campaign on what's important to New Hampshire people—problems like a workable national energy policy, decent jobs, the cost of living and adequate housing for our elderly." Conceding that the Canal issue might hurt him, he said the treaties were now "a dead letter, a fait accompli." Humphrey responded that McIntyre was "whistling in the dark" if he thought the issue was behind him. He said, "New Hampshire voters are angry. Senator McIntyre chose to follow the Carter line that to preserve the peace, America must continually yield to the hypocritical pressures of the Soviet Union and a collection of Noisy Third World countries." In July Humphrey raised economic issues, blaming McIntyre for federal spending that caused inflation and for not wanting to cut the capital gains tax.

McIntyre's mail on the treaties had run overwhelmingly against his position, and he added fuel to that fire himself with an indiscreet observation on NBC's *Today Show* about the difficulty of explaining the treaties to "the average man on the street" in Laconia, a remark the *Union Leader* did not let him forget. But the first outside validation that the issue was making an impact came in August, when someone put out the results of a poll done in July for the National Republican Senatorial Committee by the respected Detroit firm of Market Opinion Research. It reported that for McIntyre, the Canal issue "has added the first substantial negative element to his image in 16 years." The report noted that "mentions of the Panama Canal issue easily lead the list of reasons given for disapproval" of the incumbent. McIntyre told reporters the Canal issue was only "costing me some small portion of support."

Humphrey stayed on the Canal issue, complaining that Jacobson, one of his Republican primary opponents, dismissed it as unimportant just as McIntyre did. The *Union Leader* agreed with Humphrey. On July 20 Loeb's front-page editorial grudgingly endorsed Humphrey as the best of the three, a "dedicated conservative" though utterly lacking in political experience.

Humphrey campaigned tirelessly. He took only a single day off between his announcement and the September 12 primary. That was July 14, when he married a campaign volunteer, Patricia Greene. She had joined his campaign from the Boston office of the Conservative Caucus, where she was assistant editor of its newsletter, *Grassroots*.

By primary day, McIntyre was predicting that Humphrey would win the nomination to oppose him, though he still sneered at him as a "stand-in" for Thomson. Humphrey did win the primary, getting the conservative Republican vote while Masiello and Jacobson split the moderate camp. Humphrey received 35,503 votes, or 50.4 percent, to 18,371 (26.1 percent) for Masiello and 13,619 (19.4 percent) for Jacobson. A minor anti-treaty candidate, Carmen Chimento, received 2,885, or 4.1 percent.

At that point Humphrey got some very valuable new help. Terry Dolan of the National Conservative Political Action Committee came up to New Hampshire to run the campaign briefly and offer two major pieces of advice to Humphrey. The first was to broaden his campaign for the general election by using economic issues. The second was to use Boston television to reach southern New Hampshire. NCPAC also provided three of his full-time staffers, including Bill Parham as campaign manager and Craig Shirley (fresh from the primary defeat of another anti-treaty candidate, Avi Nelson of Massachusetts) as press secretary.

Not that Humphrey forgot about the Canal, though he acknowledged that no votes were left to be changed over that issue. He showed a television ad trumpeting the Canal issue. He blasted McIntyre for disregarding the views of New Hampshire voters. He said the Canal decision had weakened the nation's defenses. His flyers proclaimed, "Free the American Spirit! Halt America's Retreat—by rebuilding a tough defense and putting backbone in foreign policy—No Surrender in Panama." And Humphrey had the *Union Leader* to pummel McIntyre over the fact that he no longer owned a home in New Hampshire but did own a Florida condominium, and to denounce him for voting to table a ban on federal funding of abortions—an issue highlighted when antiabortion activists leafleted church parking lots on the Sunday before Election Day. Humphrey himself had written the flyer, proclaiming, "Gordon Humphrey believes that life is a gift from God (McIntyre would deny that right to unborn babies)." Sensing that Humphrey had a real chance to win, Reagan, Crane, George H. W. Bush, and Senator Orrin Hatch of Utah came in to campaign for him.

For his part, McIntyre never really saw Humphrey coming, never took him seriously. He attacked Humphrey as a puppet of the New Right and said he represented something different from the "gentlemen" Republicans he knew, characterized by a "sense of decency, civility, fairness and tolerance." As McIntyre campaigned, he was dogged by the Canal issue at public meetings. "You don't send me down to be a windsock," he would tell audiences. "I take every vote seriously and let me tell you how I decided."

As John Gorman of Cambridge Survey Research, McIntyre's pollster, put it in 2006, "He could not believe that someone for whom he had so little respect could defeat him." Confident that he was well ahead, McIntyre stopped using the company's paid professional interviewers for his polling, and the volunteer polling never caught Humphrey's rise. Even when Humphrey started broadcasting ads on Boston television stations, the McIntyre campaign rejected advice that he raise the money to do the same (as his friend, the Democratic candidate for governor, Hugh Gallen, was doing). He did not see the need. Dave LaRoche, McIntyre's campaign manager, said in a 2006 interview, "We were all using the frame of reference of politics in New Hampshire as they had been up to that time." On Election Day itself, McIntyre's sound trucks were not striving to turn out his vote but instead were working for Gallen, who ran and beat the despised Thomson for the governorship. "I thought we were going to beat this guy by 30,000 votes," McIntyre told the *Washington Post* in December.

There was some reason for McIntyre's confidence—beyond his contempt for his opponent and the Right. On October 27, the *Concord Monitor* reported an independent poll of 600 registered voters by a local pollster, the Blake and Dickinson company, as giving the incumbent a 56 to 30 percent lead. On November 5, Loeb's state house correspondent, Donn Tibbetts, predicted a McIntyre victory. And on election night, there was no throng of optimistic supporters gathered to celebrate Humphrey. As the veteran political correspondent Rod Paul reported, "Only two to three dozen were on hand at campaign headquarters." But that modest company had a lot to cheer. On November 7, Humphrey won with 133,745 votes (or 50.7 percent), just 5,800 more than McIntyre's 127,945.

After the election, Humphrey was equivocal about how much he thought the Canal issue had mattered. Once he said it mattered much less than economic problems like taxes and deficits. Another time he said it played a "greater role" than people thought. But reflecting on it in 2005, he had no doubts, calling the Canal "pivotal." He explained:

> It was a make-or-break issue for me and for McIntyre. You know, I won by about like a half a percent that first race. So it was a pretty close contest, and that issue cut more for us than did any other. Not that we selected it for that reason. I was way too naive at that point. I didn't understand how all that cutting or not cutting stuff works. But I felt pretty visceral about it. That's why I chose to make an issue of it. It turns out it was a good issue for us.

" I HAVEN'T FOUND ANYBODY
IN IOWA THAT'S FOR THE TREATIES "
ROGER JEPSEN ON THE ISSUE
THAT MADE THE DIFFERENCE

Conservatives have made striking claims about the electoral
potency of the Canal issue, claiming it played a significant
role in the defeats of twenty senators who voted for the treaties. They exaggerate. Besides New Hampshire, the Canal was
the central issue in no other 1978 Senate election, and in only
one in 1980. But it mattered in two other ways. It served as a
lightning rod as conservatives tried to take over the Republican
Party, sparking serious primary challenges to Clifford Case in
New Jersey and Edward Brooke in Massachusetts. And in a few
elections the Canal issue, while not dominant, was important,
important enough so that a close race would almost certainly
have gone the other way if the Panama Canal treaties had never
come before the Senate and the incumbents had never voted for
them. One of those races was Dick Clark's 1978 run for reelection in Iowa.

Clark had been a professor of history and political science
at Upper Iowa University and then the administrative assistant
to Representative John Culver. When Culver decided at the last
minute not to run for the Senate seat held by Republican Jack
Miller in 1972, Clark jumped in. He campaigned by walking
across the state on his way to a strong, upset victory with 55
percent of the vote. In the Senate, the liberal Democrat became
best known as head of the Foreign Relations Subcommittee on
Africa, fighting against Ford administration efforts to involve
the United States in the Angolan civil war.

Like McIntyre, Clark had feared that his votes for the Canal
treaties could cost him his seat. He received more than 10,000

letters on the subject. The *Des Moines Register*'s highly respected Iowa Poll showed a 56 to 30 percent margin against the treaties in March 1978. Clark wrote back to one Iowan who asked that he vote with the majority, "I firmly believe that I am in the Senate to represent the interest of the people of Iowa. At the same time, I am not persuaded that public opinion polls necessarily reflect those best interests. If that were the case, you would need nothing more than a scale to weigh the mail or a computer to record telephone calls."

Clark's situation had some clear advantages over McIntyre's. First, there was nothing weird about Iowa's statewide paper, the *Register*, except for its practice of printing its sports section on peach-colored newsprint. It was one of the country's best regional papers, unlike the *Union Leader*. It covered the news fairly and was friendly to Clark editorially. Second, while Iowa also had a Republican governor, Robert Ray was not anything like Meldrim Thomson. Ray was a classic midwestern moderate and a critic of his party's right wing.

Clark also had two major disadvantages compared with McIntyre. Unlike the New Englander, he had served only one term. Iowa's Republicanism meant that never in its history had it sent a Democratic senator to Washington for a second full term. Second, his eventual opponent, Roger Jepsen, was reasonably well known around the state. The Davenport businessman had served as a county supervisor and a state senator before four years as Ray's lieutenant governor from 1968 to 1972, though they did not get along, and he considered a run against Ray in 1972 before giving up the idea. Even so, the state's leading political writer, James Flansburg of the *Register*, initially dismissed Jepsen's candidacy, writing that "it's fair to conclude that if the Republicans thought they could beat Dick Clark this year, they'd have someone in the lists who knows something about Washington and national and international politics, agriculture and economics."

Jepsen had to defeat Ray's candidate, Maurie Van Nostrand, a former state legislator and a member of the Iowa Commerce Commission, to get the Republican nomination. Jepsen's campaign started awkwardly. He flew around the state to announce his candidacy on March 27, but after battling strong headwinds, he arrived at the secretary of state's office to file his papers only eight minutes before the deadline. At another point he risked serious trouble in a state with a high proportion of elderly voters when he called for replacing the Social Security system with private insurance and savings accounts.

Jepsen made the Canal an issue from the beginning of his race. When he first started telling reporters he intended to run, he said "it would be horrible" if the treaties were approved. He said they would be a "major issue in the campaign." When he wrote to potential contributors on March 23 saying he was about to run, he denounced Clark for "voting to give away the Panama Canal and pay $50,000,000 to a pro-Marxist, pro-Castro dictator to do it." When he actually announced in Cedar Falls, he said, "I haven't found anybody in Iowa that's for the treaties," adding, "Senator Clark hasn't even bothered to ask Iowans." He said the treaties threatened the nation's defenses and would hurt the state's farmers by raising tolls.

The treaties were a clear dividing point between Jepsen and Van Nostrand, who supported the treaties. Van Nostrand said Clark's votes for them were a welcome example of a senator who "does what he knows is right, not popular." They were not the only, or necessarily the most important, difference between the candidates in a Republican primary. Jepsen advocated a constitutional amendment to prohibit abortion, except to save the life of the mother. Van Nostrand opposed it. Jepsen's stance brought him support from Iowa's Pro-Life Action Council, which mailed out flyers and put them under windshield wipers in church parking lots on the Sunday before the primary.

Van Nostrand and Ray both attacked Jepsen as a right-winger. Van Nostrand denounced him for using "emotional issues" like the Panama Canal, abortion, gun control, prayer in schools, and the equal rights amendment. He asked, "Is Roger Jepsen a supporter of the Viguerie efforts to destroy the Republican Party and replace it with a coalition dedicated only to the promotion of its emotionally divisive causes?" He said Jepsen's "politics of hate and despair do not fit Iowa." Governor Ray said of Jepsen, "The groups I see that are endorsing him, the people who are raising money, certainly are limiting their scope. He not only has accepted, but has joined these people. They have taken a position of being far to the right in a narrow area."

Jepsen did have support from outside Iowa. A Meldrim Thomson fundraising letter, sent by Viguerie to 100,000 conservatives across the nation, asked for money for Jepsen because "Clark voted to give away taxpayers' money to Marxist dictator Omar Torrijos to take away our Panama Canal." The fund-raising appeal concluded, "This is our best chance to defeat an ultra-liberal who voted to give away our Panama Canal." Paul Weyrich's Committee for the Survival of a Free Congress sent an aide out to help run Jepsen's campaign. Two other organizations Viguerie had created, Gun Owners of America and the National Council of Senior Citizens, came out for Jepsen.

Jepsen brushed off Van Nostrand's attacks, calling them the whining of a loser. He said Viguerie was only one of many supporters, and anyway he did not get the money the mailings raised, which went to Viguerie for more mailings. He said he had not seen Thomson's letter (Thomson's press secretary said his boss had not seen it, either). From the beginning of his campaign, Jepsen had presented himself as the real challenger to Clark. One way he did it was with a full-page ad in the *Register* just after he filed, saying, "The choice in 1978 is clear. Roger Jepsen or Dick Clark. Roger Jepsen's common sense approach, accountability and responsive leadership or Dick Clark's philosophy of big government, big bureaucracy and big spending. . . . Roger Jepsen will fight for Iowa's traditional values of economy, honesty and common sense. The choice is clear. JEPSEN FOR U.S. SENATE." Jepsen said later the purpose of the ad was "to show we're in business for real."

Jepsen won the June 6 primary solidly. He carried 95 of Iowa's 99 counties with 87,397 votes, or 57.3 percent, to 54,189, or 35.5 percent, for Van Nostrand. A third candidate, Joseph Bertoche, got 10,860 votes, or 7.1 percent.

A poll taken for Clark soon after the primary by Peter Hart showed both the Canal and abortion as weaknesses for his candidacy against Jepsen. Overall, it showed Clark with a 52 to 32 percent lead. But about two-fifths of Clark's backers were classed as weak supporters. When the 694 likely voters were asked to volunteer something unfavorable about Clark, 5 percent cited the Canal issue; another 4 percent said he was too concerned with foreign affairs. Then, presented with various criticisms of Clark and asked if they were fair, only one received a plurality; 43 percent said it was fair to say "Dick Clark gave away U.S. territory by supporting the Panama Canal treaty." (Thirty-eight percent disagreed.) And when asked if there was a single issue that would decide their vote, 7 percent said abortion and 5 percent cited the Canal.

Jepsen's general election campaign involved more than the Canal and abortion. Clark's voter ratings of 100 percent from Americans for Democratic Action and 90 percent from the AFL-CIO were used to label him as too liberal for Iowa. The National Right to Work Committee ran newspaper ads attacking him over his support of the union shop. Ronald Reagan cut a television ad saying, "As a former Iowan myself, I think it's about time Iowa had a Senator who votes for Iowans"; he appeared in Ames to say Clark "thinks we must apologize for what strength we have, confess our sins to other nations. He thinks we should spend all our time trying to figure ways to demean our own nation, disarm as quickly as we can so we can bring joy to the rulers of the Third World."

Jepsen himself called for a sharp federal tax cut, the Kemp-Roth measure that was a staple of Republican races that fall and the basis of those Reagan instituted in 1981. He also announced that he was severing his ties with Viguerie, although after the election he went back to him to help retire his debt.

Jepsen's campaign and the Republican State Committee attacked Clark for his votes on such issues as school bussing, gun control, food stamps for strikers, taxpayer financing of federal elections, government spending, congressional pay raises, aid to New York City, and a new Senate office building. The campaign distributed thousands of copies of the John Birch Society's *Review of the News*, which called Clark's contributors pro-communist and said his "friends are mostly to the Left of the Marquis de Sade." Clark's campaign, on the other hand, seemed to do little more than hammer at Jepsen as "some sort of rightwing creep," as the *Register* complained.

The Canal continued to matter. A Des Moines manufacturer, Robert Dilley, put out a flyer stating, "Senator Dick Clark voted to give away the legally owned United States Panama Canal. Where do his loyalties lie? Will Alaska be next? What about Texas? Help us defeat Dick Clark before he votes to give away the United States." Weyrich and Senator Carl Curtis, a Republican from neighboring Nebraska, drove around the state in August talking about the Canal on Jepsen's behalf, getting little coverage in print but lots on radio and television. The Republican Party's state platform condemned Clark and Culver for voting for the "give-away Panama Canal treaties." Jepsen aired a radio ad telling farmers that the treaty would dramatically increase shipping costs for their corn and beans, closing the ad with the question, "Isn't it time we sent an Iowan to the Senate?" Another ad linked the Canal vote to other Clark votes that Jepsen said weakened the nation's defenses. Jepsen added the Canal to a new edition of his own flyer attacking Clark's votes. Jepsen raised the issue frequently on the campaign trail, and Clark could not avoid it. When he would do a call-in radio program, the Canal was a constant topic. Clark recalled in 2005, "I was defending it all the time."

Abortion was also a continual problem for Clark. Carolyn Thompson, chairman of the political arm of Iowans for Life Inc., told Jepsen the night he won the June 6 primary, "We're all Democrats but we're crossing over this fall." Three weeks later in St. Louis, the convention of the National Right to

Life Committee designated the Iowa race as first among the campaigns it planned to target. In heavily Catholic Dubuque, Jepsen complained in August that Clark voted three times in the previous thirteen months to subsidize abortions with federal funds. Thompson followed up with a formal endorsement on September 30, saying, "By his votes, Dick Clark has exhibited his total commitment to an unrestricted abortion policy." While Clark publicly dismissed the importance of antiabortion groups, he did go on television to state, "I don't advocate abortions. I find them very, very wrong. I would not advocate to a young woman that it's the best alternative. It's the least attractive alternative."

Polls showed a race that tightened quickly from Hart's early reading. A mid-July *Register* poll gave Clark a 49 to 39 percent lead among likely voters. Another in early September said Clark led, 52 to 40 percent. A later Hart survey, done for Clark in early October, gave Clark 57 percent (still about two-fifths of them weak supporters) to Jepsen's 27 percent. And the final *Register* poll, from October 28 through 31, found Clark with a 51 to 41 percent lead. The *Register* polls never moved significantly from July through October.

The *Register*'s Flansburg had a different impression. He wrote on October 29 that the consensus of Iowa politicians was that the race was even. Peter Hart, Clark's pollster, told Carl Leubsdorf of the *Baltimore Sun* that the impact of abortion on Catholic Democrats might be underestimated in polls. Jepsen remained confident. On October 24, he told Republicans in Sioux City, "It's going good, it's on target." He said, "After the Nov. 7 election, our erstwhile senator can retire and go soak his feet in the Panama Canal."

The main development of the final weekend was the energy shown by anti-abortion activists. They put out 300,000 flyers showing an eighteen-week-old fetus sucking its thumb with the headline "See Why This Little Guy Wants You to Vote on Tuesday, Nov. 7." Most of the flyers were distributed by mail or placed under windshields at church parking lots on the Sunday before election, but some were distributed inside churches, despite instructions from Iowa's Catholic bishops that they be kept out. The Clark campaign's response—flyers urging people not to vote on single issues—was ineffective.

On Tuesday, November 7, Jepsen won—by 26,532 votes. He got 421,598 votes, or 51.1 percent, to 395,066, or 47.9 percent, for Clark. Another 7,990 votes were scattered among minor candidates. The impact of abortion got most of the attention in postelection analyses, especially in the national press, which saw an important story in the rising influence of the right-to-life movement. The *Register* reported that it conducted a "study" of voters, apparently a sort of exit poll, about which it released no methodological details, and announced that 8 percent of Jepsen's voters said they voted for him because of abortion. That was about enough to make the difference, if only that survey had had a surgical degree of precision that even the best exit polls lack. Peter Hart resurveyed voters who had told his interviewers earlier that they supported Clark and found that nearly a quarter of them had switched to Jepsen and 10 percent had not voted at all. A quarter of the switchers, or about 3 percent of the electorate, said they had switched because of abortion. Half as many said it was because of the Canal. But Hart's survey, while measuring why people switched, did not account for the fact that many Iowans—as his earlier polls made clear—had held the Canal issue against Clark early on. In the end, neither Hart's work nor the *Register*'s "studies" offer a certain statistical way to measure the impact of these issues on the election.

As John F. Kennedy once said, "Victory has 100 fathers." While he was talking about blame for the failed invasion of Cuba at the Bay of Pigs and continued, "but defeat is an orphan," the saying applies to elections, too.★ In a close election, any cause or faction can claim, plausibly, that it provided the margin of victory. The *Register*'s postelection editorial, gracelessly titled "The Best Man Lost," said, "Clark's courageous votes on the Panama Canal treaties and abortion made him vulnerable to voters who felt strongly about these issues. Jepsen's pitch on these emotional subjects evidently paid off."

Jepsen would not have won his 26,532-vote margin without the abortion issue. In the end, it probably mattered most. But he would not have won without Clark's votes for the Panama Canal treaties, either.

★ The other 1978 election that conservatives like Phillips insist turned on the Canal issue was the Colorado Senate race. Floyd Haskell, a colorless moderate-Republican-turned-Democrat, had somehow squeaked through to win a seat in 1972, but on a range of issues he was much more liberal than the Colorado electorate of the time. He was challenged by a young, three-term conservative Republican congressman, Bill Armstrong.

Haskell voted for both treaties, although he joined McGovern in threatening to vote against the second pact if nothing was done about the DeConcini

---

★ The quotation, from an April 21, 1961, news conference, is usually cited erroneously, with victory given "a thousand fathers."

provision. He said emotional conservative opposition to the treaties them-selves reflected the idea that "we were giving away a piece of American folklore."

Armstrong denounced the treaties, saying before the vote on the first: "We would be yielding control of an important national asset to which we have a legal and moral right in exchange for a few vaguely worded promises." He complained, "This isn't just a bad bargain. It is no bargain at all." And in the fall he attacked Haskell for voting for them.

But he put far more emphasis on "big spending, big government, big taxes" and insisted that Haskell had cast the deciding vote against an impor-tant tax cut. Rowland Evans and Robert Novak, the conservative columnists, praised Armstrong for putting more emphasis on the proposed Kemp-Roth 30 percent income tax cut than any other Republican, and the *Rocky Mountain News* said he had been running on inflation ever since he announced. "This wasn't the only issue in the campaign," Armstrong wrote me in 2006, "but it was by far the most important."

The campaign was hardly bitter, even though Haskell said his challenger "represents a dedicated, forthright fringe group outside the mainstream." When the results came in, Haskell sent Armstrong a telegram saying, "We discussed the issues and clearly the majority of the people of the state agree with you."

The Canal issue probably helped Armstrong, but by no stretch of the imag-ination did it provide his margin of victory, for he won by 150,349 votes. Arm-strong got 480,596 votes, or 58.7 percent, to Haskell's 330,247 votes, or 40.3 percent.

★ The Panama Canal was a secondary issue in Maine's race between the in-cumbent, Democrat William D. Hathaway, and his challenger, Republican Bill Cohen, who had won three terms in the House. Hathaway, a wounded prisoner of war after being shot down in World War II, had upset Margaret Chase Smith, a fixture in Maine politics, in 1972. But he had not been coming back to Maine regularly, and Cohen, after playing a major part in making the House effort to impeach Nixon bipartisan, began the campaign ahead in the polls and never faltered.

Other issues mattered more, especially Hathaway's support for Indian land claims and the Dewey-Lincoln dam. But the Canal played a role, largely a tactical one. Maine veterans' groups—Hathaway's natural constituency because Cohen had no military record—opposed the incumbent because of his support of the treaties. William J. Rogers, a past national commander of the American Legion and from Maine, campaigned for Cohen, and Hathaway was made unwelcome when he appeared at a Veterans of Foreign Wars convention. That veterans' opposition made it hard for Hathaway to narrow the gap with Cohen.

Considering his later internationalist role, Cohen's opposition is a bit surprising, though it was low-key. "I went a bit easy on the issue," he said in a 2005 interview. "I didn't have to vote, and I had tremendous respect for Howard Baker. I thought it was probably a bad idea." Although Rogers contended Cohen's opposition came "long before the vote," in fact Cohen hinted rather than stated his opposition, at least until after the treaties were adopted. He wrote in December of his "serious reservations" and in March told constituents he was still "evaluating" the pacts. In May he said, "Had I been a member of the United States Senate this spring, I would have voted against the treaties."

Cohen made a radio ad in early November quoting the editorial endorsement in the *Bangor Daily News*: "Whether the issue is the Dickey Dam, Panama Canal, the land claims case, gun control, inflation, or taxation, Sen. Hathaway seems hopelessly out of touch with the times and the public priorities."

This was another race where the Canal played a role but hardly influenced the result. When the ballots were counted, Cohen had 212,294 votes, or 56.6 percent, and Hathaway got 127,327, or 33.9 percent. Others, especially Hayes Gahagan, a conservative with New Right support hoping to deny the moderate Cohen a victory, got 35,551 votes.

★ As their support for Gahagan showed, New Right conservatives were at least as anxious to punish moderate Republicans as Democrats. So no election result in 1978 excited the conservatives more than the Republican primary in New Jersey, where a thirty-four-year-old former Reagan aide, Jeff Bell, defeated Senator Clifford Case, a seventy-four-year-old moderate seeking his fifth term.

Bell had a lot of issues to use against Case, from tax cuts to a generalized "too liberal" attack. But the Canal was important for him, too. Case was the senior Republican on the Foreign Relations Committee and a strong supporter of the treaties. Bell argued that was a typical "elite" attitude, out of touch with the ordinary New Jersey voters, whom state polls showed opposed the treaties. It also gave Bell a big break in terms of exposure when a Philadelphia television station invited him and Case to debate the issue. Case, like most incumbents who think they have nothing to fear, stayed away, but the station put Bell on anyway to argue with Sol Linowitz, giving Bell more exposure than he got elsewhere.

Reagan declined to join the campaign against Case, an incumbent Republican. Nevertheless, Bell not only caught Case by surprise, but about the only outsider who predicted his victory was Weyrich, who told CBS News four days before the primary, "There are millions of voters out there who have demonstrated that under the right circumstance, they will vote for a Republican candidate if they are given a clear-cut liberal-conservative choice. They are reluctant, to come into a party, I think, that doesn't necessarily represent their point of view or has no point of view, or has, worse yet, sort of an elitist country club point of view."

Bell did not get millions of votes, but the 118,555 he did get were enough to edge out Case and his 115,082. Patrick J. Buchanan crowed, "Bell's astonishing upset of Cliff Case is a political event of more significance than any other this election year."

Bell's general election campaign drew contributions from across the country from conservatives like Ernie Angelo Jr., a Reagan backer from Midland, Texas, who told the *New York Times* that Bell's primary victory suggested "the Northeast may at last be rejoining the American mainstream." And Reagan pitched in to help. But Bell was still heavily outspent by Bill Bradley, the Democratic candidate and former New York Knicks basketball star and Rhodes scholar.

In fact, the primary was only an interesting interlude. Bradley might have had to share labor support with Case. But his much greater energy and the fact that after four terms Case was still generally unknown in the state would almost certainly have enabled Bradley to beat Case, just as he beat Bell, when the results were 1,082,960, or 55.3 percent, for Bradley to 844,200, or 43.1 percent, for Bell.

★ The other major Republican target of the New Right of 1978 was Edward W. Brooke III, the first African American ever popularly elected to the Senate and, like Case, a truly liberal Republican. Brooke had voted against three of President Nixon's Supreme Court nominees, had opposed the war in Vietnam, and was the first senator to call for Nixon's resignation. He had supported federal funding of abortions and, after weeks of apparent indecision, had supported the Canal treaties.

Avi Nelson, one of the early conservative radio talk show hosts, ran against Brooke and made the Canal a major issue. On Bunker Hill Day, June 17, he appeared with Governor Thomson of New Hampshire at the battle monument in Charlestown. Thomson asked, "What would New Hampshire's John Stark, who urged his comrades at the Battle of Bennington to 'live free or die' think of the 12 New England Senators who recently voted to give away that vital national security link between the oceans—the Panama Canal." He answered his own question: "Certainly he would have looked upon them and our President as treasonous to the cause of liberty."

A bitter divorce led to accusations that Brooke had committed perjury in an effort to make his financial liabilities seem greater than they were, and a probate judge ruled in mid-June that he had testified falsely. It took six more weeks of headlines before the district attorney announced he would not prosecute. Moreover, as Jack Germond and Jules Witcover wrote in the *Washington Star*, Brooke might have been vulnerable even without the Canal and divorce issues: "He has earned a widespread reputation for spending as little time as possible in Massachusetts, splitting it instead between Washington and his home in the Caribbean."

Brooke got past Nelson but with considerable difficulty. He won the primary by 17,963 votes, with only 53.3 percent. In the general election, he faced a strong Democratic candidate for the first time and lost to Paul Tsongas by 202,964 votes. Tsongas got 55.1 percent of the vote. Nelson's campaign and the Canal issue damaged Brooke. But with the financial questions from the divorce still hanging over his head and Tsongas, backed by Senator Edward M. Kennedy, campaigning hard, Brooke probably would have lost even if Nelson had stayed out.

★ No serious Republican challenged Howard Baker in Tennessee. But the general election struck a few sparks. One Baker aide, Tom Griscom, called it "much closer than it should have been." A major fund-raiser, Joe Rogers, deserted him over the treaties.

But Baker was helped by the fact that people thought of him as a potential presidential candidate, even though Barry Goldwater had said the day after the second treaty vote, "As far as a presidential nominee, I think he's dead. Not just because of this, but the leadership role he took in it incensed a lot of

Republicans." Baker also spent a lot of time at home after the treaties were passed. The *Tennessean*, which in 1972 had made him the first Republican it endorsed, backed him again, saying "he does not deserve the criticism that has been leveled against him by his opponent on this issue."

His Democratic opponent, Jane Eskind, tried to make an issue of the Canal. "It is incumbent upon a senator to represent the people," she insisted. At another point she said that Baker had also failed Tennessee by not winning a guarantee that the Tellico Dam would be built despite environmental concerns over the future of the snail darter: "The truth is that Howard Baker—who had the power and the influence to give away the Panama Canal—had the power and the influence to keep the Tellico Dam for Tennessee. He failed." (The dam was eventually built.)

Baker met the issue head-on. His campaign literature said his amendments were what made the treaties acceptable. And he told reporters that his polling showed 56 percent support for the amended treaties. Opposition based on the treaties, he said, was a "myth."

Despite Griscom's discomfort, the margin was 176,416 votes. Baker got 642,644, or 55.5 percent, to Eskind's 466,228, or 40.3 percent. That was below the 61.5 percent he had received in 1972, when Nixon swept the state, but it was about the same as the 55.7 percent he received in 1966, also an off-year election.

★ Another Senate race where the issue might have mattered was Sam Nunn's in Georgia. Herman Talmadge, the veteran senator, had provided welcome political cover for the freshman, Nunn, by promising to vote however Nunn did (though Nunn thought Talmadge expected him to vote no). Even so, Nunn's pollster warned him it would cost him 20 percent of the vote, and forty to fifty Georgians followed him around the state carrying signs saying, "Once we had a canal. Now we have Nunn."

But Representative Larry McDonald backed out of a threatened challenge, and neither Nunn's primary nor his general election opponents were formidable. John W. Stokes, the Republican candidate, told the *Atlanta Constitution*, "People all over the state are still chomping at the bit about the Panama Canal. They say they are not going to vote for Sam Nunn, and I don't think they would have any reason to lie to me about it." But he said he only had $6,000 to spend, and ended up with only 16.9 percent of the vote.

If, instead of Stokes, he had faced a "strong, well-financed opponent," Nunn said in 2007, "it might not have defeated me, but it would have come close."

★ Where the New Right was active, the Canal issue played a role in some House races, though it hardly affected party control of that chamber. One interesting race was the contest for Wyoming's at-large seat. Dick Cheney, Ford's chief of staff, ran and won. As he told Craig Shirley in 2004, "I campaigned against the Panama Canal treaty—a ready-made issue for me," even though the deal was essentially the one Ford had sought, and the deal he supported once Carter had made it.

16

The New Right arrived at the political bazaar as the terms and conditions for doing business were changing dramatically. Two federal laws, passed in 1971 and 1974, and one Supreme Court decision, in 1976, imposed limits on how much individuals could give candidates and promised real enforcement of those limits and those on how labor and business could do business in campaigns.

Two New Right operations, the Committee for the Survival of a Free Congress and the National Conservative Political Action Committee, played important roles in that emerging marketplace. NCPAC (pronounced "nick-pack") defined the role of independent expenditures, which the Supreme Court had encouraged and the American Conservative Union used to help Reagan in 1976. The Committee for the Survival of a Free Congress chose a quieter path, concentrating on training and advising conservative House candidates.

Both groups were political action committees, or PACs, a creature whose population exploded in the late seventies. These organizations, especially those with business interests, grew in number from 608 to 1,633 between 1975 and 1978. Their spending grew from an estimated $36.9 million ($20.5 million of that going to candidates for the House and Senate) in the 1975–1976 election cycle to a recorded $77.8 million (with $35.5 million going to House and Senate candidates).

The first, and for many years the most effective, political action committees were created by organized labor. Their history traces back to the group called Labor's Non-Partisan League, which brought unions into American politics as a serious force for the first time in 1936. The name, which lives on in the PAC of the machinists' union, reflected the idea that labor was for Roosevelt, not the Democratic Party. The founders—John L. Lewis of the mine workers, Sidney Hillman of the men's clothing workers, and Major George L. Berry of the pressmen—dreamed of creating a labor party someday. Then, in 1943, Congress prohibited contributions from union treasuries (as it had, at least in theory, for corporations in 1907). The Congress of Industrial Organizations responded by setting up the first PAC, which would receive voluntary contributions. Many individual unions followed and created their own PACs.

Business had been slow to organize PACs, for two reasons. One was that even though the 1971 campaign law expressly allowed corporations and unions to organize political action committees, the law still barred government contractors from contributing to candidates for federal office, directly or indirectly. The second was that since there were no effective, enforceable limits on contributions, businesses gave money through individual contributions, often reimbursed from company funds.

When the 1974 law eliminated the contractor ban and imposed clear reporting rules and enforceable limits on individual contributions, corporations started organizing PACs. Their numbers increased from 89 in 1974 to 433 in 1976, to 784 in 1978, and to 1,204 in 1980. Over the same period, labor union PACs grew, but much less rapidly, from 201 to 297.

But even though corporate PACs gave about twice as much to Republicans as to Democrats, that hardly satisfied the New Right, which regarded the Republican leadership of Congress as too accommodating to Democrats. Using the New Right's expansive definition of "liberal," Viguerie wrote in 1981, "In the 1976 elections about 70% of big business' political action committee (PAC) donations went to liberals." Or, as Paul Weyrich, a theorist of the Right, put it in 1980, "Where we supported the tough conservative, the business PAC was always for the establishment, the moderate candidate." In 1976 business had given four dollars to incumbents for every dollar it gave a challenger, making it no vehicle for an overhaul of Congress. Weyrich complained in 1979 that businessmen were "too stupid" to see that even if an incumbent did them a favor on one issue, he might be voting "against their interests 90 percent of the time."

That is where conservative political action committees came in. (The liberal National Committee for an Effective Congress had been founded in

Paul Weyrich testifying before the Senate Armed Services Committee
(Paul Hosefros/*New York Times*)

1948.) One of the first was the Committee for the Survival of a Free Congress, created in 1974. It was headed by Weyrich, a hot-tempered thirty-two-year-old former disc jockey, reporter, and Senate aide. From his years with Senator Gordon Allott of Colorado, he had come to know Joseph Coors, the beer baron, and he persuaded Coors to contribute $250,000 to launch the Heritage Foundation in 1973. But, he told Scripps Howard writer Richard Starnes in 1977, "After a year I left Heritage precisely because it was prohibited from doing political things by its tax-exempt status." In 1974, again with Coors's financial help, he launched his new outfit, which he conceded to Starnes had "the worst-sounding name for a political committee it was possible to find."

In 1974, Weyrich's awkwardly named committee helped seventy-one conservative candidates, mostly Republicans. It is not clear just how much help it provided. Americans for Democratic Action said the Weyrich organization gave $42,000. But a 1975 fund-raising letter for Weyrich's group, signed by Senator Carl Curtis of Nebraska, said it "raised and distributed $194,000." Both said there were seventy-one candidates. Many lost in that overwhelmingly Democratic year.

By the 1975–1976 election cycle, with the aid of Viguerie's direct-mail fund-raising operation, the committee gave $245,259 to 117 House and Senate candidates. Since most of those it helped were challengers to incumbents, again there were considerably more losses than wins. But one of those who won was Dan Quayle of Indiana, the future vice president. He upset a veteran Democratic member of the House, Representative Ed Roush, with whom local Republican officials had felt comfortable.

The committee was doing more than helping candidates directly. It published a well-regarded newsletter on races around the country. It also compiled its own set of ratings of members of Congress. Unlike other groups, which picked out 20 or 30 key votes by which to judge lawmakers, in 1977 the committee tallied 315 "major" House votes and 249 in the Senate to establish its "Conservative Register." The ratings system set a high standard for lawmakers to meet; anyone with less than 55 percent correct votes was labeled "left wing"—a label even James O. Eastland, the conservative, racist senator from Mississippi, could not avoid. At 48 percent, Eastland fell into the "moderate liberal" category. By contrast, Americans for Democratic Action gave him a 10 percent rating—very conservative by its lights, and the American Conservative Union gave him a 61 and called it a "favorable" rating. (Jesse Helms did get a 90 in the Conservative Register, and 100 from the ACU.) In all, the committee found that 70 percent of the House and 68 percent of the Senate counted as "left wing" or worse. In the House, 136 were labeled radical; in the Senate, 26 were.

Throughout the year, Weyrich's biggest focus was on House elections. Finding a different sort of candidate was an important task. Weyrich told Time, "In the past, we conservatives have paraded all those Chamber of Commerce candidates with the Mobil Oil billboards strapped to their backs. It doesn't work in middle-class neighborhoods."

The real test was ideological. Candidates seeking support from the committee had to fill out a seventy-two-point questionnaire to measure the depth of their conservatism. Then, if their race did not seem either hopeless or a sure thing, they were invited to attend campaign schools lasting several days, preferably accompanied by their campaign manager. Campaign schools were popping up all over the country, conducted by parties, unions, and interest groups. Their faculties, which included conservative members of Congress, taught as many as twenty courses.

What made the Weyrich schools unique was that there was one lesson that candidates had to accept if they wanted any more help from the committee—an approach to precinct organization. It was called the "Kasten Method," after the approach taken by Robert Kasten in races for the Wisconsin state senate and later the U.S. House of Representatives in the seventies. As Weyrich explained it in 2007, Republicans in the past had often focused their efforts only on Republican precincts. "Our plan required that every precinct be considered, not just safe ones." He said a campaign worker would get as much credit for meeting the 26-vote target he had been set in an inner-city precinct as someone who met his quota of 300 in the suburbs. Kasten and his staff taught that course, and the schools were often held in Milwaukee.*

After candidates and aides completed the course and returned to their races, Weyrich would send field men out to check on how things were going and to help out. He might pay a $500-per-month salary for someone in the campaign. The visits, the staff salary, and perhaps a waiver of the school's $350 tuition fee all counted as "in-kind contributions." They counted, as valued by the donor, against the new $5,000 limit allowed PACs for any election, a primary or a general election. Weyrich preferred the in-kind approach to giving cash to candidates, though he did make direct cash contributions, too. In the 1977–1978 cycle, for example, the committee gave House candidates $71,431 in cash and $126,794 in "kind."

That was an unusual balance. Most PACs gave mostly cash, and in fact most campaigns preferred it. The most generous of the corporate PACs, the International Paper Company's organization, gave $116,460 in cash and nothing in "kind." The United Automobile Workers PAC gave $803,785 in cash and just $6,500 in "kind." But the National Committee for an Effective Congress, the liberal political action committee on which Weyrich patterned

---

* Some Republican campaign officials scoffed at Weyrich's insistence on this method. Russ Evans, who headed the 1976 and 1978 campaign operations for the National Republican Congressional Committee, said the Kasten system would not succeed where there was an entrenched Democrat because enough precinct workers could be enlisted. Evans observed in a 2007 interview, "When you drink his Kool-Aid, you have to follow his organizational requirements."

his own organization, showed a pattern similar to Weyrich's. It also sought to train and assist inexperienced campaigners, and it gave $56,146 in cash and $77,250 in "kind" to House campaigns in the 1977–1978 cycle.

Sometimes the efforts of Weyrich's committee paid off. Daniel Crane, Phil's younger brother, was running in downstate Illinois for a House seat that a conservative Democrat, George Shipley, had held for twenty years before retiring. Crane, a dentist, was running against an attractive state legislator, Terry Bruce. Between late June and Election Day, the committee's field staffers paid ten separate visits to his campaign, valuing them at $2,125.09 on its reports to the Federal Election Commission. The committee also paid $250 toward the salary of George Windhorst, who coordinated Crane's volunteers. T. R. Reid of the *Washington Post* wrote, "The Crane camp put together a volunteer organization that dug up Republican voters everywhere—even in the traditionally Democratic counties—and saw to it that they turned out to vote." The Kasten system worked; Crane got 86,051 votes, or 54.0 percent, to Bruce's 73,331.

Sometimes the Weyrich efforts failed. His view of an ideal candidate could often differ from that of the voters in a given district, and incumbents of that era almost always had more money to spend than did challengers. For example, David Crane, a third brother who was a psychiatrist and a lawyer, was running in Indiana for the second time against David Evans, a former teacher. In 1976, Evans had won comfortably, with 55.0 percent of the vote. The next time around, Weyrich's people paid David Crane's campaign eighteen field visits, reported as a $2,972.65 in-kind contribution, starting in November 1977. The committee also paid $1,000 toward a staffer's salary in the summer of 1978.

David Crane paid attention to the Kasten precinct strategy. He outspent Evans and campaigned heavily on television and in newspaper ads, blaming Democrats and Evans for inflation while condemning the Panama Canal treaties and the SALT negotiations. On some occasions, reported the *Indianapolis Star*, he portrayed Evans "as a fence-straddler who tried so feverishly to stay on both sides of the issues that he ended up falling on his dignity." But it was not enough. David Crane lost again. Evans got 66,421 votes, or 52.2 percent, to his challenger's 60,630.

Another losing committee effort, one not decided until weeks after Election Day, was in eastern South Dakota. Leo K. Thorsness, a Republican and a Medal of Honor winner who spent six years as a prisoner of war in Vietnam, had lost in 1974 to George McGovern, when he retained his Senate seat after losing forty-nine states, including South Dakota, in his 1972 presidential run. That campaign brought Thorsness statewide name recognition, but for some South Dakotans an image as a harsh-speaking carpetbagger. In 1978 Thorsness tried for an open House seat that had been held by Larry Pressler, a moderate Republican. Pressler in turn was running for the Senate seat held by retiring Democrat James Abourezk. And the final piece of the political musical chairs game was that Tom Daschle, an Abourezk aide, was the Democratic nominee for Pressler's House seat.

Thorsness's 1978 campaign emphasized the conservative coalition-building that was another of Weyrich's themes, who worked hard to enlist evangelical Protestants, at the time traditionally apolitical, into campaigns. Weyrich explained the opportunities for coalition-building this way: "Most liberal incumbents just happen to be pro-abortion gun-controllers whose biggest thrill in life is to figure out how to tax their neighbor on the one side in order to send the kids of the neighbor on the other side across town on a school bus."

In the Thorsness campaign, the main allies were one of the oldest conservative political organizations, the National Right to Work Committee, founded in 1955 to work to ban labor contracts requiring workers to join a union, and one of the newest, South Dakota Right to Life, Inc., the state voice of the growing antiabortion movement. Both organizations campaigned for him, and Thorsness took part in an antiabortion demonstration in Brookings, outside a Daschle fund-raising event.

Thorsness's own nearly successful last-minute ad blitz denounced Daschle for agreeing with his former boss, Abourezk, on the Panama Canal treaties and for taking labor PAC money (illustrated with a photograph of George Meany, head of the AFL-CIO, with a cigar). But seven field visits from Weyrich's committee staff, starting in February and valued at $2,387.12, plus staff salaries paid totaling $1,719 and a $500 contribution, were not quite enough to put Thorsness over. Recounts that lasted more than a month left Daschle the winner in a recount, by 139 votes. (That was a landslide compared with the 14-vote margin the first official canvass showed.)

While Weyrich's group emphasized in-kind contributions, it worked with other conservative PACs that gave cash. As Weyrich wrote in 1980, because "most of the newer special interest groups relate to conservative issues," coalitions developed "around some candidates." Three special elections for vacant

House seats in 1977 proved good opportunities, when conservative groups successively backed three Republican winners, Arlan Stangeland in Minnesota, Jack Cunningham in Washington, and Bob Livingston in Louisiana.

Weyrich's group did support some incumbents, but usually with small cash contributions. The exception was Congressman Larry McDonald of Georgia, the John Birch Society official who topped the Weyrich's Conservative Register with a 93 percent rating (the ACU gave him 100). Seeking a third term, McDonald faced an intense challenge from a retired businessman, Smith Foster, who spent his own money freely and charged that McDonald was a "counterfeit Congressman." The incumbent responded that Foster was a "counterfeit conservative" who would sell out to labor. McDonald failed to win a majority in the August 8 primary, only narrowly edging Foster, and was forced into an August 29 runoff primary.

The Committee for the Survival of a Free Congress weighed in with a $2,000 contribution the day before the runoff and sent its field staff to help on five occasions in August, valuing those visits at $1,944.71. The turnout was higher for the runoff than for the first primary, a rare event, and McDonald won with 45,789 votes, or 51.5 percent, to Foster's 43,188.

Those races illustrate how the Committee for the Survival of a Free Congress operated in an election cycle that was probably its most important. Other ideological PACs gave more money, but except for the National Committee for an Effective Congress (NCEC), few provided much on-the-ground campaign help.

Some were able to give a much bigger proportion of their contributions out as donations (see Table 1). The National Rifle Association's Political Victory Fund gave out 60 cents of each dollar it collected. The Conservative Victory Fund, associated with the ACU, gave 35 cents, and NCEC gave 19 cents. Weyrich's committee gave away, in cash or in kind, only 12 cents out of each dollar it raised.

None of the ideological PACs approached the bottom-line efficiency of labor or business groups, which could use payroll checkoffs to collect money and union or corporate funds to manage their operations. At the International Paper Company, 77 cents of each dollar collected went out as a contribution. The United Steelworkers gave out 89 cents of every dollar collected (see Table 2).

Weyrich wrote in a paper for Michael Malbin's *Parties, Interest Groups and Campaign Finance Laws* that the problem of high costs for PACs like his was the

TABLE 1 Selected Political Action Committee Activity in 1977–1978 Election Cycle

Name of PAC	Receipts	Contributions to Candidates	% of Receipts	Independent Expenditure	% of Receipts
Ideological PACs					
Citizens for the Republic	$3,114,514	$431,586	13.9	$0	
National Conservative Political Action Committee	2,842,851	220,980	7.8	20,671	0.7
Committee for the Survival of a Free Congress	2,023,121	241,233	11.9	684	*
Gun Owners of America	1,449,270	178,634	12.3	0	
National Committee for an Effective Congress	1,051,658	204,189	19.4	0	
Conservative Victory Fund	775,959	273,104	35.2	0	
John Connally Citizens Forum	722,993	77,427	10.7	0	
Fund for a Conservative Majority	606,466	30,300	5.0	0	
NRA Political Victory Fund	605,790	365,961	60.4	58,330	9.6
Council for a Livable World	566,862	28,441	5.0	0	
National Women's Political Caucus Campaign Support	135,666	14,100	10.4	0	

*Indicates less than 1 percent.

Source: Federal Election Commission.

1974 law's $5,000 limit on contributions to PACs. Without the act, he wrote, his committee "could have persuaded several major contributors to back its work and then established another kind of fund-raising program, avoiding direct mail altogether. The act, however, took the large contributors out of the political process. Consequently CSFC had no alternative but to turn to direct mail to seek out the small contributor. It is vastly more expensive, especially in the nonelection year, to raise funds from small contributors."

"It is ironic," he wrote, "that the election reformers who are now busy devising ways of taking Richard Viguerie out of the political process have only themselves to blame for putting him there in the first place. Their 'reform' law created the circumstances that made this sort of operation the only alternative for most kinds of noncorporate or nonunion political action."

TABLE 2 Activity of Selected Corporate, Labor, Trade/Member/Health, and Cooperative PACs in 1977–1978 Cycle

Name of PAC	Receipts	Contributions to Candidates	% of Receipts	Independent Expenditure	% of Receipts
Corporate					
DARTPAC (Dart Drugs)	$282,109	$116,811	41.4	$81	*
AMOCO Political Action Committee	265,644	157,800	59.4	0	
Voluntary Contributors for Better Government (International Paper)	225,315	173,856	77.2	0	
Labor					
AFL-CIO COPE Political Contributions Committee	1,443,385	898,541	62.3	0	
UAW-V-CAP	1,432,855	976,900	68.2	536	*
United Steelworkers Political Action Fund	673,832	601,930	89.3	0	
Trade/Member/Health					
Realtors Political Action Committee	1,909,310	1,133,078	59.3	0	
American Medical Political Action Committee	1,657,885	1,649,695	99.5	48,189	2.9
Automobile and Truck Dealers Election Action	1,461,493	973,175	66.6	0	
Cooperatives					
Committee for Thorough Agricultural Political Education (Associated Milk Producers, Inc.)	917,493	446,361	48.7	0	
Trust for Special Political Agricultural Community (Dairymen, Inc.)	598,438	168,300	28.1	0	
Agricultural and Daily Educational Political Trust (Mid-America Dairies)	374,273	232,800	62.2	0	

*Indicates less than 1 percent.

Source: Federal Election Commission.

17

The National Conservative Political Action Committee took a different approach. NCPAC was the most famous, and to its enemies the most notorious, of the conservative PACs. While it often collaborated with the Committee for the Survival of a Free Congress and other groups in supporting a particular candidate like a Jeff Bell when he ran for the Republican Senate nomination in New Jersey in 1978, it came to stress nothing as prosaic as precinct organization. It became known for high-visibility attack ads. Those ads were harsher in tone than many candidates were comfortable broadcasting themselves, though by today's minimal standards they seem routine.

The independent expenditures were one reason for the attention NCPAC received. Perhaps even more important were the quotable, iconoclastic comments about activities from its executive director, John T. (Terry) Dolan:

"We could elect Mickey Mouse to the House or Senate," he told KUTV in Salt Lake City in 1980.

"I don't think there is anything wrong with fear," he explained to ABC News that year.

"Our goal is the destruction of the campaign laws as they are presently constituted," he told the *New York Times* also in 1980.

"It's a stupid law," he told Myra McPherson of the *Washington Post.* "They're going to take me kicking and screaming to jail before I stop my activities."

In the spirit of the Mickey Mouse boast, he elaborated to McPherson:

Groups like ours are potentially very dangerous to the political process. We could be a menace, yes. Ten independent expenditure groups, for example, could amass this great amount of money and defeat the point of accountability in politics. We could say whatever we want about an opponent of a Senator Smith and the senator wouldn't have to say anything. A group like ours could lie through its teeth and the candidate it helps stays clean.

NCPAC was founded in 1975 by Charles Black, then an aide to Senator Jesse Helms; Roger Stone, an alumnus of the less than criminal "dirty tricks" side of the 1972 Nixon campaign; and Dolan, who had the least experience but perhaps the most imagination of the trio.

Dolan, always known by his middle name of Terry, came from an anticommunist Catholic family that stopped voting for Democrats when Dwight Eisenhower ran for president in 1952. Before that, an uncle, Jack Dolan, had run in a Democratic congressional primary in Massachusetts in 1946—the primary won by another veteran of the South Pacific, John F. Kennedy. Terry's family lived in Connecticut, where his father managed a Sears, Roebuck store. Terry was always active in politics and leafleted for Richard Nixon in 1960—when he was nine. Terry and his brother Tony, who was eleven, sneaked under the barricades to shake Nixon's hand when he campaigned in Connecticut. Terry graduated from Georgetown University, where he was active in Young Americans for Freedom, and from Georgetown Law. Tony Dolan, who served President Reagan as chief speechwriter, recalled in a 2007 interview that Terry's main political motivation was that "he really resented big government. He saw government as a threat." He said Terry had "a certain Irishness—a capacity for anger."

NCPAC planned to offer campaign services, much as Weyrich's committee did, though precinct organization was not as dominant an element of its curriculum. Conservatives often lost, it said in a 1975 prospectus, because of a "serious lack of technological training and assistance in many areas of their campaigns." For conservatives to succeed, it said, they "must begin now to recruit candidates, train and place campaign staffers, and assist candidates through financial and in-kind contributions such as opposition research, voter surveys, demographic materials, field staffs, campaign consultation and other types of assistance." Its first assistance, in 1975, was provided to at least twenty legislative candidates in Virginia, who got survey data on their districts and campaign advice, valued by NCPAC at $50,000.

In the 1976 congressional elections, NCPAC gave $343,867 to House and Senate candidates. It was able to give that much in large part because Black—who had gone off to work in the 1976 Reagan campaign—asked Reagan at the Republican convention to sign a fund-raising letter. Reagan wrote, "Through NCPAC, we conservatives are using expert organization to defeat those politicians who spend your tax dollars as though there were no tomorrow. The ones who are trying to impose these liberal ideas and morality on you and your family." It raised $800,000, a huge sum for the organization.*

For the most part in its early years, NCPAC was an unremarkable PAC, giving money and polls done by Arthur Finkelstein, the able conservative pollster, conducting campaign schools, and helping conservative candidates find capable staff.

NCPAC made its first use of independent expenditures toward the end of that 1976 campaign, several months after the ACU's ads in support of Ronald Reagan's presidential campaign. It reported expenditures in support of seven House candidates, with its biggest effort on behalf of John Burcham, a Republican candidate in Washington's Maryland suburbs. NCPAC spent $6,000 for four half-page ads in the *Washington Post* and *Washington Star* and $4,885 to run a thirty-second commercial six times on local television. The newspaper ad said "GLADYS SPELLMAN IS ONE OF THE BIGGEST SPENDING LIBERALS IN CONGRESS" and "John Burcham will fight inflation." The television ad said that Spellman, a freshman, voted for a congressional pay raise Burcham would have opposed. Dolan told the *Post* he had chosen Spellman as a target because the race was close and she was "the most obnoxious about her radical viewpoints" of the freshmen House members in the Washington area. But the popular Spellman beat Burcham for the second time, raising her share of the vote from 52.6 percent in 1974 to 57.7 percent in 1976.

An independent expenditure in a Virginia campaign first made NCPAC controversial in 1977. A liberal, labor-backed candidate, Henry Howell, somehow won the Democratic nomination for governor. NCPAC created a Virginia subsidiary called Independent Virginians for Responsible Government,

---

* That mailing, according to Ann Stone, was also used to "prospect" for possible donors for a future Reagan campaign for president. At the time of the mailing Stone was the political director of Viguerie's direct-mail operation and was married to Roger Stone.

which produced letters and television ads attacking Howell over school busing, public employee unions, and gun control. Each of the ads, however, was
inaccurate. For example, the busing ad said Howell advocated busing Virginia
children into the overwhelmingly black schools of the District of Columbia
when in fact he had once spoken of D.C. children being bused into Virginia.
The Republican candidate, John Dalton, called on the NCPAC subsidiary to
withdraw its ads so that Howell would not have "an opportunity to martyr
himself." Withdrawing the ads was easy enough because no television station
had been willing to run them. The two campaigns then attacked each other
furiously, showing no embarrassment about inaccurate charges of their own.
Dalton won by 157,983 votes, getting 55.9 percent. He became the state's
second Republican governor since Reconstruction. He succeeded Mills Godwin, who had switched parties to become a Republican and defeat Howell in
1973.

The independent expenditures that became NCPAC's trademark flowered
in 1979, though the idea did not originate at its headquarters in Arlington,
Virginia, but 2,040 miles away.

In Boise, Idaho, Don Todd had run a losing campaign for Allen Larsen, a
Republican candidate for governor in 1978. Larsen, a Mormon stake president, won an upset victory in the primary but found himself in trouble in the
general election after he told a reporter he believed it was possible to legislate
morality. Todd recalled in a 2006 interview, "It got so people thought he was
going to try to pass a law against people staying up late."

Todd concluded that they had lost because "our candidate became the issue." Jake Hansen, his partner in the Larsen campaign, said, "If we could do
that to Frank Church, we could beat him." Church, an old-fashioned western
liberal from a conservative state first elected in 1956, was now chairman of
the Senate Foreign Relations Committee after managing the Panama Canal
treaties on the Senate floor.

Todd, a former executive director of the Idaho Republican Party, said they
started with "$400 in leftover postage from the Larsen campaign. It was still
on the meter. We sent out a fund-raising letter to Larsen contributors." Then,
out of ignorance, they broke the law, taking Federal Election Commission
lists of contributors to other conservative candidates and sending them letters asking for money. "We didn't know it was illegal," Todd said.

They named their organization the Anyone But Church (ABC) committee
and worked quietly for a couple of months, without "press releases, without

anybody knowing we were in existence. We wanted to build our contributor base before we went public. We knew we wouldn't get favorable coverage, we'd get killed in our crib," Todd said in 2006.

Then on January 22, 1979, Todd announced he was sending out 10,000 fund-raising letters to pave the way for Church's defeat. He wrote, "You and I know about his past record, how he led the fight on the Senate floor to give away the Panama Canal, his actions in regard to Communist Cuba, Southeast Asia and now Taiwan." He asked, "What will be left if you and I allow him to serve eight years as chairman of the Foreign Relations Committee?" The message was, "We will not promote any one candidate to run against Church, but we will lay a solid base for whoever does. When we say ANYONE but Church, that is exactly what we mean!"

There was some hostile reaction from Idaho Republicans. Steve Ahrens, a columnist for the Idaho Statesman in the state capital of Boise, wrote, "Republicans around the legislature this week were generally horrified when ABC hit the news, viewing it as exactly the wrong approach to the tactical problem of defeating a powerful, veteran senator like Church. They grimaced at the sarcastic title, implying that everyone in Idaho is better qualified for the U.S. Senate than Church, a low blow indeed." He continued, "One conservative Republican legislator said whoever the party candidate is, ABC will be a 'millstone' around his neck. Another legislator called it an 'embarrassment.' One joked Church must have hired Todd to stage this."

That spring the ABC committee broadcast its first television advertisement. It showed Idaho state representative Jim Golder standing at a missile site and saying, "These silos aren't filled with missiles any more. They are empty" because Church "has almost always opposed a strong national defense. He led the fight to give away our Panama Canal. And he voted to slash national defense procurement." In fact the silos were empty because they had held Titan missiles, which had been replaced in the Pentagon armory, though not in those particular silos, by Minuteman missiles. Church had voted for the Minuteman. The ABC committee broadcast the ad only three times, paying fifteen dollars each time for use during ABC's Good Morning America. But the ad, though of poor quality on 8 millimeter film, was picked up by most stations in Idaho and used in news stories about the ABC effort, and got national air time as well.

Steve Symms, a congressman who eventually ran against Church, shed crocodile tears in August when he told a television audience that if he ran, he would not ask the ABC committee to go out of business. "It may be danger-ous, maybe it will cost Steve Symms the election if he gets into it," he said, "and if that's the case, so be it."

By that time Dolan and pollster Finkelstein had been convinced that the "anyone but" approach was a shrewd way to make a high-visibility impact on the 1980 elections, to get started building up the negatives for selected Demo-crats long before there were Republicans chosen—or even announced—to run against them, and also an effective way to raise money by offering an opportunity to fight several liberal candidates at once. Todd's approach was adopted, and indeed NCPAC adopted him and his one-target PAC. On July 1, 1979, NCPAC absorbed the ABC committee as the ABC Project of the National Conservative Political Action Committee.

NCPAC had already spent money in March on newspaper ads in South Da-kota attacking McGovern, the 1972 presidential candidate who was running for his fourth term in the Senate. McGovern had supported Carter's formal establishment of relations with China. A sketch showed McGovern hand-ing the United States to a Chinese soldier. In August Dolan announced that Church, McGovern, Birch Bayh of Indiana, John Culver of Iowa, and Alan Cranston would be his organization's targets, and that ads attacking them were about to begin. "We picked them," he explained, "because they are the most distasteful, the most liberal, the most radical and the most vulnerable." Tom Eagleton of Missouri was added to the list in May 1980.

There was one constant about their targets, Dolan explained in a June 1980 interview with Rod Gramer of Boise's *Idaho Statesman.* "In each of the targeted campaigns we have, every single one of these guys, when we ask 'What is the major failing?' the Panama Canal comes up as either number one or two" in Finkelstein's polls. "The America people think the Panama Canal was per-haps one of the most important issues that ever came up in the Senate, cer-tainly in recent times," he said.

Over the next year and a half, NCPAC made television and print ads at-tacking the six senators, frequently recutting the same ad with a different target. A woman named "Verna Smith" appeared as a housewife from Sac-ramento against Cranston and from Indianapolis against Bayh. In each she was shocked to discover that the National Taxpayer's Union and other groups did not give her senator 100 percent ratings, but only 7 or 8 percent. To the music of "Sweet Georgia Brown," the theme of the Harlem Globetrotters, a black basketball team, a young white man in a red, white, and blue uniform dribbled a basketball while an announcer denounced Culver for "visiting countries around the world, all at taxpayers' expense." The same ad was used against McGovern. California assemblyman Pat Nolan sliced a large baloney and said, "One very big piece of baloney is Alan Cranston telling us he's fighting inflation. The price tag on that baloney is $46 billion dollars. That's how much deficit spending Cranston voted for last year alone. That means more inflation and more taxes for you and me. So, to stop inflation, you'll have to stop Cranston first." Nolan also did an ad at a gas pump attacking Cranston, saying, "Cranston has a chauffeured limousine in Washington and a private gas pump. He doesn't worry about the price." Different faces and voices did the baloney ad against Church, Culver, and McGovern.

Besides the Golder ad against Church, the Panama Canal issue was also raised in ads against Eagleton and Culver. In one, a voice asked, "Did you know Tom Eagleton voted to give away our Panama Canal?" A man who was listening to that and other questions about defense then threw away an Eagleton campaign button. In the other, a ten-second ad in Iowa attacked Culver and Jimmy Carter. A voice proclaimed, "When you vote on Tuesday, remember the Panama Canal [as a pencil checked Reagan's name on the ballot], a part of America's heritage and a vital link in our national defense. Remember John Culver [as a pencil checked the name of his opponent, Charles Grassley] led the battle to give it away."

NCPAC also campaigned against its targeted senators with newspaper ads and direct mail. For example, in Iowa its Committee for Another Responsible Senator called for a vote for Grassley because he and Culver differed on tax cuts, "big government bureaucracy," "tax paid abortions," cutting national defense spending, growth in overall federal spending, and the Panama Canal. Then it reprinted the ad and sent it in the mail, asking for money to run it again. Dolan sent out a fund-raising letter for his Iowa operation's name, calling the incumbent an "APPEASEMENT ADVOCATE." The Dolan letter claimed that NCPAC had softened up Culver with its early attacks while Grassley was seeking the Republican nomination. NCPAC attacked Eagleton, saying he had voted for aiding a leftist regime in Nicaragua and against funding the neutron bomb; in fact it had both votes wrong. Similarly, an Anyone But Church ad accused Church of voting for a congressional pay raise when he actually opposed it. Todd's office blamed NCPAC headquarters for that error.

There were some disputes about how effective the NCPAC attacks were. Some candidates, like McGovern, confronted them angrily, giving them more attention than they might have got on their own. Press conferences to announce new ads, sometimes with a very slight buy of advertising time, got free attention when newspapers covered them and television news programs showed the ads as part of their stories. Finkelstein said the ads put Church and McGovern on the defensive, and George Cunningham, a top McGovern aide, said those efforts had cost McGovern about 20 points on a favorability index. "It was like a pack of jackals around an elk," he told *Congressional Quarterly*. "They pull him down, then the bear comes in and eats him."

Finkelstein said heavy press coverage undoubtedly exaggerated the impact of New Right efforts. But he said the impact was still real. And he contended that while there was some backlash against outside groups telling people how to vote, he said it never rebounded against the Republican candidates. Yet in Idaho, Bill Fay, an aide to Symms, contended that by the end, NCPAC's efforts actually cost Symms a few percentage points. Dan Quayle, moving up to the Senate by ousting Senator Birch Bayh, agreed on November 11, 1980, just three days after Election Day. He said efforts by NCPAC and the Moral Majority hurt Republican Senate candidates in South Dakota, Idaho, and Iowa. Republican candidates still won in those states, he said, because Ronald Reagan's landslide pulled them through.

NCPAC did some studies of its campaigns' effectiveness. Michael J. Robinson, then director of the Media Analysis Project at George Washington University, was given access to that polling. He reported in particular on a study that measured attitudes toward Eagleton in Springfield, Missouri, before and after a May–June radio and television blitz. Those ads argued that the more people looked at his record, the less they liked it. On national defense, energy, taxes, and economics, the polling data showed the "ads caused drastic changes in his public image," Robinson wrote in 1981. For example, before the ads were broadcast, 42 percent of respondents said Eagleton was doing a good job on national defense. Afterward only 10 percent did.

My own judgment is that the New Right attacks, and NCPAC's in particular, mattered in the 1980 election, but it is easy to overstate their impact. One reason for my caution is that the press exaggerated the New Right effort by taking at face value the accurate, but misleading, independent expenditure totals reported by NCPAC. They are misleading because fund-raising costs, down to the pay of "cagers" who opened envelopes replying to fund-raising appeals, were included among the independent expenditure totals reported to the Federal Election Commission. Cautious accounting dictated that they be included, because the mailings themselves generated opposition. But they made the effort seem more formidable than it was.*

For example, NCPAC's reports to the FEC said that independent spending against Church reached $305,524. But only $20,263 is clearly identified in the reports as for air time or newspaper ads. A few thousand more may have been lumped into some other expenditures, but the impact is not the same as buying a quarter million dollars' worth of air time, which in Idaho in those cheaper days might have exceeded what was available for stations to sell. (The costs of press releases and new conferences, which also produced negative publicity for the incumbents, are largely buried in the reports.) The largest apparent share of independent spending that went directly into air time and newspaper ads was in Eagleton's case; NCPAC reported spending $101,794, and apparently spent $38,367 on air time and newspaper ads. For Bayh, the total was $159,534, with $26,740 clearly buying advertising. For Culver, the total was $197,996, with $25,382 clearly spent on advertising. For McGovern, running in a state whose low population made advertising very cheap, there was a total of $178,745, with $7,716 clearly for advertising. Against Cranston, NCPAC reported spending $194,139, with only $3,585 clearly spent on ads attacking him.

Poring over Federal Election Commission reports shows how much of a supply chain was behind the frontline attacks on a candidate. NCPAC reported the following items in its anti-McGovern effort for the month of January 1980: $3,712 for printing, $2,049 for mailing, $819 for postage, $37 for shipping, $937 for rental of mailing lists, $2,264 for "list rental and direct mailing fees" (not separated), $50 for a WATS telephone line, $350 for "production services," $34 for video equipment rental (perhaps to show a television spot at a press conference?), $3 for recording, and $272 for personal expenses and petty cash. There was just $2,201 for time buying and ad placement.

Besides its independent spending against its six target senators, NCPAC also spent on the presidential race. Its first effort was against Edward M.

---

* The ACU's 1976 reports did not follow this practice. Its FEC reports showed a total of $256,218 spent on air time and newspaper space (most of the spending was for radio ads) for independent spending in support of Reagan's campaign for the nomination. Only another $15,801 for travel, mailing, and computer services was attributed to those pro-Reagan efforts. While the North Carolina effort may have been the most important, the ACU also spent $33,000 helping Reagan carry Texas and $35,000 on a losing effort in Ohio.

Kennedy. On the November day when the last Kennedy brother went to Fa-
neuil Hall in Boston and announced that he was challenging President Carter
for the Democratic presidential nomination, NCPAC ran a full-page ad in
the *Washington Post* to announce its "Kennedy Truth Squad." It said that the
liberal media should ask Kennedy tough questions, and it offered several,
including:

> You have been in the Senate for 18 years, and yet not one major piece of leg-
> islation bears your name. . . . Your personal background shows very little
> to be proud of in leadership qualities, particularly under pressure. With
> this type of record, what makes you think you have the leadership abilities
> to be president?
>
> What makes you think an *extreme liberal* like yourself is able to be a good
> president?
>
> Would Jack Kennedy vote for Ted Kennedy? He supported strong de-
> fense spending. . . . You have a 0% rating from the American Security
> Council ranking you as the most anti-defense member of the Senate. You
> favored the Panama Canal Treaties, SALT, and establishing diplomatic re-
> lations with Cuba. You even voted against the same tax cut your brother
> proposed as president. Don't you think this shows the similarities between
> Ted and Jack Kennedy go no further than the last names?
>
> Chappaquiddick. Will you consent to an unedited interview to discuss
> the entire affair? Since you have nothing to hide, will you take a lie detector
> test during this interview?

It is impossible to tell from the FEC reports how much was spent on actual
advertising out of the $247,918 NCPAC said it spent against Kennedy. A No-
vember 1979 item for advertising expenses totaling $23,616.90 could be for
time buying and newspaper space, but it could also represent, at least partly,
the costs of preparing the ads. Nor is it clear why Dolan much cared how Kennedy fared against Carter. Both Richard Viguerie, who handled the mailings,
and Roger Stone, who was working at NCPAC until he left for the Reagan
campaign shortly before the anti-Kennedy effort began, recalled in interviews
in 2007 that they believed the effort was primarily intended to raise money.
They pointed out that Kennedy's name was the best vehicle to raise money
from conservatives. An indication of that direction for the anti-Kennedy effort
is clear in the reports. In November, $43,903 was spent on postage, out of the
total of $71,928 in independent spending against Kennedy. In December, the

Terry Dolan presents President Ronald Reagan with a card pledging support from the National Conservative Political Action Committee, May 16, 1983. (Ronald Reagan Library)

single biggest item out of a total of $24,870 was for payroll. That money went to the "cagers" who opened the letters responding to the mass mailing of November.

NCPAC also ran one more major independent expenditure campaign. Unlike some of his colleagues in the New Right, such as Weyrich, Viguerie, and Phillips, Dolan never wavered in his allegiance to Reagan. NCPAC reported spending $1,859,168 to support Reagan's presidential candidacy. Here significant amounts did go into television advertising, with a reported total of $209,990 for time buying for the pro-Reagan advertising.

Gerald Rafshoon, who produced Carter's television ads, believed one NCPAC spot was particularly damaging in the South. The spot showed photographs of Carter's appointees as an announcer declared: "In 1976 Jimmy Carter said 'Why Not the Best?' Let's look at what he gave us. Andrew Young, who called Iran's Ayatollah Khomeini a saint, forced to resign after lying to the President. Bert Lance also forced to resign. Peter Bourne, the Carter drug

TABLE 3 Selected Political Action Committee Activity in 1979–1980 Election Cycle

Name of PAC	Receipts	Contributions to Candidates	% of Receipts	Independent Expenditure	% of Receipts
Ideological PACs					
National Congressional Club	$7,873,974	$56,104	0.7	$4,616,641	58.6
National Conservative					
Political Action Committee	7,648,540	231,414	3.0	3,377,391	44.2
Fund for a Conservative Majority	3,163,528	143,082	4.5	2,078,023	65.7
Citizens for the Republic	2,357,684	242,475	10.3	0	
Americans for an					
Effective Presidency	1,920,377	13,000	0.6	1,270,208	66.1
Committee for the Survival of					
a Free Congress	1,647,556	135,123	8.2	0	
National Committee for an					
Effective Congress	1,570,788	426,872	27.2	0	
Gun Owners of America	1,414,951	183,480	13.0	119,891	8.5
Americans for Change	1,072,549	17,250	1.6	711,856	66.4
NRA Political Victory Fund	1,044,879	434,303	42.3	441,891	41.6
Women's Campaign Fund	694,080	72,763	10.5	0	
Life Amendment PAC	625,748	19,621	3.1	65,536	10.5
Conservative Victory Fund	550,147	300,977	54.7	0	
Handgun Control Inc. PAC	170,589	6,300	3.7	43,055	25.2
National Women's Political Caucus					
Campaign Support Committee	48,198	11,500	23.9	0	

Source: Federal Election Commission.

expert, forced to resign after supplying drugs to a White House staffer. And the list goes on. If you want a President whose judgment you can trust, then vote for Ronald Reagan for President." Rafshoon told a postelection conference conducted by Kathleen Hall Jamieson at the University of Maryland that he believed the ad was a successful effort to incite racist opposition to Carter because of his ties to the black former UN ambassador.

Jamieson, the leading authority on the era's campaign commercials, considered another NCPAC ad as the most "damaging" to Carter. This one contrasted Carter's campaign promises with reality. It showed the words Carter used in a 1976 debate with Ford: "By the end of the first four years

TABLE 4 Activity of Selected Corporate, Labor, Trade/Member/Health, and Cooperative PAC in 1979–1980 Cycle

Name of PAC	Receipts	Contributions to Candidates	% of Receipts	Independent Expenditure	% of Receipts
Corporate					
North Western Officers Trust Account (Chicago & N.W. Transportation Co.)	$ 668, 021	$ 85,600	12.8	$ 0	
Sunbelt Good Government Committee (Winn-Dixie)	400,844	254,350	63.5	0	
AMOCO PAC	385,494	193,575	50.2		
Labor					
UAW-V-CAP	1,792,406	1,424,231	79.4	143	*
Machinists Non-Partisan Political League	1,029,920	855,408	83.1	26,085	2.5
AFL-CIO COPE	1,008,240	780,565	77.4	768	0.1
Trade/Member/Health					
Realtors Political Action Committee	2,739,879	1,536,273	56.0	70,198	2.6
American Medical Political Action Committee	1,728,392	1,351,685	78.2	172,397	10.0
Automobile and Truck Dealers Election Action	1,273,857	1,039,776	81.6	0	
Cooperatives					
Committee for Thorough Agricultural Political Education (Associated Milk Producers, Inc.)	1,323,567	733,789	55.4	0	
Special Political Agricultural Community Education (Dairymen, Inc.)	630,065	221,908	35.2	0	
Agricultural and Dairy Educational Political Trust (Mid-America Dairies)	514,740	270,650	52.6	0	

*Indicates less than 1 percent.

Source: Federal Election Commission.

of the next term we can have the unemployment rate down to 3%." The announcer stated, "The current national unemployment rate is 8 percent. During the four years of Jimmy Carter's term one million more Americans were put out of work." Then the ad showed Carter saying, "I keep my promises to the American people," and then the words "promises, promises, promises" echoed before the announcer commented, "We trusted Jimmy Carter once. Can we afford to trust him again?"

NCPAC's ads were not the biggest independent expenditures on behalf of Reagan. Two ad hoc organizations, Americans for Change and Americans for an Effective Presidency, were formed specifically to make ads to help Reagan. Americans for Change, created by Harrison Schmitt, a Republican senator from New Mexico, sent cassettes to 6,000 prospective donors to show what their contributions could produce. Americans for an Effective Presidency was created by the agency headed by Doug Bailey and John Deardourff that had produced Ford's commercials in 1976. One of its ads, shown on different Ohio stations, was tailored by market by showing local factories where jobs had been lost during Carter's tenure. Each of these groups spent almost two-thirds of its receipts on independent expenditures. And Helms's PAC, the National Congressional Club, spent $4,616,641, or 58.6 percent of its receipts, to help Reagan. The Fund for a Conservative Majority spent heavily to boost Reagan in the New Hampshire and Florida primaries after George H. W. Bush had upset him in Iowa and Reagan was running low on cash (see Table 3). Among nonideological PACS, only the American Medical Association, with $172,397, went in much for independent spending (see Table 4).

But the NCPAC ads may have had some impact. They were shown heavily in the South, including Alabama, where Reagan won by 17,462 votes, and Mississippi, where he defeated Carter by 11,808 votes. In neither state did the presidential campaigns advertise heavily. NCPAC's logic was simple and nonconspiratorial. A couple of years later, Craig Shirley had become Dolan's spokesman, and he told Jamieson what Dolan had told him: "We read in the newspaper that the Reagan strategy was to go North. So we went South."

18

After leading the fight against the treaties, the American Conservative Union expected to resume what it considered its rightful role at the front of the fight to change America. The issue had raised a lot of money and given the organization thousands of new names. Contributors were classed as members, and by November 1978, the ACU was claiming 325,000. The organization continued to fight the Canal treaties, urging pressure on members of the House to get them to vote against the implementing legislation. There were also ambitious plans, some patterned on the work against the treaties. For example, the ACU made a film opposing Carter's efforts to win ratification of SALT II, a new arms treaty with the Soviet Union, and announced that it would show it on television as it had the attack on the Canal pacts. The film even included the previous year's enemy, Howard Baker, among the on-air critics. The ACU also set up a speaker's bureau to send critics around the country attacking the treaty.

Representative Robert Bauman, the Maryland Republican who succeeded Philip Crane as chairman in 1979, gave an interview to *Human Events* and said what the ACU was "going to do now is more of the same." He continued: "Over the years we have devoted ourselves to the issues. We've created issues. We've been able to mobilize public opinion on things such as the Panama Canal treaties, the SALT treaties, things in which conservatives are deeply interested. And the fact we're regularly quoted in the press and that people look to us for the conservative position, I think, is evidence that we have succeeded."

"We have a rather ambitious and wide-ranging plan now for dealing with many issues before the Congress and before the state legislatures ranging from opposition to the D.C. amendment, to major things such as the SALT treaties," he said. "And with a large budget and several hundred thousand people who support us, I think we have a bright future."

Bauman was whistling in the dark. As early as July 1979 the organization was in deep financial trouble. That large budget, more than $3 million, was one reason. The bottom line was based on the assumption that the revenue level reached during the Canal effort could be maintained the next year. As the organization painfully discovered, people who contribute because of a television appeal are not very good prospects for direct mail. David Keene, then an ACU board member and subsequently its long-term chairman, observed in 2007 that the Canal issue was a double-edged sword. He explained, "The canal issue was a great boon for us. It raised a lot of money. Afterwards, there was a letdown and it almost destroyed us."

The ACU's state affiliates, which were financially independent, did keep functioning in about a dozen states from Maine to California. (The North Carolina conservatives even had separate county organizations.) They rated state legislators, pushed conservative issues at the state level, and occasionally dealt with presidential politics. Seeking to help Ronald Reagan, the Florida Conservative Union ran an ad before that year's primary, with pictures of Mr. Peanut and George Bush, saying:

> The same people who gave you Jimmy Carter now want to give you George Bush. . . . The purpose is to control the American government, regardless of which political party—Democrat or Republican—wins the presidency this coming November. The Trojan horse for this scheme is Connecticut-Yankee-turned-Texas-oilman George Herbert Walker Bush—the out-of-nowhere Republican who openly admits he is using the same 'game-plan' developed for Jimmy Carter in the 1976 presidential nomination campaign.

The Texas Conservative Union picked up on the theme two months later, accusing Bush of having been a member, like Carter, of the Trilateral Commission.

But in early 1980 Bauman told the ACU's national board that the organization's books were all wrong: "We have had to do a total reorganization of the record keeping and reporting." The direct mail effort itself was proving costly, with the ACU paying 82 cents for each dollar raised. Not only that, but a dispute with Bill Bonsib, the organization's direct mail vendor, ended up in court. He won a judgment of $123,264 and threatened to sue individual board members for more.

By 1980, the ACU was doing very little other than worry about money. That summer, Becky Norton Dunlop, the group's deputy executive director, told another conservative group to go ahead and plan unilaterally for the next year's CPAC event. She wrote to Robert Heckman, executive director of Young Americans for Freedom, "As you know, the ACU has discussed little other than finances in recent days. In that light, I would recommend that you and the YAF Board make a decision with or without consultation of the ACU staff and board regarding CPAC. Set the date that is best from your perspective. I can assure you that I will wholeheartedly back your decision with ACU Board members." The conference, the ACU's signature event, eventually was pulled together.

Even with the organization's longtime favorite, Ronald Reagan, campaigning for president, the ACU was a bystander in the 1980 elections. It compiled its annual ratings of members of Congress but lacked the $7,000 needed to publish them. It stopped publishing *Battle Line*, saving $10,000 a month. The inactivity hurt the fund-raising, as conservatives gave money to organizations that were more active for their cause. The ACU staff was cut almost to nothing in September.

Though the group was not doing anything to help Reagan, his staff came through to rescue the ACU. It provided a mailgram signed by Reagan:

> Without your support today, ACU could go out of business by Election Day. This is absolutely true. And it would be devastating to me personally. I need ACU if I am elected President. ACU is the key to my plans to change the direction of our government. Because patriotic Americans like you have supported ACU in the past, I must ask you to respond immediately—and make an emergency contribution. . . . The ACU budget has been slashed to the absolute minimum. . . . If ACU closes its doors the liberals will literally dance in the streets.

As Dunlop noted at the time, "It was the first letter in several months that showed a healthy profit," as did a follow-up mailing.

Beyond the realities of fund-raising and the failure to understand that the Canal issue was unique in its appeal, the ACU undoubtedly suffered from the lack of a full-time chairman. Bauman, in his fourth term and a likely Senate candidate in 1982, was a fixture on the House floor, working to trip up the Democrats on procedure. He helped lead opposition to federal funding for abortions and to the equal rights amendment. His most frequent utterances were, "Mr. Speaker, I object!" The Speaker, Thomas P. O'Neill Jr., said of him: "He's tough, and he certainly irks the leadership when he tries to get things done."

In October 1980, Bauman was interviewed by the *Baltimore Sun* about the ACU's troubles and insisted that he had not been "close to the problem in the last few weeks." He had another problem.

In October the Justice Department charged him with soliciting and performing oral sodomy on a minor in early 1980. He pleaded not guilty, said it happened when he was drinking heavily, and entered a six-month rehabilitation program after which the charges were dropped. But the conservatives did not give him that long. Weyrich demanded that Bauman resign from Congress and from the chairmanship of the ACU. Weyrich asserted, "It is impossible to defend his alleged actions." He said, "We hope and pray that he will, in fact, repent and redeem himself. However, the cause which he has helped to represent is greater than any one individual."

Bauman, who said some years later that he was gay, had previously sponsored legislation specifically authorizing employers to discriminate against gays and another measure to deny veterans' benefits to those discharged for homosexuality. He resigned the chairmanship of the ACU, though he stayed on the organization's board for a few years. Representative Mickey Edwards of Oklahoma was elected as chairman in November. Bauman did not quit the House, but the voters in his heavily Republican district on Maryland's Eastern Shore voted him out of office weeks later.

The ACU's leadership problems had not begun with Bauman. The faulty assumptions about how the Panama Canal fund-raising levels would last had been set under Philip Crane, before his term as chairman ended in February 1979. For his last several months in office, Crane was focused not on the ACU but on a presidential campaign that produced more than a little tension at the office, where most hearts were with Reagan. It sometimes seemed that the organization's monthly, *Battle Line*, was promoting Crane himself, featuring him far more frequently than it had singled out M. Stanton Evans, his predecessor. His campaign never got very far, though at times it symbolized the continuing dispute within the Right—between social issue conservatives and economic conservatives.

Crane, a college history teacher with what authors Jack Germond and Jules Witcover called "collar-ad good looks," had won a special election to the House from Illinois in 1969 when Representative Donald Rumsfeld resigned to join the Nixon administration. His presidential ambition was openly discussed in his congressional office almost immediately.

Crane was a hero to many conservatives. He had stumped for Goldwater in 1964 and traveled thousands of miles in the late sixties to speak to young conservatives joining the movement through groups like Young Americans for Freedom and the Intercollegiate Society of Individualists.

He had also campaigned hard for Reagan in 1976 but turned on him after the choice of Richard Schweiker as a vice presidential candidate. He began talking publicly about running in July 1978, counting on the prominence among conservatives that he had gained from the Canal fight and his youth (he was forty-seven to Reagan's sixty-seven) to make him a viable alternative to Reagan. He insisted he was not running against Reagan, telling reporters that there was "a very good chance" Reagan would not run. Most conservatives did expect Reagan to run, but some felt he would choose not to be a candidate again, or that his age (he would turn sixty-nine in 1980) would keep him from conducting a vigorous campaign.

The difficulty with this argument was that Reagan had told Crane, "On a scale of one to ten, I'm at ten and a half" on running again, though he insisted he had made no final decision. Crane also said he had assured Reagan that he would not let his candidacy divide the party so that a moderate would be able to slip past them—a risk the Union Leader foresaw as it began attacking the idea as a "disaster" even before Crane formally announced. A July 26 editorial said he would split conservative forces and let a liberal or a moderate win, Loeb argued.

That announcement came on August 2, 1978, in Washington. Crane explained that he began so early to overcome the advantage other candidates had in name recognition. And he insisted he was not making his age an issue against Reagan. On policy matters, he sounded like Reagan, pledging "a commitment to our future and a restoration of the American dream to its proper custodian, the American people. As a free people, liberated from excessive government, we can achieve and together embark on the greatest and most exciting productive century our country has ever known." He also attacked the Carter administration for proposing tax increases, cutting defense spending, and failing to curb the federal bureaucracy.

His allies cheerfully made the comparison with Reagan. Paul Weyrich said some conservatives were cooling toward the Californian and added, "He has tarnished his relationship a little bit with some of the activists. . . . It's activists who tend to determine where the effort is made in a presidential campaign. And I think that you'll find that Crane may be able to pick up some of these people."

Although Crane had the field to himself until John Connally announced on January 24, 1979, the press did not take him seriously, except for William Loeb, whose *Union Leader* savaged him on the front page as a drinker (many years later Crane was treated for alcoholism) and a womanizer. Though the article "The Two Faces of Congressman Crane" was based on sources like "common knowledge" and what an associate said Crane had "once told a friend," Loeb's accompanying editorial piously insisted that the article did not run—on the day Crane came to address the New Hampshire legislature— "solely because we are supporting former governor Ronald Reagan for the Republican nomination for the presidency." Loeb said it was his newspaper's duty to profile presidential candidates because the general press and television let them off easily.

But within conservative ranks, the direction of the campaign was very important. Viguerie, who was handling the direct mail, and Weyrich wanted the campaign to build on social causes such as the burgeoning right-to-life movement. *Human Events* reported in May 1979 that when the campaign was being conceived in the summer of 1978, "it was decided that—to try to derail Reagan—Crane would be projected by the New Right as the front-running Conservative Movement candidate and would seek special ties to single-issue constituencies such as anti–gun control organizations, right-to-work groups and pro-life organizations."

But when Arthur Finkelstein, the pollster, joined the campaign in December, he urged a different focus. *Human Events* reported that "Finkelstein almost immediately began to clash with self-styled 'New Right' leaders because he disagreed with their emphasis on precinct organization, and he did not attach prime importance to dealing with single issue constituencies—such as abortion, gun control, and bussing, preferring Crane to emphasize the economic issues his polls showed were paramount with the voters." Those were also the issues Crane was most comfortable with. The candidate did not disagree with the New Right groups on the substance of social issues, but he cared more about economics. One of his pet ideas was that the United States should return to the gold standard.

Weyrich left the campaign in February 1979 and complained that Crane had not taken advantage of his opportunities. In 2007, Weyrich said his departure was not over any dispute concerning issues, but because the campaign was chaotic, Crane was not able to be a "national candidate," and he did not want to waste his time. But Finkelstein and Rich Williamson, Crane's former top aide in Congress who was running the campaign, did not have long to savor Weyrich's departure. Arlene Crane, the candidate's bossy wife ("I'm probably the strongest woman I've ever met," she told the *Chicago Tribune*) drove them out for not paying enough attention to her and her ideas about how the campaign should be run. Viguerie was still around, but there were intense arguments over his charges, whether he would stay, and whether the campaign owed him as much as he said it did. By March 31, 1979, Crane had piled up $822,022 in debts, much of it to Viguerie's companies. Jerry Harkins, who had been Crane's administrative assistant when he was first elected to the House, took over as campaign manager.

Viguerie quit the campaign on August 7 and announced that he would volunteer for Connally, raising money through direct mail and seeking to convince his friends on the Right to back the former Texas governor. He had no visible impact. Terry Dolan of NCPAC, for example, said he had told Viguerie he disagreed because Connally was hardly the best conservative candidate. "I think both Phil Crane and Ronald Reagan have indicated they deserve support from conservatives more than John Connally," Dolan said.

Crane might as well have quit, too. He campaigned, appeared in debates, but never got as many as one out of twenty-five Republicans in any state to vote for him before he dropped out on April 17, 1980. His best showing while he was campaigning was 3.2 percent in Georgia on March 11. After everyone but Reagan had quit, on June 3, he somehow got 8.2 percent in New Mexico.

★ The other conservative organization with a real membership, the Conservative Caucus, did not quit the Canal battle when the Senate approved the treaties. Shrewdly, it focused on the fact that Senate ratification of the treaties was not the end of the fight. The House still had a chance to vote, though not on the treaties themselves, but on legislation to implement them. The Carter administration, preoccupied with the Senate, had paid little attention to the House, where there had always been strong opposition to giving up the Canal.

The Conservative Caucus launched "Project Mayday," named for the international distress call. It sought to force a vote by March 31 on a House resolution by Representative George Hansen of Idaho that would seek to undo the treaties by asserting that no property in the Canal Zone could be transferred without a specific act of Congress—that is, by both houses. March 31 was the date on which transfer would take effect. "March 31 is Mayday for those of us who want to fight," Phillips wrote his members, "when bloodshed is not necessary, using our constitutional prerogatives, to preserve America's crucial strategic interests at the Isthmus of Panama." If passed, the Hansen resolution would be an argument in court against the validity of the treaties—on the basis that the Constitution's provision that Congress (meaning both Houses) had the power to dispose of government property had been violated. Since the House leadership had no use for the resolution, the only way to force floor action was with a discharge petition—a petition requiring the signatures of 218 members. The effort came close, but failed. Discharge petition signatures are secret until the number 218 is reached (which hardly ever happens); 191 congressmen announced they supported the petition.

Phillips then turned to the argument that if the implementation legislation itself could be defeated, that could be used as a constitutional argument against the treaties. The administration's proposed legislation was being handled by Representative John Murphy, the New York Democrat who headed the Merchant Marine Committee and had strongly opposed the treaties. The Carter administration at first opposed and then accepted his bill as the best it could get. It sought to limit costs to the United States by requiring that toll revenues be used to reimburse American costs. (The administration had greatly underestimated those costs during Senate treaty consideration.) It also put the U.S.-Panama commission that would operate the Canal through 1999 under Pentagon control. But even that plan ran into trouble in the House, which voted on May 17 by only a 200 to 198 margin to consider the legislation. Phillips was elated by the close vote, sending out thousands of mailgrams saying that defeating the Murphy bill would keep the Canal from falling "under the control of a Communist government closely allied with Fidel Castro." But when House leaders lobbied hard, the Murphy bill was passed a month later, 224 to 202, after the defeat of a series of damaging conservative amendments to make the legislation tougher on Panama.

Phillips did not lose heart, printing the roll call and telling his members to keep lobbying their representatives because the "decisive vote" would not come until a House-Senate conference report came to the House floor in September. "Contrary to what Jimmy Carter, the State Department and their friends in Congress are saying," he wrote in July, "the Carter-Torrijos Canal treaties will not take effect if Congress votes against the transfer of U.S. Territory and property and refuses to appropriate funds for the Payaway."

When the conference report did come to a House vote on September 20, the opponents startled the administration by defeating the measure, 203 to 192. President Carter told some congressmen that he felt partly to blame because he had not realized the House might vote the measure down and so had not made personal phone calls to members.

That vote sent the bill back to the House-Senate conference, which tinkered with it and sent it back to the House. On September 26, 1979, Murphy insisted that defeat would led to the Canal being shut down, and Bauman, the senior Republican among the House conferees, agreed, though he said personally he would vote no: "For the continued operation of this canal we need in place some implementing legislation, and this is the only implementing legislation left."

Hansen complained that being told by Murphy and Bauman that the bill had to be passed amounted to making the House into a "parrot" for the president. He said the real issue was "Do we have the guts in the House of Representatives to do what the American people want—what we know is right—what must be done to preserve this nation?" Phil Crane joined in, saying, "We in this body, each and every one of us, are the ones who ultimately will make the decision as to whether our canal is given away. . . . This is not the time that the United States should be retreating."

Before the vote Jim Wright, the majority leader, told his colleagues, "At least a score, probably 30 members," had told him, "I want that bill to pass. I know it is in the best interest of the United States, but my constituents misunderstand it and I can't vote for it." If members believed that, the Texan continued, "you sell your constituents short." Wright continued, "If you really do not think they possess the intelligence to understand it," then "you really do not believe in the fundamental premise of a representative democracy."

In the end, the measure passed, 232 to 188. Twenty-five members who had opposed the bill six days earlier voted in favor of the latest version; the most notable switcher was John Rhodes of Arizona, the minority leader. Phillips published the roll call, with a separate box identifying the thirteen Democrats and twelve Republicans who changed sides, and announced that not long before the 1980 election, the Caucus would spend $1 million to mail 12.5 million households in fifty House districts information on how their representative had cast this "watershed vote."

19

The Panama Canal was never central to the presidential election in 1980. Ronald Reagan did not talk about it much, and Howard Baker never got far enough to test whether it would be critical to his chances. But it was there as an undertone.

Baker's unique courage in talking a stand he had been told would deny him the nomination was noted immediately after the vote on the second treaty, even as his chances were disparaged. On April 18, 1978, Barry Goldwater told CBS News, "As far as a presidential nominee, I think he's dead. Not just because of this, but the leadership role he took in it incensed a lot of Republicans. But again, I have to admire the courage of the man for having done it."

Baker did not agree, or at least put on a brave face, telling Tennessee reporters, "I don't think the canal issue will be the determining issue by 1980. Voters will more likely be concerned with issues like the economy and arms limitation. And I'm sure that if there is a political future after the 1978 elections for me, that a vote for the Panama Canal treaties at that time is going to look a lot better than a vote against it."

But he promptly made it clear that if he was with Carter on the Canal, he was against him on a range of other foreign policy issues. Baker worked with Senator John Tower of Texas, who headed the Senate Republican Policy Committee, to craft a lengthy indictment—a "catechism of fault-finding," the *Washington Post* called it—that all thirty-eight Republican senators signed and issued on May 3. In summary, it said, "In 15 short months of incoherence, inconsistency and ineptitude, our

Howard Baker, after supporting the Canal treaties, argued against the SALT II treaty at the Senate Foreign Relations Committee, October 17, 1979. (AP Images/Chick Harrity)

foreign policy and national security objectives are confused and we are being challenged around the globe by Soviet arrogance."

After he won reelection to the Senate that fall, Baker led an informal Republican gathering in Easton, Maryland, to make a major assault on Carter's SALT II arms reduction negotiations, winning a vote that the arms talks be considered in light of other problems with the Soviet Union. The Carter administration had been arguing against such "linkage" of arms control and other issues. That February 1979 conference bound no one, but twenty-four of the twenty-six Republican senators present supported the resolution. And Baker, who had supported Carter even after Panama on issues like selling fighter planes to Egypt and Saudi Arabia despite being urged that opposition would win Jewish votes, said he thought the concept that bipartisanship in foreign policy, the idea that "politics stops at the water's edge," was obsolete. Speaking of Senator Arthur Vandenberg of Michigan, who led Republican support for President Truman's policies just after World War II, he told the *New York Times*, "Vandenberg was right in his time, but I think we're right in our time."

Baker had hoped the SALT II treaty would come to the Senate floor in 1979 and allow him to campaign for the presidency from the arena he knew best. But Carter stopped pushing the treaty, and it did not reach the floor. Possibly because of that expectation, Baker did not work hard on the nuts and bolts of campaigning and organization. He stayed on as minority leader and campaigned only on weekends. That enabled George H. W. Bush, the other main alternative to Reagan, to get a long head start in Iowa. Baker considered and rejected advice from consultant Doug Bailey that he resign from the Senate to demonstrate that he was totally committed to the campaign.

Still, he was a plausible alternative to Reagan when he finally announced his candidacy on November 1, 1979. A *New York Times*/CBS News Poll taken at that point put Baker at 13 percent, more or less tied with John B. Connally of Texas, who had 15 percent; Reagan had 37 percent of the Republicans polled. Bush had only 3 percent. With Connally a figure associated with both Lyndon Johnson and Richard Nixon but with no roots in the party, Baker was plainly the less conservative alternative to Reagan.

But he lost that standing just three days later at a "straw poll," an event even more meaningless than the *Times*/CBS News survey or any other pre-primary poll taken months before people vote. Republicans in Maine, seeing the publicity that the Iowa GOP had won for straw polls, decided to hold one. With strong support from Senator Bill Cohen, it seemed likely that Baker would come out on top. So Baker scheduled his first formal campaigning so that he would end up in Portland on Saturday, November 3, and claim a victory. He flew in with fifty reporters on a chartered plane. Unfortunately for him, the Bush campaign, led by Josie Martin, a twenty-two-year-old state legislator from New Hampshire who registered college students for the event, narrowly won. Bush got 466 votes, or 34.9 percent, to Baker's 33.4 percent. On a slow news day, the story led the front page of the *New York Times*, and the Bush campaign used photocopies of the story to raise money. David Keene, who was working as Bush's campaign director after being eased out of the Reagan circle, had expected to lose the event, whose importance Baker's side had promoted. But he said that Saturday night, "Remember all that stuff we were saying earlier in the week about this not being important? We were wrong."

Baker shook up his staff, worked hard in Iowa, and Bailey and his partner John Deardourff made one superb television commercial showing Baker facing down an Iranian student over the seizure of the U.S. embassy in Tehran where fifty-three embassy personnel were held hostage. Baker was occasionally challenged by audience members over the Panama Canal treaties, but because he never established himself as the leading moderate, the impact of the issue was never tested.

Bush, a war hero and former congressman, ambassador to the United Nations, Republican national chairman, head of the U.S. mission to China, and CIA director, did become the alternative to Reagan. A narrow victory in the Iowa caucuses propelled him to the top of national polls. But he failed to capitalize on the opportunity and establish who he was and what he stood for. Reagan won in New Hampshire and then took most of the remaining primaries to lock up the nomination.

★ The treaties did come up in Reagan's campaign, but only in the course of attacking the SALT II arms control treaty Carter was seeking. Reagan would say, "The president said we must ratify the SALT II Treaty because no one will like us if we don't. He said we should give away the Panama Canal because no one would like us if we didn't. It is time to tell the President: We don't care if they like us or not. We intend to be respected throughout the world."

But staying away from the issue was the plan.

On April 18, 1978, Reagan had been in Japan, meeting officials and businessmen, when the Senate ratified the second treaty. Pete Hannaford and Richard V. Allen, a foreign policy specialist who had worked on the 1976 Republican platform, were traveling with him and brought the news. Allen recalled in 2006, "He took it hard. He may have said 'Damn,' which was strong for Reagan." But there was nothing to be done about it; the treaties would soon be the law of the land.

So Reagan made a statement to the Associated Press, saying, "It is no secret that I feel the treaties are flawed." He complained that the will of the American people had been ignored, and that the Senate had not judged the treaties on their merits but approved them because the administration said if they were rejected, then Carter's prestige would suffer. "I hope my misgivings will not be realized. But I cannot help but be disappointed by what has happened. I feel it is a loss to the people of the United States and perhaps the people of all the world."

He was a bit less grumpy three weeks later when he appeared on CBS's *Face the Nation* and said, "I thought that the Panama Canal issue was an issue with the people of this country, and I think the people felt that way, too. I hope that it's over as an issue—that particular one. I really mean that. I hope that all of the things that many of us feared would follow adoption of those very flawed treaties will not take place, for our country's sake. I'm not sure that they won't yet."

That was his basic posture in 1979 and 1980, though once in a while he slipped up. Campaigning for the Connecticut primary in March, he said that as president he intended "to get the canal back." When reporters asked how, he said he did not know. In Oklahoma the same month, he said that if Panama were to "step over the line just once in violation, we'll step in." Again it was not clear what he meant.

He was a bit more specific in an October interview with Gary Schuster of the *Detroit News*, saying that although he had no plan to revoke the treaties if he were elected president, "You can never say never." He elaborated, "I think it's something that has to be watched very closely."

He continued, "You can't say that down the road there might not be some differences with regard to the treaty or some violation on the other party's part. And you've got to keep your option open to what you would do in that event. Suppose, for example, that—heaven forbid—but suppose there should be some alliance by way of Cuba or the Soviet Union or something that would put that in the hands of people who would not keep it open to world commerce. In that case, I think you'd declare the treaty null and void." When reporters challenged him about the story, he responded, "You guys keep asking hypothetical questions at me, I give you hypothetical answers."

It was the same relaxed mood he would use to great effect when he debated Carter five days later and rebuffed a Carter attack over Reagan's opposition to Medicare and national health insurance with a dismissive "There you go again." Both answers avoided the point, but if Reagan was at a disadvantage on facts, he was miles ahead on style and reassurance.

★ The one place where the Canal affected the 1980 election was that it worked against Howard Baker being chosen as Reagan's running mate. His name had been on lists of potential candidates, with pundits frequently saying he would help Reagan most. Conservatives campaigned intensively against that idea and claimed credit when he was not picked. In June, when the vice presidency was the only element of suspense left to the Republican effort, *Human Events* wrote that Baker "is such an anathema to the Right that his selection would seriously deflate Reagan's hard-core supporters and possibly prove fatal to the presidential campaign."

Viguerie's *Conservative Digest* devoted most of its July issue to a denunciation of Baker. The cover, showing Baker in a yellow dunce cap, read, "Why Howard Baker Flunks the VP Test. And No, It's Not Just the Panama Canal." John Lofton, the magazine's new editor, denounced Baker and insisted his views were different from Reagan on the Canal, the philosophy of the Republican Party, big government, abortion, homosexual rights, the equal rights amendment, the minimum wage, welfare, and at least a dozen other issues.

Inside, the magazine contained brief quotes from twenty-five conservatives calling Baker everything from "unprincipled" (Terry Dolan) to "unacceptable" (several answers) to "ineffective" (Mike Thompson of the Florida Conservative Union). He was criticized on the Panama Canal issue and abortion, and several critics argued, as did Alan Ryskind of *Human Events*, that if Baker was picked, "conservatives will not work hard for Reagan." But there was almost equal condemnation of Bush, and Viguerie said in a 2005 interview that the magazine should have both of them on the cover in dunce caps.

Afterward, when Reagan had gone through a bizarre flirtation with the idea of having former president Ford as his running mate and then picked Bush, the magazine boasted, "Conservatives, with the New Right in the forefront of the effort, prevented Tennessee Sen. Howard Baker from gaining the number two spot on the GOP ticket." But there was no cheering for Bush; the magazine published an article in the same issue titled "Bush Blunder."

Viguerie and friends gave themselves too much credit. Reagan liked and respected Baker, despite their differences over the Panama Canal, but he was not impressed with Baker as a campaigner. Above all, he wanted someone who would work hard in the fall campaign, and that desire recommended Ford and ultimately Bush, even though Reagan did not particularly like him. Bush had fought on as hard as he could until the end, and he was strong in states where Carter was vulnerable, like Pennsylvania. Reagan knew that Baker would provoke strong opposition over the Canal and other issues, but he was never intimidated by New Right leaders. But they may have thought he was, especially when he met with them at the convention. He told them Baker was not being considered.

There is one other reason that Baker was not chosen. He told Reagan in late June that he did not want the job. He said he would like to be president, but not by succeeding on someone else's death. To aides, he also said he did not want the job because vice presidents had nothing to do, and he also did not want to go through the experience of waiting out a decision he could not affect, as he had when Ford passed him over in 1976. He went on *Face the Nation* a few days later and said he did not want to be asked to run for vice president and did not expect to be asked. "My political landscape is littered with positions on controversial issues, whether it's the Panama Canal, or revenue-sharing, or fiscal responsibility, or national defense policy." He said he did not think a controversial record like his would be an asset in a vice presidential candidate.

One last reason, which Baker spoke of directly to Reagan but only brushed on *Face the Nation*, was the hope that the Republicans would pick up enough Senate seats (they then held forty-one, including one independent) to gain a majority. He thought it was becoming a real possibility and wanted to work to make that happen. He told the television audience he wanted to concentrate on "my campaign to be Majority Leader of the Senate."

"THEY NEVER WANTED TO SEE ANOTHER PANAMA CANAL AD"

THE NORTH CAROLINA SENATE CAMPAIGN

20

In none of the 1980 elections that fulfilled Baker's hope was the Panama Canal more dominant than in the North Carolina Senate race. Robert B. Morgan, a well-known former state legislator and attorney general, was seeking reelection to a seat he had won with 62 percent of the vote in 1974, when he succeeded Sam Ervin. He was opposed by John P. East, a well-regarded professor of political science from East Carolina University. East had run token Republican races for Congress and for secretary of state but had never held public office. He was Jesse Helms's candidate.

Morgan came to the Senate in 1975 and signed on to that year's Thurmond resolution insisting the "United States should maintain and protect its sovereign rights and jurisdiction over the canal." When he got a heavy load of letters about the Canal that year, he would tell constituents, "Certainly, I can see no reason for us to turn over control of the Canal to the Panamanian government. We built it, we paid for it in American dollars and lives, and we have a treaty which gives us the right to control and operate it."

But he soon found a reason. Senator Daniel K. Inouye of Hawaii, the chairman of the newly created Senate Select Committee on Intelligence, sent committee members around the world to visit stations of the Central Intelligence Agency during the Christmas recess in 1976. Inouye sent Morgan to Panama, where the CIA station chief showed him around, pointing out the vulnerabilities of the Canal to sabotage. Morgan spent a week there, meeting Panamanian leaders and seeing how well

Senator Robert Bob Morgan (U.S. Senate Historical Office)

the Americans lived. For Panamanians entering the Zone, he said, the experience must have been like the way he felt driving Interstate 87 through Fort Bragg, and finding himself under the jurisdiction not of his state's police, but of MPs.

So he recalled telling Carter, when the president called the next August to ask senators to postpone making a decision on the treaties until they could be briefed, "Mr. President, you don't have to talk to me. I've been down there and I can see we're never going to have tranquility down there until we do something. You've got my vote."

Even before he indicated publicly where he wanted to go, he told the North Carolina State Bar Association on October 28, 1977: "Our relationship with Panama on the future of the Canal is a festering sore and affects our relations not only with Latin America but with the rest of the world. Our global position as a world leader and as a moral standard bearer is seriously weakened by maintaining this vestige of colonialism."

After discussing the issues his constituents had raised, from communist influence to American weakness, he said:

> We have basically three options to choose from in dealing with the Panama Canal. We can do nothing, by which I mean refuse to consider any new treaty. I believe this would be a mistake. It would be wrong and it would antagonize the people of Panama and throughout Latin America. If there were guerilla activity, and we sent more troops to Panama, it would antagonize people throughout the world and create great divisions in this country. And what if a few well-trained guerillas sabotaged the locks and succeeded in closing the Canal? We would have the land, but the Canal would not be open, and we need that more.
>
> We could choose to just give the Canal back to Panama, with no restrictions or conditions. Some people feel this is the only just action the U.S. can take. But I don't think that this is in the legitimate interest of the United States, which must be recognized and protected, or in the interest of the rest of the world.
>
> Or, we can try to find a course which returns the Canal to Panama but which also protects the rights of the United States. This is what I support.

Morgan said some issues still needed to be clarified, but once the Baker-Byrd amendments were passed, he kept his word to Carter.

In 1979, Helms chose East, who had worked on the effort to make the 1976 platform as awkward for President Ford as possible, as a challenger to Morgan. East said he promised "solid and substantial" support through various elements of the senator's political machine, which was run through the Congressional Club. There would be enough, East said in October, 1979, to assure "a very competitive and very exciting campaign." He said Helms "regards Morgan's Canal vote as the crucial one." That explained, he said, why

Helms would break with senatorial courtesy and openly oppose another senator from his own state.

East, who told a reporter that he loved Plato and liked Cicero, Saint Augustine, Saint Thomas Aquinas, and Edmund Burke, had a naive sense of what he was getting into, commenting, "This is not to say that Senator Helms will be out running a very negative campaign against Robert Morgan. That would not be done. He wouldn't do it."

North Carolina has been no stranger, before 1980 or after, to dirty campaigning, usually over race, and Helms was involved with a lot of it. But this time, the Canal was the emotional issue that dominated a bitter campaign.

When East announced his candidacy on January 26, 1980, he said,

> Sadly, in recent years, we have witnessed the rapid erosion of America's traditionally strong position in the foreign policy and defense area. The recent events in Iran and Afghanistan are only symptoms of this erosion. My opponent, Robert Morgan, has contributed heavily to this policy of weakness which in recent history began with our giving up the Panama Canal. Mr. Morgan voted for this legislation, costing the American taxpayers millions of dollars, to fund our relinquishing the Canal. More recently, Mr. Morgan voted to confirm Sol Linowitz as an American negotiator in the Middle East. Incredibly, Linowitz is the man who negotiated the Panama Canal Treaty.

Tom Ellis and Carter Wrenn, the top officials at Helms's Congressional Club, ran the campaign. They sent out letters on Congressional Club letterhead, signed by Helms, asking people to send money to help East win. They raised about $2 million, and the National Republican Senatorial Committee, seeing an upset in the making, chipped in with $252,000, all the law allowed it to give. While the Congressional Club was doing millions of independent spending for Reagan, its lawyers advised that it could not be "independent" if it was running East's campaign, so it made no independent expenditures on his behalf.

Morgan campaigned in traditional North Carolina fashion, appearing at one barbecue event after another. East was rarely seen in public early in his campaign, and few voters knew that he was confined to a wheelchair, as a result of polio he contracted while serving in the marines in 1955. Instead his campaign was based mainly on television ads, with East outspending Morgan on television by about three to one. Wrenn said in 2006 that he believed

90 percent of the campaign's advertising was about the Canal. "I had people calling me and saying they never wanted to see another Panama Canal ad," Wrenn said. So in the last two weeks they added spots about Nicaragua, textiles, and tobacco. There were four or five different Canal spots, which have not survived.* One ad pictured the Canal and a U.S. aircraft carrier. Morgan saw it before it was broadcast and said that East apparently did not know that carriers were too wide to fit in the Canal.

There were other commercials too. One showed a car with bumper stickers for East and for Reagan, with the message "Ronald Reagan needs John East in the Senate." Another, with a red X over a picture of the projected B-1 bomber, said, "Robert Morgan has joined the liberal parade against the B-1 bomber. . . . Today there is a new parade to make the United States superior in defense again. The parade is going East. Elect Ronald Reagan and John East." (The references to Reagan enabled another Helms-inspired group, Americans for Reagan, to pay part of the cost as an expenditure for Reagan but independent of his campaign.) Still another East ad said Morgan "voted to give your Panama Canal away, voted to give Panama millions of dollars to take it and then voted to give $75 million to the Marxist government of Nicaragua." The pictures of Morgan in the ads were unflattering; Dr. Raymond Wheeler, a Charlotte physician and a former president of the Southern Regional Council, an organization dedicated to moderation on issues of race, said they made Morgan appear "as a Mafia-type figure."

As Morgan explained in a paper he issued to denounce those charges and others on September 15, he had regularly voted in favor of developing the B-1 bomber in 1975 and 1976. "To charge that Senator Morgan is weak on defense is ludicrous," it said of the navy veteran of World War II and Korea. The paper pointed out that Morgan voted with Helms against a 1976 measure to give whoever was elected president that year the decision on whether to cancel the new long-range bomber. But that provision became law, and in 1977 Carter decided to cancel the project and rely instead on cruise missiles. Morgan then voted against spending any money to build prototypes of the bomber, as did other previous supporters of the B-1, including Senator John Stennis of Mississippi, chairman of the Armed Services Committee. The $75

---

* Morgan, in a memo written January 5, 2004, asserted, "The Congressional Club had someone at every TV station to pick up the tapes on election eve. We have made concerted efforts to obtain them but have been unable."

million for Nicaragua was sought by Carter in hopes of diluting Soviet and Cuban influence on the Sandinista regime, which had overthrown the Somoza family dictatorship in 1979.

The state's leading newspapers, the *Raleigh News and Observer* and the *Charlotte Observer*, were both critical of East's ads. The Raleigh paper said of the spot about the Canal and Nicaragua: "This is such an incomplete and misleading treatment of the issues that they could appeal only to people who scarcely paid any attention to the subject." Rich Oppel, editor of the Charlotte paper, called East's ads "a collection of clichés and half-truths." He said they "converted hawkish, conservative Morgan into a dove-like big spender."

A similar message for East was conveyed in flyers. One showed Helms reflecting on how the future survival of America could depend on electing those "who are willing to fight for the survival of all we hold dear." When the flyer was opened, it compared "The Liberal Politicians" (Carter and Morgan) with "New Leaders for America" (Reagan and East). It said Carter and Morgan favored giving away the Canal and paying Panama to take it, aiding Nicaragua, building a new "posh" Senate office building, and raising gasoline taxes by 350 percent and opposed the B-1 bomber, "American Defense superiority," right-to-work laws, and control of deficit spending. Reagan and East, it said, opposed what Carter and Morgan favored and favored what they opposed. A similar flyer pictured Morgan with Edward Kennedy. And East himself sought to drive home the point, telling a reporter that Morgan "is typical of the McGoverns, the Churches, the Bayhs and the Culvers"—four of the senators on NCPAC's hit list.

East's campaign set the agenda. Wherever Morgan went, he was forced to defend his votes on the Canal, the B-1, and aid to Nicaragua, whether it was on call-in programs or at public meetings. Morgan tried to counterattack against the Congressional Club on June 21 when he announced he was running for reelection, saying at a Raleigh news conference, "What you have is that the opposition party has been taken over by a private club and the club will run the campaign." He predicted, "It promises to be a campaign that will be filled with innuendo, smear and accusations that are as silly as they are vicious." Later, after he had seen the ads against him, he labeled Ellis a "master of deceit."

Helms also brought race and religion into the campaign. In East's hometown of Greenville in late October, he said, "Our polls show these races are winnable. But Andrew Young's been down here organizing the black vote,

Senator John East, shortly after being sworn in by Vice President Walter Mondale, January 1981 (George Tames/*New York Times*)

and it will come out and it will elect unless we get our people out. Now, how bad do you want Ronald Reagan and John East?" Enthusiastic applause greeted his warning about the potential influence of Young, the black ex-congressman and ex-ambassador to the United Nations. Morgan also wrote in 1999 that the Ku Klux Klan tore down his signs and made a bonfire of them. Years later, Morgan quoted approvingly from Wayne Greenhaw's *Elephants in the Cottonfields: Ronald Reagan and New Republican South*. In his book, Greenhaw quoted Larry Grant of the White Knights of the Ku Klux Klan as telling a Raleigh rally, "We put out more than fifty thousand pieces of literature in country stores from one end of the state to the other." It is not clear just what literature Grant referred to, but thousands of copies of the John Birch Society's *Review of the News* did appear in towns across the state. The October article suggested Morgan was corrupt and denounced his "Far Left votes" on abortion, the debt ceiling, compulsory airbags, a consumer advocacy agency, and eleven other issues, of which it said the Panama Canal was "especially important." It said, "Conservatives believe that no Senator who voted to give away our Panama Canal can ever again be trusted consistently to fight for America's interests."

Religion came in when Helms, in a television ad endorsing East, said, "What we need is a real American in the Senate. A real Christian in the U.S. Senate." That offended Morgan, a Baptist who had denounced the growing influence of Reverend Jerry Falwell's Moral Majority. In the spring, Morgan urged Baptists to remain true to their historic commitment to keep church and state separate and not to invoke religion "on matters upon which reasonable persons may differ." He warned that American colonial history showed that "every group that gained state power harassed those who differed and persecuted dissenters."

Public polling consistently showed Morgan with a comfortable lead. As late as the third week of October, a *Charlotte Observer* poll found him with a 52 to 32 percent advantage. But Finkelstein, who was working for East, never found Morgan over 50 percent and at the end, according to East, found it a "dead heat," though East released no numbers.

On Election Day, Finkelstein was proved correct. East won by 10,401 votes, receiving 898,064 votes, or 50.0 percent, to Morgan's 887,663, or 49.4 percent. A fringe candidate got the other 11,948 votes.

The East campaign had succeeded in portraying Morgan as too liberal, despite the fact that his voting record was viewed more favorably by the

American Conservative Union than by Americans for Democratic Action. For his six years, ACU rated him 50 percent right. ADA gave him only 27 percent.

The Canal issue was central to that portrayal. Tom Ellis said it would have been "impossible" for East to win without it. "It was THE issue." And Jesse Helms told an audience in Burlington not long before Election Day: "Only one North Carolina Senator voted to give away the Panama Canal, and it wasn't Jesse Helms."

21

Frank Church was clearly the most logical target for the anti-treaty forces. He not only had voted to turn over the Canal but also had led the floor fight eloquently and carefully handled Dennis DeConcini to keep the second treaty from imploding. And unlike Robert Morgan, he could never be called a conservative; the ADA rated Church's 1975–1980 term at 57 percent liberal; the American Conservative Union gave him only a 14 rating as a conservative.

Church had sought morality in American foreign policy well before Carter started talking about it. In the mid-seventies, Church ran two major investigations of how the country operated abroad. One probed the bribes paid by American firms, especially Lockheed Aircraft, to get contracts. That led to a law against such bribes, the Foreign Corrupt Practices Act. The other was a wide-ranging investigation by a special committee into the CIA and the FBI. It revealed assassination plots against foreign leaders like Patrice Lumumba of the Congo and domestic political surveillance. That probe led to the creation of permanent select committees in both houses to look over the intelligence community's shoulder.

In 1976 Church returned to the Senate after an unsuccessful run for the Democratic presidential nomination, an effort crippled by the delay he needed to wind up his pathbreaking intelligence investigation. He was uncomfortable in dealing with the Carter White House, which he thought still bore a grudge over his 1976 campaign. Church's timing had given it the air of a "stop Carter" movement. Although initially reluctant, he

undertook a trip to Cuba at Carter's urging in August 1977. He won the release of almost 100 family members of U.S. citizens but stumbled at his departure by saying he had "found a friend" in Fidel Castro, a bumbling gaffe
his political foes used relentlessly.

But when Carter wired him that same month to say a Canal agreement
was imminent, Church replied, "Please count on my support in the weeks to
come." He said so with foreboding, as did McIntyre and Clark. His widow,
Bethine Church, said in a 2006 interview that he told her he was sure it would
cost him reelection when he ran for a fifth term in 1980. He said he understood the stakes. "We'll only discuss this once," she recalled him saying.
"The Panama Canal is going to lose me the election. It's just going to add to
the many things that people have thought I shouldn't do. It's going to lose me
the election, but remember, it's the right thing to do."

Church was then the second-ranking Democrat on the Foreign Relations
Committee, and the chairman, John Sparkman of Alabama, was no longer
sharp. So Church played a leading role in committee deliberations, warning
Carter of the need for clarity so firmly that Carter once slammed down the
phone on him.

On the Senate floor, he defended the treaties eloquently from the day the
debate opened. He told his colleagues:

Back in 1903, this was a very different world. Half a dozen major powers
controlled the whole world. There was a single empire, the British Empire,
upon which the sun never set, exercising its jurisdiction over one-third of
the land area of the globe. . . .

In the 75 years that have followed, we have seen the most extraordinary
transformation. The empires have melted away like so many icebergs in
the spring. . . .

There is no way to preserve the past, no matter how nostalgically we
might cling to it. The interests of the United States will be protected
through a new arrangement with Panama which reflects the realities of the
present. And even as our own national pride naturally is identified with the
heroic achievements of the earlier years, when we managed to construct
a canal that at the time was the greatest single engineering undertaking
in history, even though we may still think of the Panama Canal in terms
of our conquest of malaria and yellow fever, and Teddy Roosevelt and
the White Fleet and the Big Stick, those are days that related to a period

of empire, when great nations did as they pleased, with little hindrance. Those memories have nothing whatever to do with the realities of 1978.

Retaining American jurisdiction over a canal zone in a little country where we assert all the prerogatives of a colonial power is an anachronism which the world no longer accepts, and which the Panamanians cannot accept. For us to persist in this claim upon a little country would be to invite recrimination, hostility and resentment that will extend beyond Panama, and will affect our relations with all of the other republics of South America throughout the hemisphere.

David McCullough, the historian of the Canal, wired congratulations for a "magnificent" speech, and the capital was impressed with Church's leadership. Idaho, however, was unimpressed with his stand, let alone his leadership. And for all his fervor in Washington, Church did little to make his case at home, keeping references to the treaties in his newsletters to a minimum. Still, more than most senators Church did fire back when constituents' letters irked him. After the first treaty had been approved, Cameron Fuller of Post Falls, Idaho, wrote him, "I've prayed night and morning now for many months that He 'the Lord' would strike you dead if you voted to give away our Canal in Panama. I now realize that it is His wisdom that you should be allowed to live as a traitor and so be known to all men." Church replied, "The Lord did not strike me dead when I voted for the first of the two Panama Canal treaties, and I'll take my chances without fear when I vote for the second. Could it be that the Lord is on my side?"

By 1979, Sparkman had retired, and Church he had become chairman of the Foreign Relations Committee. That position was once held by his childhood hero, William E. Borah, a progressive Republican whose thirty-two years had made him the only senator from Idaho to serve longer than Church. Borah, a Republican, had opposed involvement in European wars in the late thirties, an isolationist view Church had endorsed as an eighth grader whose letter to the editor warned that America would be a "sucker" if it got involved. When Church was critical of the war in Vietnam in 1965, Lyndon Johnson suggested he was following Borah's example.

The chairmanship brought him the issue of the SALT II treaty, which Carter had submitted to the committee. Church's support of the treaty brought more criticism, and the prestige of the chairmanship cut no ice back home. A June 1979 poll taken by Lance Tarrance for Steve Symms, a four-term Republican congressman who had yet to announce his candidacy, found that 44 percent of those surveyed said Church was "in step with Idaho," but 48 percent saw him as in step with Washington. About a fifth of those who said he was out of step with Idaho cited the Canal.

Church's own polling was at least as discouraging. Peter Hart found that only 27 percent of respondents supported the Canal treaties, while 63 percent disagreed. Fifty-one of that 63 percent disagreed strongly, as did two-thirds of weak Church voters and the undecided. Hart concluded:

> Frank Church's support of the Panama Canal Treaty continues to hurt. Any thoughts that this issue would fade once the treaty was ratified must be dismissed. In Idaho, and in other states as well, Panama obviously remains a symbolically important issue to a great many voters. We believe there is no way for Frank Church to 'get right' on this issue, and that the only course is to get voters' attention centered on other foreign policy issues.

But, as Bethine Church recalled, her husband resisted the advice and tried to make up for not talking about the treaties much in Idaho when they were pending in the Senate. He told her, "I'm not going to vote for it and not have the people of Idaho understand why I voted." In essence, he gave a pared-down version of his Senate speech, taking seven or eight minutes, whenever the issue came up, which was often:

> While all the other empires were melting away, we've maintained a strip across Panama, 10 miles wide and 50 miles long, over which we exercised full jurisdiction, imposed our own laws. It was a colony, by any standard, by any definition. Now, if Mexico were up here in Idaho, holding a strip of land on either side of the Snake River, and we couldn't go from one side to the other without being subject to the Mexican police, Mexican troops and Mexican courts, we wouldn't put up with it for one minute. Yet, the Panamanians had to put up with it for about 75 years, because they were a little country and there wasn't much they could do.

He even insisted on airing a television commercial on the subject, but aides got it off the air after a couple of days.

Church had always had to worry about the conservative Idaho electorate. But as the only Democrat ever reelected to the Senate from the state, he had managed by balancing superior constituent service, opposition to gun control, and support for the sugar beet industry against unhappiness with some of his foreign policy stands and his environmentalism.

For much of 1979, Church was running hard, though without a declared opponent. Instead, he found himself running against assorted independent groups, of which NCPAC's Anyone But Church project, run by Idaho Republican Don Todd, was the most active. As Church traveled around Idaho during the August congressional recess, the ABC committee attacked him over the Canal, the SALT II treaty, and the charge that his investigation of the CIA was a "witch-hunt" that weakened the agency, which led to the fall of Iran and lines at gas pumps. "Every town he'd go in, we'd have an ad in the newspaper or on the radio station making a new allegation about him," Todd said in 1979. "Church must have thought the world was coming apart, although it was only in the town he was in."

Another local group, the Idaho Committee for Positive Change, insisted its purpose in a fund-raising letter was merely to inform voters: "Understand, we are not talking about a negative, anti-Church campaign. What we are talking about is voter education. The voter has a right to know." Then it issued a pamphlet citing Human Events, the John Birch Society, and the ACU to show that Church had not told the truth about the Canal treaties.

He was also attacked by antiabortion groups, local and national, and by a Washington-based outfit called the Committee to Defeat Union Bosses, which tied his Canal votes to the stand of the AFL-CIO. The National Pro-Life Action Committee put out flyers showing him (and McGovern, Bayh, and Republican Jacob Javits, along with a sixteen-week-old fetus), with the headline "These politicians are running for re-election in 1980. . . . While this little one is running for his life right now." It said the four had "consistently voted pro-abortion." Stop the Baby Killers, another new antiabortion group headed by Idaho's other Republican congressman, George Hansen, said Church and others "think it's perfectly okay to slaughter unborn infants." In fact, Church supported a constitutional amendment to allow states to regulate abortions, but not an amendment to ban them entirely.

The pace of attacks created a political storm. Church was especially provoked by an ABC project ad saying he wasted taxpayer money on the treaty implementation law, on a loan to bail out New York City, and by voting himself a $13,000 annual pay raise (which he actually voted against). He held a press conference to accuse the ABC committee of "using the well-known big lie technique." He declared: "Those of you who are old enough will remember that Adolf Hitler said in *Mein Kampf* that if you tell a big lie and tell it often enough, people will believe it. And I think that is the technique they have employed."

Church also made a blunder that roused both liberals and conservatives. On August 30, 1979, he received a call from the State Department telling him that the press was about to reveal there was a Soviet combat brigade in Cuba. In 1962 he had denied the presence of missiles in Cuba and suffered grave political harm at the revelation that the missiles were real. This time, he thought he had to get out in front. He called an 8:30 P.M. news conference at his home and announced a "buildup of Soviet ground troops to brigade strength." He demanded their removal and said SALT II could not be ratified unless they were removed. (It turned out later that the troops were no addition to Soviet forces, but successors to units that had been there since the missile crisis of 1962.) Liberals in Washington blamed Church for torpedoing the treaty. Symms, sounding more and more like a candidate, asked why it had taken Church so long to discover that the Soviet Union was a threat. He also tried to protect himself from the Right by some surprising Senate votes against the confirmation of two liberal nominees for the federal appeals court in Washington—Abner Mikva, hated by the handgun lobby, and Patricia Wald, denounced by the antiabortion groups.

When Symms finally announced his candidacy on April 7, he hit Church hard on the Canal and other foreign policy issues, declaring: "Frank Church has designed and advocated a weak and vacillating foreign policy which gave away the Panama Canal, negotiated an unequal, unverifiable SALT II Treaty, cancelled the B-1 bomber and cut the naval shipbuilding program. He, more than anyone else, presided over the emasculation of our nation's first line of defense, the CIA." He also attacked him over budget deficits and big government.

Symms was one of the most conservative members of the House. For his eight years, the ACU (on whose board he sat) had rated his voting record at 100 percent five times. His average was a 97. Americans for Democratic Action agreed, giving him a 4 percent liberal rating overall. He had lost battles in Congress with Church over wilderness areas, which Symms opposed as an infringement on capitalism. He had entered politics after marine service, which disappointed him when the Cuban missile crisis ended without combat. He came home to Idaho, grew apples, and published "The Idaho Compass," an antigovernment newsletter, before winning the House seat in 1972.

Throughout 1980, while the publicly released polls fluctuated, they always made it clear this was a close race. And the three-way race, among Church, Symms, and ABC and other ad hoc groups, stayed rough. Church called Symms a tool of the oil industry, a potential "Senator from Exxon." He suggested Symms used his office to provide "special legislative aid" for Nelson Bunker Hunt, a billionaire silver speculator, all the while making $10,000 himself on silver futures trading. He called Symms a do-nothing congressman who "has yet to pass—or repeal—a single bill."

Church had even more zest for the fight against the ABC Project. "Is Idaho up for grabs?" he asked in a mailing across the state. "Can one of our seats in the U.S. Senate be taken over by a handful of political gunslingers in Virginia?" He said NCPAC's "Idaho front" was "pouring hundreds of thousands of dollars into a massive media campaign designed to misrepresent my record and distort my positions on issues." Citing the inaccuracies in ABC ads, he said, "They care nothing about Idaho, her people, or her problems. They know I work for only one special interest, Idaho's, and they want me replaced by someone who will toe their line." But he was defensive, too. The last page of the seven-page mailing was a Q & A on the Panama Canal, illustrated with a picture of him "meeting in Panama with John Wayne, a strong supporter of the new treaty."

ABC kept running ads. One featured retired Lieutenant General Daniel Graham, former director of the Defense Intelligence Agency, charging that Church's investigation had weakened the intelligence capacity of the United States. James McClure, the Republican who was Idaho's other senator, went even further. After Symms (caught by ABC News) prompted a supporter at a rally in Grangeville to ask about the CIA, Symms turned to McClure, who accused Church of getting Richard Welch, the CIA station chief in Athens, killed. McClure falsely accused Church of naming agents and said the station chief had told him, "He's going to get some of our people killed." McClure said, "Two weeks later that man was dead. The man I was talking to had been assassinated." In fact Church's investigating committee neither sought nor received names of agents.

Other groups weighed in. An Idaho Moral Majority publication called *Christian Citizens News* said Symms's record on family issues was 100 percent and Church's was 33 percent. It printed a twenty-seven-item questionnaire that Symms had answered appropriately and Church had ignored. One of its local leaders, Rev. Buddy Hoffman, told Haynes Johnson of the *Washington*

Frank Church (right) and Steve Symms debate, October 23, 1980
(*Idaho Statesman* photo, Boise State University Library)

Post that churches were registering new voters because "Church represents the trouble we're in today" and has "a very sad voting record on abortion."

Thousands of copies of the John Birch Society's *Review of the News* were sent across the state. Its article, after denouncing Church for the Canal treaties, said: "One of the secrets of Frank Church's success as a 'Liberal' in a Conservative state has been his care to stay on the right side of a few sensitive issues such as gun control and school prayer. On other key issues of concern to his Conservative constituents he tends to vote with Conservatives a time or two when an issue is already settled in favor of his 'Liberal' friends—and then to cite those votes throughout a campaign."

At the Republican state convention in June, Symms mocked Church's claims of being a "heavy hitter" in getting bills passed. "How many home runs can Idaho and the nation afford?" he asked. "Senator Church scored a home run when he led the fight to pay away the Panama Canal, but that was one time when if he'd listened to the people in Idaho, they'd have told him he ought to make a sacrifice fly." And when the candidates debated on October 23, Church said: "I know I was laying my job on the line" by supporting treaties. Symms insisted it was "not in the best interest of the country to give away the Panama Canal."

With about three weeks to go, Peter Hart reported to the Church campaign that their messages were beginning to get through. For example, Church was preferred on effectiveness by 61 percent, to 16 percent for Symms. And his poll showed the race vote choice effectively even, with 47 percent for Symms and 46 percent for Church. But Hart warned, as he had all along: "The one issue that continues to work against Church relates to national defense and the Panama Canal Treaty. . . . We would recommend that Church continue to concentrate on his positive message and the contrast between him and Symms, rather than allowing the Panama Canal issue to dominate the campaign in the final days." That was not under Church's control. A newspaper ad from Symms that ran in at least eighteen newspapers, many of them small-town weeklies, showed a billboard with the message:

Whose Leadership Helped Push the Panama Canal Treaty Through?
FRANK CHURCH'S
It's Time Idaho [and the U.S.A.] Had a Better Friend

Of course there was a blizzard of last-minute ads on the air and in newspapers. A Symms ad had William F. Buckley Jr. and Senator McClure, Church's Idaho colleague, attacking Church over the CIA investigation. A Church ad said Symms had "zero accomplishments." A Symms ad said Symms, not Church, had staved off gun control. A Church ad said Symms voted against veterans and servicemen. An organization called the Replace Church Committee said Church had passed too many laws. The pro-Church Idaho Voters Association said Symms only voted no. And so on. And so on.

There was one more that people remember. Don Todd had some money left over in the ABC bank account, so he taped a fifteen-second television commercial and played it incessantly over the last few days: "Now that all the shouting's over, remember the Panama Canal—built with American blood and treasure. Frank Church voted to give it away."

There were many reasons for the result: a stagnant economy, antiabortion leafleting at churches the Sunday before Election Day, Ronald Reagan's popularity (he got 66 percent in Idaho to 25 percent for Carter and 6 percent for John Anderson)—and the Panama Canal. When the votes were counted for Senate, Symms had 218,701 and Church 214,439.

The margin was 4,262 votes. Church had been right.

22

Herman Talmadge had to be concerned about reelection in 1979 and 1980. Though Georgia had never elected a Republican to the Senate, Talmadge, a Democrat, had recently been through very public treatment for alcoholism and an equally public and bitter divorce. Even worse, his ex-wife had revealed how he lived off cash stuffed into his pockets by constituents. That led to a sixteen-month investigation by the Senate Ethics Committee, harsh coverage in the Atlanta newspapers, and ultimately to an 81 to 15 vote in the Senate denouncing him. The resolution read, "It is the judgment of the Senate that the conduct of Senator Talmadge is reprehensible and tends to bring the Senate into dishonor and disrepute and is hereby denounced." The particulars cited were false expense claims, unreported gifts, using campaign contributions for personal expenses, and filing inaccurate reports on his 1974 reelection campaign.

Until the divorce led to revelations that he stashed $100 bills given him by constituents in an old overcoat, Talmadge had rarely made headlines. He was not a flashy senator. His most prominent moments came when he sat on the Senate Watergate Committee, but he left the attention-getting to Sam Ervin and Howard Baker, rarely saying much. He was chairman of the Senate Agriculture Committee, an important position for Georgia, and the second-ranking Democrat on the Finance Committee, perhaps the Senate's most powerful committee.

Still, after he beat back a 1980 primary challenge by Lieutenant Governor Zell Miller, then a liberal, the conservative Talmadge had reason for confidence. Cambridge Survey Research,

Pat Caddell's polling firm, reported on a mid-September poll showing Talmadge with a 55 to 32 percent lead over Mack Mattingly, his Republican challenger:

> Herman Talmadge appears to be in decent shape heading into the last months of his campaign for re-election. He has a solid 25 point edge over his Republican opponent, and has won back much of his primary opposition including even some of those who favored Zell Miller in the runoff. His opponent is still not well known, and draws only fair marks from those Georgians who do recognize him. Talmadge has maintained the base of support—lower status, older Democrats in south and central Georgia—that has backed him in this year's primary and throughout his career and is also winning a solid vote from black Georgians.

Mattingly, who got into politics as a result of his admiration for Barry Goldwater, quit his job as an IBM salesman in 1979 and ran hard for eighteen months. He actually announced on September 28, 1979, at the Kiwanis Club of Jesup, a hamlet about seventy miles southwest of Savannah. He told the Kiwanians that he had filed with the Federal Election Commission, he blamed Washington for inflation, and he called for an across-the-board tax cut. He would later add "strong leadership in the defense posture in this country" as a critical issue, and he would criticize Talmadge for voting against spending any more money on the B-1 bomber. As he campaigned, he stressed economic issues, mainly tax cuts and the budget deficit. He also hit Talmadge hard on absenteeism, emphasizing that in 1980 Talmadge had missed more than half the votes in the Senate.

But there was also lingering anger over the Panama Canal treaties, often linked to the SALT II pacts. A typical constituent message to Talmadge, from James A. Rose of Kennesaw, read: "I firmly believe, and expect to vote for you next year; however, if you vote for SALT II I will have to reconsider my position. Your voting of the Panama Canal giveaway, the whispering campaign that has followed it, is actually costing you more votes than your hearing by the Senate Committee. Nobody believes much good can come out of the Senate anymore anyway."

Sam Nunn, Georgia's junior senator, had overcome the Canal problem he feared, winning reelection easily in 1978. But Nunn carried no other baggage, and his opponent had no money. The national Republican Party, however, put plenty of money behind Mattingly. One of his television ads raised the Canal issue in the course of complaining that Talmadge would not debate. Showing a picture of Talmadge, the ad's announcer said: "Herman Talmadge says he won't debate Mack Mattingly." The announcer said it was because, if he did, Mattingly would ask him questions like "Why did you vote to give away the Panama Canal and to kill the B-1 bomber?" The announcer asked, "How about it, Mr. Talmadge, will you debate Mack Mattingly?" A fake Talmadge voice, with faked moving lips, said "No thanks," and the announcer closed by saying, "Herman Talmadge didn't vote for you. Why should you vote for him?"

Mattingly had an even more inventive way of raising the issue. As he traveled Georgia's back roads, he would take a list of twenty-three questions he said should be raised in the debate Talmadge would not join. He would tack them on a door or a bulletin board and explain to reporters, as he did when opening a headquarters in Dalton, "Now don't y'all let Herman Talmadge come to Dalton and leave without answering these questions." Mattingly would tell reporters he was following the tradition of Senator Richard B. Russell, who had used the same technique in running against Talmadge's father, Eugene Talmadge, in 1936. The small-town papers picked up on the tactic and especially on the question "Why did you vote to give away the Panama Canal?"

Mattingly felt the issue mattered. He recalled in a 2007 interview, "It was a thorn in his side. It got us some votes." T. Rogers Wade, a former Senate aide who chaired the 1980 Talmadge campaign, agreed, because "it probably threw some cold water on some of his supporters" in small towns. So did Sam Nunn, who said in a 2007 interview that he believed it had damaged Talmadge's chances and that he had seen a poll at the time saying that "5 to 10 percent of the vote were swayed on that issue."

Five percent would have been more than enough. Mattingly won by 27,543 votes, getting 803,676, or 50.9 percent, to Talmadge's 776,143, or 49.1 percent.

★ The Canal was a part of the 1980 campaign against George McGovern in South Dakota. He recalled, in a 2006 interview, that "I couldn't have a Q & A in South Dakota without its coming up." His support of the treaties was attacked in flyers. His Republican opponent, James Abdnor, used it, among many other complaints, in ads just before Election Day and boasted on television that he had "stood firm against the giveaway of America's vital shipping lanes in the Panama Canal." McGovern was bothered enough to issue a flyer of his own, saying that Panamanian operation of the Canal had proved successful. He even made a television commercial, in which retired admiral Gene LaRocque stood in a flight jacket in front of a ship and missiles and stated:

> I spent thirty-one years in the Navy from combat at Pearl Harbor to defending the Panama Canal. George McGovern voted for the Panama Treaty. It was a tough decision, but militarily the right one. Today, America's defenses in Panama are stronger, the canal is earning more revenue than ever, and Castro's influence is down. The Joint Chiefs of Staff supported the Panama Treaty. They believe in a strong America and so does George McGovern.

Then an announcer's voice added, "George McGovern, for a strong defense."

But NCPAC's attacks, issued through its South Dakota project, People for an Alternative to McGovern, focused most heavily on other issues like tax cuts, gasoline costs, and McGovern's "globe-trotting." NCPAC undoubtedly softened him up in 1979 and early 1980. McGovern conceded that it had hurt him, saying in May 1980, "I'm always answering negative questions: 'Is it true you're a pal of Fidel Castro, that you sold the Panama Canal to the Communists, that you want to kill the unborn.' It's all these off-the-wall right-wing ideas. They've been running this stuff for two years, and there's no question it creates a negative mood."

The NCPAC attacks may have produced a backlash. McGovern hammered away at the "outsiders," mocking some of Dolan's outlandish comments. Dolan's claim that he could elect Mickey Mouse was featured in a McGovern television spot. Abdnor said NCPAC had hurt him more than McGovern and filed a suit against the organization.

The heaviest issue used against McGovern was abortion. Right-to-life groups backed Larry Schumaker, a college mathematics teacher who moved back from Texas to enter the race after twenty years away from South Dakota. He ran in the Democratic primary against McGovern and got a surprising 38 percent. The antiabortion groups then hammered at McGovern for refusing to support a constitutional amendment to prohibit abortion; their ads called him "anti-family" and a "baby killer."

McGovern, reflecting in a 2007 interview on his defeat, said the Canal "mattered, but not as much as some of the other issues. The abortion issue mattered a lot more." The Canal, he said, "could have been decisive," but only if the election was "razor thin." It wasn't. Abdnor won with 190,594 votes, or 58.2 percent, to McGovern's 129,018 votes, or 39.4 percent.

★ The Panama Canal was also around as an issue in the Iowa Senate race. Peter Hart, polling for the incumbent Democrat, John Culver, reported in October 1979: "One foreign policy issue not to emphasize is the Panama Canal Treaty. Only 30% of Iowa voters strongly or mildly agree with the Treaty, while 50% disagree, 33% of them strongly. Disagreement is strongest among voters in the 50–64 age group, who in most respects are strong Democrats. Only among strong Culver voters do we find a plurality for the Treaty; when we turn to weak Culver voters, the vote is 52%–31% against." And Lance Tarrance and Associates, polling for Republican Charles Grassley, pointed out in August 1980 that 45 percent of Iowans either supporting Culver or undecided said they would be less likely to vote for him if they knew he had supported the treaties. Twenty-eight percent of that group said such knowledge would make them more likely to vote for Grassley. Twenty-eight percent of that group said such knowledge would make them more likely to vote for Culver.

In Iowa the NCPAC affiliate called itself the Committee for Another Responsible Senator and ran ads and then sent them to possible supporters to raise money to show them again. One cited the Canal, along with tax cuts, bureaucracy, abortion, federal spending, and defense spending. An earlier mailing, signed by Terry Dolan, had asked recipients to send money to help Grassley win the Republican primary, attacking Culver on a range of issues but not mentioning the Canal.

The Moral Majority, headed by Rev. Jerry Falwell after Weyrich helped him create it, was another player in Iowa, and the combative Culver eagerly took them on. "I have searched the Scripture," he told an ecumenical meeting in Des Moines in late October, "but I can't find anything saying Jesus Christ opposed the Panama Canal Treaty or favored the Kemp-Roth tax cuts. Yet I get a zero in Christian morality from the Moral Majority because I didn't. They're trying to manipulate sincere people on religious grounds. Well, the Scriptures aren't political and the New Right is not the New Testament." Grassley, no orator, told the same meeting that he opposed abortion, the SALT II treaty, and hospital cost containment legislation. He said taxes should be cut, military expenditures increased while the budget was balanced.

Grassley won comfortably, with 683,014 votes, or 53.5 percent, to Culver's 581,545 votes, or 45.5 percent.

★ In three other 1980 Senate races the Canal might have mattered to the result, but the evidence is too slim to count them. In Wisconsin, Senator Gaylord Nelson, a veteran Democrat, lost to former congressman Bob Kasten, by 40,824 votes out of more than 2 million. Kasten criticized the Canal treaties in the spring and summer when he was seeking the Republican nomination, but he made hardly any use of it in the fall when voters were paying more attention. Instead he attacked Nelson over small business, inflation, and Nelson's opposition to tax cuts. A television ad charged that Nelson was "out of touch" with Wisconsin, which could have appealed to people who thought he failed to represent his state when he voted for the treaties. David Obey, then a young congressman and a Nelson supporter, said in a 2007 interview that he thought the issue "hurt Gaylord, it hurt all of us." But the issue itself came up rarely, if at all, in the fall campaign, except when Kasten told an interviewer from the *Madison Capital Times* that while he would have voted against the treaties as written, he favored the "eventual return" of the Canal to Panama.

In Indiana, NCPAC used the Canal issue a bit against Birch Bayh, a Democrat seeking a fourth term in a conservative state where his biggest previous share of the vote was 51.7 percent in 1968. This time he only got 46.2 percent. He received 1,015,962 votes, but Representative Dan Quayle received 1,182,414 votes, or 53.8 percent, a landslide compared with Bayh's margins in earlier years. Quayle stressed inflation and the argument that it was time for a change—the same argument Bayh used to defeat Homer Capehart in 1962, when the challenger denied Capehart a fourth term. There is no chance that the Canal issue was responsible for Quayle's 66,452-vote margin. Bayh himself credited Reagan's landslide (defeating Carter by 411,459 votes) for his defeat. "I could have had another million dollars and no Panama treaty and it wouldn't have made a difference," he said in a 2006 interview.

In Florida, Senator Richard Stone, a Democrat running for a second term, was ousted in an October 7 runoff primary. Bill Gunter, the state treasurer, hit Stone over the Canal issue and won by 40,408 votes. Though Gunter had other issues to use against Stone, the Canal may have decided the Democratic race. The general election then pitted two foes of the treaties, Gunter and Paula Hawkins, a Republican consumer advocate. Hawkins got 1,822,460 votes, or 51.7 percent, to Gunter's 1,705,409 votes, or 48.3 percent. But even though the Canal may have cost Stone the Democratic nomination, it is far from clear that he would have won the general election if he was the nominee. Any race between Gunter and Stone was sure to be bitter; they had been political enemies for years. Florida's late primary and runoff made uniting a divided party almost impossible. With Reagan beating Carter by 627,476 votes in Florida, Hawkins probably would have won over Stone no matter what the issues were.

23

Ronald Reagan's landslide victory on November 5, 1980, carrying forty-four states with 489 electoral votes, had coattails for Congress not seen since 1964 or repeated since. Republicans added 33 seats in the House, for a total of 192. The Democrats, with 243 members, still had a majority of 51, but it was a frightened majority that was often wary of challenging Reagan.

More important, Republicans won twelve Democratic-held Senate seats, the biggest party shift since 1958. Their caucus grew from forty Republicans and Harry F. Byrd Jr., of Virginia, an independent, to fifty-two Republicans and Byrd—the first Republican majority since 1955. The last three Republican presidents, Gerald Ford, Richard Nixon, and Dwight Eisenhower in his second term, had to contend with Democratic majorities in both houses. That gave them a ready excuse when their legislative initiatives failed. Ronald Reagan had a chance to govern.

Howard Baker, who had risked his political future by supporting the Canal treaties, became Senate majority leader because at least five of the Republicans, Gordon Humphrey, Roger Jepsen, John East, Steve Symms, and Mack Mattingly, had won their seats by using the Canal against Democrats who voted for it. Without them, there would have been only forty-seven Republicans (plus Harry Byrd). Robert Byrd would still be majority leader.

Baker's becoming majority leader was not a certainty on Election Night. New Right leaders said he was too accommodating, on the Canal and other issues. For example, Weyrich called him a "roll over and play dead type of Senator." Such criticisms were potentially more important than one might think because many of the new senators felt they owed their election to the New Right. So, early on the morning after Election Day, about 6:30, Baker met with Ron Mc-Mahan, his longtime press secretary, and James Cannon, his chief assistant in the minority leader's office. They had heard rumors that Paul Laxalt, as Reagan's first friend in the Senate, would seek the leader's role. Baker decided the way to deal with that was to call him directly. He woke Laxalt before dawn in a Nevada hotel. Baker asked Laxalt if he would nominate Baker to be leader. Laxalt probably never coveted the hard work of the leader's job. He agreed to nominate Baker and said Baker could announce it. That settled who would be majority leader.

The successes of Reagan's first years in the White House have many roots, starting with his own determination to cut taxes, eliminate federal programs, and increase defense spending. He came into office as a popular replacement for Carter, and that popularity was renewed and intensified after he was shot and nearly killed by John Hinckley on March 30, 1981.

Divisions among House Democrats also helped Reagan. But having control of the Senate was crucial. Having disciplined majorities in both houses would be even better for a president, as the one-party control George W. Bush enjoyed after the 2000 election showed. But having one house provided three major advantages for Reagan. First, a majority leader controlled the schedule—which bills came to the floor, and when, and which did not. Second, committee chairmen came from the majority party, and those Republicans wanted to help Reagan, just as the Democratic chairmen of 2008 want to thwart George W. Bush. Third, this majority and its leaders could provide advice on how to get things accomplished, knowledge Reagan's old allies did not bring to Washington.

Scheduling sounds boring. But in a body where it sometimes seems that nothing can be accomplished without unanimous consent, the majority leader's power to set the Senate agenda—on his own—is a striking exception. A leader schedules votes to achieve an effect, to pass a bill, or perhaps to embarrass a president. The first lesson on that power came in Reagan's first weeks in office. There is a statute that prescribes how high the national debt can be, a sort of legislative version of King Canute ordering the incoming tide to retreat. Every so often the law must be changed when the increasing debt bumps up against the old ceiling. For years Republicans had voted against increasing the debt ceiling to protest the budget deficits they blamed on

Democratic Congresses. Without a change, the government would be barred from spending money, that is, barred from functioning.

The debt limit of $935 billion was to expire on February 18, 1981. Baker did not schedule the vote to raise it—to $985 billion—right away. "I counted votes and found out we didn't have the votes," he said in a 2007 interview. Republicans, new and old, were reluctant to break a party habit and vote to raise the debt limit. As Reagan wrote in his diary about another debt increase later that year: "All of us have been against it in the past because the Dems used it to continue their deficit spending. Now we are trying to end such spending. . . . But we're still paying for their sins. If we can't borrow—we'll be out of money." Democrats enjoyed the Republicans' embarrassment after years of being taunted by the former minority. "We didn't nearly have the votes until the president had hot-boxed a number of senators," Baker said in the 2007 interview, "and I had indoctrinated young freshmen on the responsibility of leadership." Those methods of persuasion finally worked, and the bill passed, 73 to 18, on Friday, February 6, Reagan's seventieth birthday. He noted in his diary, "Received a great present—our own Sens. who had held out on debt ceiling turned around and we carried the day."

Baker also used the Senate rules to force some domestic spending cuts. Under a procedure known as "reconciliation"—which took spending decisions away from the always generous Appropriations Committee and its subcommittees—the leadership forced through a budget reconciliation bill. It combined reduced appropriations for $35.2 billion in a single measure. Reconciliation bills cannot be filibustered. Byrd, who had become minority leader and generally surprised Baker with his willingness to cooperate, was furious. A master of Senate procedure and a high-ranking member of the Appropriations Committee, Byrd told Baker, "I'll never let you do that again." As things turned out, Byrd could not thwart Baker and the Republican majority; reconciliation bills were passed in 1982 and 1983.

Committee chairmen set agendas, too, and influence bills from their committees. In the end, the five-year, $749 billion tax cut measure of 1981, which reduced the top income tax rate from 70 percent to 50 percent, had only eleven votes against it. But Bob Dole, who was chairman of the Senate Finance Committee, said in a 2007 interview that the bill was much more sweeping than it would have been if Russell Long, the Louisiana Democrat, had remained as chairman. "Russell Long was a great chairman and very persuasive," Dole said.

Although escaping from what had seemed to be a permanent minority status had surprised many Republicans (and Democrats*), the chairmen made a difference. There was Dole at Finance. Orrin Hatch of Utah, as chairman of the Labor and Public Welfare Committee, got block grants through to consolidate health programs, measures that Edward M. Kennedy would have squelched if he had been chairman instead of the ranking minority member. Strom Thurmond, as chairman of Judiciary, pushed through a tougher crime bill and supported more conservative judges than Joseph Biden of Delaware, his ranking member, would have tolerated.

And the Republican majority's advice was welcomed. Except for James A. Baker III, the former Bush campaign manager whom Reagan had picked to be his chief of staff, there was very little Washington experience among the first people chosen for top jobs. That was the main reason Nancy Reagan, Mike Deaver, and Stuart Spencer urged Reagan to hire Baker, who had run campaigns against him. When Senate Republican leaders met with Reagan's top aides one evening in December 1980 to learn what they had in mind as a legislative agenda, the senators came away unimpressed, sensing that the Senate was going to have to guide the Reagan administration through the legislative forest.

Reagan's diary has repeated examples of how Senate advice mattered and was taken seriously. In April 1981, Howard Baker warned him to delay announcing a planned sale of AWACS surveillance aircraft to Saudi Arabia until an economic program had been voted on. Reagan called the advice "sound." In July the majority leader warned him that he could lose on a proposal to eliminate the minimum $122 monthly Social Security that went to anyone who had ever paid anything into the system. Reagan weighed the advice and decided to fight. (Ultimately he lost.) In 1982 he reluctantly took the advice of Baker and others that some modest tax increases were necessary to get spending cuts he wanted.

While both Howard Baker and Bob Dole, who succeeded him as majority leader in 1985, said in 2007 interviews that they wondered if the Reagan team ever realized how important the majority was to their success, James Baker, the chief of staff, had no doubts. He said in a 2007 interview that having "a

---

* On Election Night, when Baker called Dole to tell him that Republicans had won a majority and Dole would be chairman of the Finance Committee, Dole asked, "But who's going to tell Russell Long?"

Senate majority made all the difference in the world in getting the 1981 Reagan economic program through the congress." Without it, he said, there might have been a small tax cut, but no spending reductions. Moreover, the Senate majority's control of the schedule made it possible to "block Democratic initiatives with which we disagreed before you ever got to a veto situation."

Reagan understood, too. Not long before Election Day, 1982, Richard Wirthlin, Reagan's pollster, came in to report that he thought there was an 80 percent chance Republicans would hold the Senate. "It will be disastrous if we don't," Reagan wrote in his diary.

★ Ronald Reagan was president for eight years, and the general public (especially those who considered themselves conservative) liked him and thought of him as a conservative. But before he could be sworn in, the New Right conservatives were complaining. At first they complained of his appointments. On November 14, Richard Viguerie said, "These people represent a philosophy that was tried and proven to be a failure. The vast majority of them are people who for 15 years minus four months have opposed Ronald Reagan every step of the way of his political path." In the December issue of *Conservative Digest*, Howard Phillips laid out a series of steps Reagan would have to take or else conservatives would have to "disassociate ourselves from the Reagan White House in order to salvage our cause." His demands included $200 billion in domestic spending cuts, an end to government subsides of "leftwing activists," and getting tough with Cuba and the Soviet Union. And on Reagan's fifth day in office, the *New York Times* reported that he was under attack over appointments that indicated he did not plan to "carry out his conservative campaign pledges." Terry Dolan said: "It's mind-boggling that conservative, pro-Reagan activists are being bumped off job lists, while people who have no commitment to Ronald Reagan are being given jobs." He continued: "To say that Ronald Reagan has to employ country-club, silk stocking George Bush Republicans is garbage. That didn't win him the election. He won by broadening the base to the ethnics, the blue-collar vote, the born-again Southern Democrats." In fact, the only New Right activist employed by the Reagan administration was Morton Blackwell, who was made the White House liaison to conservatives.

They would complain, on and off, for much of Reagan's tenure. Frequently the occasion for their anger was a compromise or deal, struck by the Reagan administration when it did not have the votes to get all it wanted. From his days of negotiating for the Screen Actors Guild, Reagan understood compromise. As he said in a slightly different context—discussing conservative purist members of Congress—"Some I talked to are dedicated (they say) to what we're trying to accomplish but they won't vote with us because the budget compromise isn't *exactly* to their liking. A compromise is never to anyone's liking—it's just the best you can get and contains enough of what you want to justify what you give up." Reagan was usually not bothered by conservative complaints. On February 26, 1982, he wrote in his diary, "Richard Viguery [sic] held press conference along with John Lofton and blasted me as not a true conservative—made me wonder what my reception would be at the Conservative Dinner. I needn't have worried—it was a love fest. Evidently R.V. & J.L. don't speak for the rank and file conservatives. Speech was well received."

The New Right conservatives had other problems. Richard Richards, Brock's successor as chairman of the Republican National Committee, told reporters that NCPAC should stay out of campaigns where Republicans told them they were not wanted. NCPAC also had problems with Democrats. Democrats on its 1982 hit list were not taken by surprise. In Massachusetts, Edward M. Kennedy's aides scared television stations out of running Dolan's spots. They told station managers that they might face libel actions or other difficulties if they ran the ads—which, unlike candidate advertisements, they had no obligation to run. The Democratic Senatorial Campaign Committee urged all embattled Democrats to use that tactic to make it hard for NCPAC to broadcast "the typical heavy-handed NCPAC media barrage, long on hyperbole and short on accuracy, consciously designed to whip up fear and animosity throughout the electorate." Democrats were successful enough in this tactic that NCPAC sued seven Democrats, and the television stations they had dealt with in Dallas, Fort Worth, Tulsa, Springfield, Massachusetts, Baltimore, and Billings, Montana, accusing them of conspiracy. The suit got nowhere.

Because of this tactic, it is not clear how many of NCPAC's ads actually got on the air in the 1981–1982 cycle. It did run some spots attacking Paul Sarbanes, a Maryland Democrat seeking a second term. One showed a ship in one of the Canal's locks, with the announcer saying, "This is the Panama Canal. Paul Sarbanes led the fight to give it away." Then it showed Baltimore harbor and said Sarbanes took no stand on dredging it. Finally the announcer suggested, "Maybe Paul Sarbanes is more interested in liberal positions like giving away the Panama Canal than saving the Baltimore harbor." Sarbanes won easily. The Canal issue did not work in 1982. Four years had passed since the vote, and a lagging economy was helping Democrats. In 1978 and 1980 the economy had helped Republicans, the Canal issue was fresher, and several of the defeated candidates were in fact, as the Right charged, more liberal than their states.

24

The Canal itself was almost forgotten, especially by Reagan, a man who did not look backward. He never mentioned the Canal to Howard Baker, neither in Baker's four years as majority leader nor in his sixteen months as Reagan's chief of staff in 1987 and 1988. And when Reagan met in 1982 with Panama's then president Ricardo de la Estrella and said he was "looking forward to a warm working relationship between the two countries," the occasion never made it into his diary. The only time Reagan appears to have mentioned the Canal in public was in a 1986 national television speech when he said communism in Nicaragua would enable the USSR and Cuba to "threaten the Panama Canal." But, as promised in 1978, the Canal stayed open to ships of all nations, if they were not too broad of beam. Neither Cuba nor the Soviet Union interfered.

Panama, but not the Canal, made headlines in the United States first in 1979 and then in 1989. The first time was when Torrijos repaid President Carter's Canal stance by inviting the deposed Shah of Iran to Panama. The Shah had been in the United States for medical treatment, and Carter believed the hostages seized by students in Tehran would not be freed until he left. No European country wanted him. Then, in 1989, the United States invaded Panama to arrest Manuel Antonio Noriega, Panama's dictator and Torrijos's intelligence chief in the days of the treaties' ratification, on an indictment for cocaine trafficking. Unlike Torrijos, who had been a popular dictator before he died in a mysterious airplane crash in 1981, Noriega was despised, and the public generally welcomed the

The Panama Canal from the Pacific, with the Miraflores locks in the foreground and the Pedro San Miguel locks in the distance, January 1978 (Howard Baker)

American soldiers. A CBS News Poll of Panama showed that 92 percent of Panamanians approved of the invasion.

In 1998, the year before the last American soldiers were to leave, the United States made an effort to use Senator Nunn's reservation to reach an agreement on setting up a multinational counternarcotics center in Panama. But Panama's resistance to the idea of having any American troops left behind killed that idea. In 1999, Panama's recently elected president, Mireya Moscoso, traveled to Washington to ask President Bill Clinton to attend the ceremonies marking the transfer of the Canal to her country. Moscoso, the widow of Arnulfo Arias, the president whom Torrijos had deposed in 1968, had agreed to change the date of the ceremony to December 14, rather than December 31, to avoid the distraction over the new millennium that would begin on January 1, 2000. When she met Clinton at the White House on October 19, he showed little interest in her invitation, not even saying he hoped to go. He deflected her request with the excuse that "I frankly don't know if I can come to the transfer ceremony. About every four years we have a big argument with the Republican Congress—and it appears that we are reverting to what happened last time, when the fight continued into the Christmas season."

Jimmy Carter urged Clinton to go. So did the State Department. American ambassadors in Latin America asked him to attend. He took his time before answering. Eventually Madeleine Albright, the secretary of state, agreed to go. Then, on December 9, she decided—despite an argument with the president's national security adviser, Samuel R. Berger—that she had to cancel and stay in Washington to meet with Israeli and Syrian leaders. She telephoned Moscoso on December 13. According to a State Department memo on the conversation: "The Secretary spoke to President Moscoso this morning. The Secretary apologized for her inability to attend tomorrow's ceremony. President Moscoso said it was a terrible shame that neither the President nor the Secretary would be able to come."

There was a widespread assumption in Washington that fear of political attacks from Howard Phillips (who did attend the ceremonies) and other conservatives kept high officials away. Maria Echeveste, who had been a top White House aide dealing with Hispanic affairs, reflected that view in a 2005 interview when she commented, "Nobody wanted to touch this with a ten-foot pole." But my sense, after exploring the issue with many of those involved (except Albright, who refused to be interviewed), is that nobody in the government cared enough to go. They did not get to the point of worrying about political repercussions.

Well, not quite nobody. The highest-ranking government official in the American delegation was William Daley, the secretary of commerce. Rodney Slater, secretary of transportation, went, too. Bob Pastor, the former NSC aide who had become a professor at Emory University, and former senator Dennis DeConcini, who had nearly torpedoed the treaties, were on hand. Television newsmen from the United States criticized the delegation's makeup. ABC's anchor, Peter Jennings, pointed out, "The President was conspicuously absent." NBC's Jim Avila said, "Today, President Clinton ignored the Canal, refusing Panama's invitation to celebrate the turnover, insulting the country the United States military helped create to make the canal possible." More important, Panama made it clear that it felt snubbed. David Gonzalez of the *New York Times* quoted one Panamanian official involved in the planning of the ceremonies: "No big names, no midlevel, nothing. No rock stars. Madeleine Albright is the Bruce Springsteen of Foreign Affairs. It looks like we're getting Barry Manilow instead."

The ceremonies did get former President Carter. After a choir sang Beethoven's "Ode to Joy," Carter, Moscoso, the king of Spain, and assorted Latin American leaders chugged down beside the Miraflores locks in one of the locomotives that pull ships through the locks, looking like a dressed-up version of the opening frames of the *Beverly Hillbillies*. Carter noted that the Canal had been "both a source of pride in the United States and a symbol of subjugation to many citizens of Panama." He spoke of the difficulties of ratifying the treaties, noting the number of senators who lost elections after voting for them. He recalled: "In both nations there were citizens who made deliberately false statements, exaggerated real differences and predicted future catastrophes—all designed to mislead citizens and inflame latent passions. There are still a few of them in my nation today." But after ratification in 1978, Carter said, the transfer had been "harmonious," and there was "mutual respect between our two nations, a canal that is secure and superbly managed by an independent authority, real and firmly established democracy in Panama." Carter signed a document and said, "It's yours." Ships blasted their horns. Fireboats sent geysers of water into the air.

The Canal was almost Panama's. The last dozen American soldiers were packing to leave. The actual transfer would be accomplished by a low-key exchange of papers, signed for the United States this time by Louis Caldera, secretary of the army. At the stroke of noon on December 31, President Moscoso raised Panama's flag over the Canal headquarters. "The Canal is ours," she shouted. (To avoid protest demonstrations, the Stars and Stripes had been lowered the evening before and not raised that morning.)

★ Panama got the Canal and is developing the engineering to build a third set of locks wide enough so that supertankers and even American aircraft carriers can fit. A variety of onetime opponents of the treaty, from Paul Laxalt to Philip Crane to George W. Bush, say things have worked out much better than they expected. The Canal, after all, has operated pretty much the same under Panama control as under the control of the United States.

But if the Panama Canal battle left the Canal itself unchanged and undamaged, it left marks on American politics. The uproar over the Canal foreshadowed the single-issue attacks over intense, emotional issues from abortion to gun control to same-sex marriage that have become a constant refrain in elections for offices high and low. It is not a long conceptual leap from suggesting that a McIntyre or Church is a dupe of the Soviet designs on the Canal to Saxby Chambliss's 2002 ads suggesting that Senator Max Cleland, a triple amputee from Vietnam, was soft on terrorists, Saddam Hussein, and Osama bin Laden because he voted against the Bush administration on some elements of the bill creating the Department of Homeland Security.

Of course, attack ads were invented long before the Canal was dug, let alone surrendered. Handbills attacking John Adams as a supporter of a monarchy, or his son, John Quincy Adams, whipping a crippled veteran, were staples of the 1796 and 1828 campaigns. And the famous "daisy" television ad of 1964 smeared Barry Goldwater as the candidate who would blow up the world. Moreover, the Canal ads, unlike the attacks on the Adamses and Goldwater, had some literal truth to them. The target senators had voted to give up the Canal. Their argument, that they had voted that way to ensure continued use of the waterway, was too complicated to sell, especially on television.

Nor was the Canal issue a constant in the television campaigns against pro-treaty senators. It appeared more heavily in print ads and in fund-raising appeals. Here the drumbeat of attacks on the treaties in the winter of 1977–1978 made only occasional reminders necessary later. People who hated the idea of giving up the Canal remembered the senators who voted that way.

But one real innovation that sprung from the Canal campaign was the Don Todd–NCPAC approach of beating up on an incumbent long in advance of an actual election, expecting to weaken him for whoever eventually decides to run against him. Before Church or Culver had Republican nominees to face, NCPAC was hammering them on the Canal and other matters. That approach is common today. The conservative Club for Growth ran television ads in August 2005 to attack (misleadingly) John McCain over the inheritance tax in New Hampshire, where he won the 2000 presidential primary and planned to compete in the 2008 contest. In February 2007, the liberal group MoveOn.org used television to attack three senators up for election in 2008, John Warner of Virginia, John Sununu of New Hampshire, and Gordon Smith of Oregon, over the war in Iraq, calling them, inaccurately, supporters of a "surge" of troops there. By August 2007, House incumbents were under early attack, too, on issues from Iraq to taxes. Stuart Rothenberg, author of a respected political newsletter, told the *Washington Post*, "There's a sense that you can make anybody vulnerable, you can weaken any candidate no matter how strong he appears to be, by starting out early and beating the stuffing out of him."

Another Canal debate legacy is independent spending—the method that financed M. Stanton Evans of the ACU telling North Carolina voters that "Ronald Reagan would not cave in to Castro, and says American sovereignty in Panama must be maintained." The ACU's independent spending in 1976, reported as $272,059, and even NCPAC's $3,777,391 in 1980, are dwarfed (even after inflation) by current outside spending. Assuming that campaign cost inflation was twice as great as that of the Consumer Price Index, NCPAC's spending in 2004 campaign dollars would have been $18,398,792. Eight of the newest class of outside spending operations, known as 527s after a section of the tax code, spent more than that in 2003–2004. America Coming Together spent $76,270,931 to help Democrats. The Progress for America Voter Fund spent $35,437,204 to help Republicans. Even the Swift Boat Veterans for Truth, John Kerry's caustic enemies, spent $22,424,420.

From the start, independent spending has been a way around money shortages. The ACU's 1976 efforts were most useful when the Reagan campaign was nearly broke—after the federal matching grants system had stalled when the Supreme Court voided the 1974 Federal Election Campaign Act. Similarly, the 2004 pro-Kerry campaigning by the Media Fund, the AFL-CIO, and MoveOn.org came after Kerry was nearly broke, and Bush, who had not had to spend a dime to ensure nomination, was unloading on him in the spring.

Outside ads are usually negative, and with a harder edge, than candidates and sometimes even political parties feel comfortable airing. Even though they would seem ordinary today, NCPAC's attacks on Henry Howell in 1977, and on Senators Church, Bayh, Cranston, Culver, Eagleton, and McGovern in 1980, were striking and harsh by the standards of those days. Now, when hardly anything seems beyond the pale, the Swift Boat Veterans for Truth ads attacking John Kerry's war record were a message the Bush campaign would never have dared to make on its own, and the effort those anti-Kerry veterans put into months of news conferences and interviews gave their charges an air of sincerity. Yet the "distance" from the campaign may sometimes be only in the minds of the politicians. A National Annenberg Election Survey in 2004 showed that 46 percent of the public (and 23 percent of Republicans) thought the Bush campaign was behind the Swift Boat ads, while 37 percent thought the ads had been made "with no connection to the Bush campaign." Kathleen Hall Jamieson, the scholar of campaign advertising, commented in 2007: "In the absence of evidence to the contrary, viewers reasonably assume that the person who benefits from a political ad is probably its godfather."

The efforts by independent organizations are regularly deplored by editorial writers, by targeted candidates, and sometimes by the candidates they help (whatever they believe about how the outside ads' themes or tone is wrong, usually they are happy with what the ads accomplish). But it is plain that the First Amendment means independent ads are here to stay. Occasionally the "independence" may be questionable; in 1988, ads about Willie Horton, a Massachusetts prisoner who raped a woman while on furlough, hurt Governor Michael Dukakis, the Democratic presidential candidate, and its sponsors insisted they had given the Republican campaign of George H. W. Bush a clear opportunity to keep it off the air.

But most of the time virtual coordination is easy enough without violating the law. The sponsors of these ads are rarely as distant from the political process as the anti-Kerry veterans, who themselves became significant only when they found experienced help. They are usually political veterans who know how the game is played. And even when campaigns are scrupulous about not talking to the "independents," the campaigns talk to the press, and the outsiders can read. In 1980, for example, NCPAC advertised in the South because Terry Dolan read in the newspapers that the Reagan campaign was concentrating on the North. To help their strategy, published polling by news organizations is available if these groups do not hire their own pollsters. That gives them information comparable to what is available to candidates. It is easy enough these days to track where favored candidates are advertising and decide whether to reinforce those efforts or to go elsewhere.

The Panama Canal debate also transformed the Republican Party. The Canal may have been at most a minor factor in 1980 when hard-line conservatives replaced moderate Republicans, like Alphonse D'Amato defeating Jacob Javits in New York, or Don Nickles succeeding the retiring Henry Bellmon in Oklahoma. But the balance among Senate Republicans shifted dramatically with the 1978 and 1980 elections of anti-treaty Republicans like Gordon Humphrey, Charles Grassley, Bill Armstrong, John East, Steve Symms, Mack Mattingly, Robert Kasten, and Paula Hawkins—several of whom defeated more moderate Republicans in primaries. Although most of them served only one or two terms, the Republicans who eventually followed them (even after Democratic interregnums) were very conservative.

And the conservatism of Senate Republicans today reflects the change in control of the party at the grass roots. The tension continues between the economic conservatives, who wanted less control of the economic life of the nation, and the social conservatives, who wanted more control of its moral life. But the battles are won more often by the social conservatives, whether the issue is abortion before a Supreme Court chosen mostly by Republican presidents or creationism before a midwestern school board. The coalition of factions ignited by social issues from gun control to abortion, envisioned by Richard Viguerie in the seventies, has largely been realized in today's Republican Party.

The Senate is a more partisan place for many reasons, but the aftertaste of the Canal debate made it especially difficult to find common ground on foreign policy issues. As even Howard Baker, the man who saved the treaties, said in 1979, the idea that politics stopped at the water's edge had become passé. "Vandenberg was right in his time," he said then, "but I think we're right in our time." Reagan overcame that shifting perspective for a time with his immense prestige. But two decades later, it is almost beyond imagination to see the U.S. Senate getting a two-thirds vote for an even remotely controversial treaty, which is to say any treaty that could possibly be attacked as insufficiently protective of the United States' interests.

The most significant change that the Canal debate fostered was beyond the politics of parties and elections. The election of Ronald Reagan, who could well not even have run in 1980 if the Canal issue had not kept his hopes alive in 1976, amounted to a revolution. Reagan, rarely one to reflect, much less boast, did say, "We've made a difference." He cited, in his farewell address, economic expansion and improved American morale. His leadership brought the tax cuts and arms buildups he had promised, but also huge budget deficits instead of the balanced budget he promised. The deregulation he promised came, too, with many efficiencies but also a huge savings and loan industry scandal. And for all his history of bellicose talk about the Soviet Union, Reagan reached agreement with Mikhail Gorbachev on the first treaty that ever eliminated a class of nuclear weapons, the intermediate-range (up to 3,400 miles) nuclear missiles.

Reagan set agendas not only for future Republican presidents, especially the tax cuts of President George W. Bush, but for Democrats, too. "I hope we have once again reminded people that man is not free unless government is limited," Reagan proclaimed in his farewell address. Bill Clinton said, "The era of big government is over" in his 1996 State of the Union address. More concretely, Clinton's support of welfare reform would have been unlikely without the Reagan attacks on the system and the consensus he developed that the failures of welfare were self-perpetuating and doing recipients no good. Not only is the Republican Party more conservative than it was before Reagan, so is the Democratic Party. It no longer has much zest for new federal programs. It let the budget surpluses of the late nineties pass without using the money to try to tackle any major national problem, and today it seems fundamentally incapable of deciding that some issue—health care, infrastructure, global warming—requires real sacrifice in higher taxes, jobs, or even inconvenience.

The United States is, by almost any measure, a more conservative country today. But it is also one where political consensus and middle ground are rarely found. The Panama Canal no longer divides Panama.

But the fissures it opened thirty years ago have widened; they divide the United States.

NOTES

ABBREVIATIONS

ABC ABC Evening News, transcribed at Vanderbilt Television News Archive,
Heard Library, Vanderbilt University, Nashville, Tennessee

AC *Atlanta Constitution*

ACU American Conservative Union

ACU at BYU American Conservative Union Files: MSS 176, Register of the American
Conservative Union, 20th & 21st Century Western and Mormon
Americana, L. Tom Perry Special Collections, Harold B. Lee Library,
Brigham Young University, Provo, Utah

Af Author's files, Jimmy Carter Library

BG *Boston Globe*

BLCU Rare Book and Manuscript Library, Butler Library, Columbia University,
New York, New York

CBS CBS Evening News, transcribed at Vanderbilt Television News Archive,
Heard Library, Vanderbilt University, Nashville, Tennessee

CM *Concord Monitor* (New Hampshire)

CNN Cable News Network reports, transcribed at Vanderbilt Television News
Archive, Heard Library, Vanderbilt University, Nashville, Tennessee

CQWR *Congressional Quarterly Weekly Report*

CR *Congressional Record* (followed by Congress and session); CR 93:II
indicates 93rd Congress, 2nd session

CSM *Christian Science Monitor*

CT *Chicago Tribune*

DMR *Des Moines Register*

DP *Denver Post*

ECU Collection 268, East Carolina Manuscript Collection, Special
Collections, J. Y. Joyner Library, East Carolina University, Greenville,
North Carolina

FCC Frank Church Collection, Boise State University, Boise, Idaho

FEC Federal Election Commission

GRFL Gerald R. Ford Library, Ann Arbor, Michigan

HE *Human Events*

Hoover Hoover Institution on War, Revolution and Peace

Int Interview (by author unless another interviewer is indicated)

IS	*Idaho Statesman* (Boise)
Kanter	Julian P. Kanter Political Commercial Archive, the University of Oklahoma Political Communication Center in the Department of Communication, Norman
Kaufman	Burton Kaufman files
LAT	*Los Angeles Times*
LBJL	Lyndon Baines Johnson Library
NBC	NBC Nightly News, transcribed at Vanderbilt Television News Archive, Heard Library, Vanderbilt University, Nashville, Tennessee
NHSN	*New Hampshire Sunday News*
NYT	*New York Times*
RBRUGA	Richard B. Russell Library for Political Research and Studies, University of Georgia
RNO	*Raleigh News and Observer*
TCC	The Conservative Caucus
UNH	Milne Special Collections and Archives, University of New Hampshire Library
WHCF	White House Central Files
WHSF	White House Subject Files
WP	*Washington Post*
WS	*Washington Star*
WSJ	*Wall Street Journal*

PREFACE

Page ix "American pluck": Charles A. Beard and William C. Bagley, *The History of the American People* (New York: Macmillan, 1928), p. 626.

CHAPTER 1

2 *Nashville*, head of railway: David McCullough, *The Path between the Seas: The Creation of the Panama Canal, 1870–1924* (New York: Simon and Schuster, 1977), p. 356.

2 Authority demanded by Bunau-Varilla: ibid., p. 356.

2 Ten miles, permanent right to take lands: John Major, "Who Wrote the Hay–Bunau-Varilla Convention?" *Diplomatic History*, Spring 1974, p. 171.

3 Treaty text: http://www.yale.edu/lawweb/avalon/diplomacy/panama/pan001.htm, accessed 8/22/07.

3 Roosevelt, Taft: Walter LaFeber, *The Panama Canal: The Crisis in Historical Perspective*, updated ed. (New York: Oxford University Press, 1989), pp. 34–35.

4 Omaha: John Gunther, *Inside Latin America* (New York: Harper and Brothers, 1941), p. 152.

4 "United States territory" : Mabel B. Casner and Ralph H. Gabriel, *The Story of American Democracy* (New York: Harcourt Brace, 1950), p. 527.

4 "Hate" : Willis J. Abbot, *Panama and the Canal in Picture and Prose* (New York: Syndicate Publishing Company, 1914), p. 235.

4 "Real, unexpressed reason": ibid., pp. 233–234.

4 Marines: ibid., p. 234, McCullough, *The Path between the Seas*, p. 568; NYT, 7/5/1912, 7/6/1912.

4 "Ignorance," "indolent": Sue Core, *Panama Yesterday and Today* (New York: North River Press, 1945), pp. 165, 180.

4 Backward: William J. Jorden, *Panama Odyssey* (Austin: University of Texas Press, 1984), pp. 521–522.

4 1947 riots, students: LaFeber, *The Panama Canal*, pp. 79–80; NYT, 12/13/47, 12/24/47.

4 "Ten thousand boys": NYT, 12/28/47.

5 Unequal pay scale: NYT, 12/24/47; LaFeber, *The Panama Canal*, p. 83.

5 Equal pay scale: LaFeber, *The Panama Canal*, p. 94.

5 Fifty flags, employment legislation: John Major, *Prize Possession: The United States and the Panama Canal, 1903–1979* (New York: Cambridge University Press, 1993), p. 331.

5 Ridiculous: NYT, 5/3/58.

5 Milton Eisenhower: Major, *Prize Possession*, p. 331.

5 Rioting: NYT, 11/3/59.

5 Thirty injuries: NYT, 9/18/60.

5 "Puzzling": *Public Papers of the Presidents of the United States, Dwight D. Eisenhower. 1959* (Washington, D.C.: Government Printing Office, 1965), p. 773.

5 Unfair: Kaufman folder Panama VII, citing Walter W. Rostow to President Johnson, 8/12/66, LBJL, NF Country File, boxes 69 and 70 combined, folder Panama Canal Negotiations Vol. I; NYT, CT, 7/27/67.

5 "Visual evidence": *Public Papers of the Presidents of the United States, Dwight D. Eisenhower. 1959*, p. 794.

5 House resolution: LaFeber, *The Panama Canal*, p. 101.

5 Panama's flag flown: NYT, 9/18/59.

5 Pentagon objection: NYT, 9/18/59.

5 Wage increases: NYT, 4/20/60.

6 "Collusion," "bound hand and foot": Kaufman, citing Chiari to President Kennedy, 9/8/61, Panama Canal IV, R6 Planning documents for construction of an

Inter-Oceanic Sea Level Canal + Lock Canal, box 3, folder "Panama Canal Policy and Relations with Panama (1)."

6 Chiari requests: Jorden, *Panama Odyssey*, pp. 31–33.

6 Kennedy told Chiari: Major, *Prize Possession*, p. 334.

6 Memorandum, "new treaty": *WP*, 2/9/64.

6 Both flags: Jorden, *Panama Odyssey*, p. 34.

6 Disbanded: LaFeber, *The Panama Canal*, p. 106.

6 "Complete revision," "serious problems": Recording of Telephone Conversation between Lyndon B. Johnson and Robert Chiari, 1/10/64, 11:40 a.m. Citation 1711, Recordings of Telephone Conversations—White House Series, Recordings and Transcripts of Conversations and Meetings, LBJL.

6 Four Americans, twenty-four Panamanians: LaFeber, *Panama Canal*, p. 109.

6 Account of rioting: Jorden, *Panama Odyssey*, pp. 35–55.

6 Firm: Mark Atwood Lawrence, "Exception to the Rule? The Johnson Administration and the Panama Canal," in Mitchell B. Lerner, ed., *Looking Back at LBJ: White House Politics in a New Light* (Lawrence: University Press of Kansas, 2005), pp. 20–47.

6 "Not a thing has been done": recording 1711, LBJL.

7 "Being firm": Recording of Telephone Conversation between Lyndon B. Johnson and Senator Richard B. Russell, 1/29/64, 10:30 a.m., citation 1612, LBJL.

7 "Ceding some rights": Atwood, "Exception to the Rule?" p. 22.

7 "Every issue": *Public Papers of the Presidents of the United States, Lyndon Johnson. 1963–1964. Vol. I* (Washington, D.C.: Government Printing Office, 1965), p. 405; *NYT*, 3/22/64.

7 Diplomatic relations, Anderson appointment: *NYT*, 4/4/64.

7 Sea-level canal, "Entirely new treaty," "sovereignty of Panama": *Public Papers of the Presidents of the United States, Lyndon Johnson. 1963–64, Vol. II* (Washington, D.C.: Government Printing Office, 1965), pp. 1663–1665.

7 CIA officer: Kaufman folder Panama VII, citing Walter W. Rostow to President Johnson, 8/12/66, LBJL, NF Country File, boxes 69 and 70 combined, folder Panama Canal Negotiations Vol. I.

7 A few months: Robert Anderson int 5/14/79, by William J. Jorden, Jorden papers, box 21, LBJL.

7 1967 treaty: Jorden, *Panama Odyssey*, pp. 116–119.

7 Opposition from Republicans: *CT*, 6/28/67, 7/8/67, 7/10/67; *NYT*, 8/9/67.

8 State Department worry: Jorden, *Panama Odyssey*, p. 149.

8 UN: *NYT*, 3/22/73.

8 Kissinger's attention: Jorden, *Panama Odyssey*, pp. 206–207.

8 "Fresh look": *Public Papers of the Presidents of the United States, Richard Nixon. 1973* (Washington, D.C.: Government Printing Office, 1975), p. 443.

8 "Principles": *Department of State Bulletin,* 2/25/74.

9 "Invite disaster": Thurmond, CR 93:II, pp. 2854, 8832, 2/7/74.

9 "Insanity": Murphy, CR 93:II, p. 2546, 2/7/74.

9 Inspired by Roosevelt: Dan Flood to Frank Waldrop, 12/17/66 in Miles P. DuVal Papers, box 3, folder 4, Georgetown University Library.

9 Flood warned Johnson: Flood to Johnson, 1/7/64, in DuVal papers, box 3, folder 1.

9 "Surrender of sovereignty": Flood to Nixon, 5/3/74, in DuVal papers, second series, box 2, folder 9.

9 Thurmond resolution: CR 93:II, p. 8833, 3/29/74.

9 "We bought it . . . ": CR 93:II, p. 8835, 3/29/74.

CHAPTER 2

10 *Monterey,* Canal: Gerald R. Ford int 5/4/05, af.

10 Denounced Johnson treaties: CT, 7/8/67.

10 Impeachment of Eisenhower: LaFeber, *The Panama Canal,* p. 101.

10 Ford with Jorden: Ambassador Jorden's call on the Vice President, 3/14/74, Gerald R. Ford vice presidential papers, box 65, folder 3/3–3/31/74, GRFL.

10 Ford with Bunker: Ambassador Bunker's visit, 3/21/74, Ford vice presidential papers, box 65, folder 4/74, GRFL.

10 Ford with Tack: Memorandum of Conversation—Juan Antonio Tack, 4/15/74, Ford vice presidential papers, box 65, folder 4/74, GRFL.

11 "Great importance": Thurmond to Ford, Telegram from Strom Thurmond to the President, 8/14/74, White House Congressional mail file, box 25, folder Thurmond, Strom, GRFL.

11 Talking points: Tom Korologos to Ford, 8/16/74, WHCF, Subject file, box 51, folder PR 7–1, 8/15–8/16/74, GRFL.

11 Thurmond's worries: Letter from Strom Thurmond to the President, 9/11/74, National Security Advisor, NSC Latin American Affairs, Staff files 1974–77, box 6, folder Panama Canal—Congress (1), GRFL.

11 Americans for Democratic Action ratings: http://www.adaction.org/votingrecords.htm, accessed 8/23/07.

11 "Exposure to diplomacy": Yanek Mieczkowski, *Gerald Ford and the Challenges of the 1970s* (Lexington: University Press of Kentucky, 2005), p. 274.

11 Protect Nixon: Stephen E. Ambrose, *Nixon: Ruin and Recovery 1973–1990* (New York: Simon and Schuster, 1991), p. 238; Jules Witcover, *Marathon: The Pursuit of the*

Presidency 1972–1976 (New York: Viking, 1977), p. 36; Richard Reeves, *A Ford, Not a Lincoln* (New York: Harcourt Brace Jovanovich, 1975), p. 40.

12 "Our long national nightmare": *Public Papers of the Presidents of the United States, Gerald R. Ford. 1974* (Washington, D.C.: Government Printing Office, 1975), p. 2.

12 Cable to Panama: Kissinger to Jorden and Bunker 8/9/74, af.

12 Dozens: Brent Scowcroft int 3/23/06, af.

12 Seen as Ford's commitment: Jorden to Kissinger, 8/13/74, af; WP, 5/19/76.

12 Treaty by 1975: Bunker to Kissinger, 11/7/74, National Security Advisor Presidential Country Files for Latin America, 1974–77, box 6, country file Panama (1), folder State Department telegrams to Sec State—NODIS, GRFL.

12 Standpoint of national defense: Frank Coxe to Robert Morgan, 3/3/75, Robert Morgan papers, box 411, folder I, ECU.

13 Thurmonds and Floods: NSC Memorandum of Conversation, box 11, folder 5/12/75 – Ford, Kissinger, pp. 3–4, GRFL.

13 State versus Defense: Jorden, *Panama Odyssey*, p. 277.

13 New instructions: Ellsworth Bunker and William D. Rogers to Kissinger, 2/6/75, National Security Advisor Presidential Country Files for Latin America, 1974–77, box 6, folder Panama (2), GRFL.

13 Bunker: National Security Council meeting files, box 1, 5/15/75, GRFL.

13 Kissinger, Schlesinger, Clements: National Security Council meeting files, box 1, 5/15/75, GRFL.

14 "I've had some experience": National Security Council meeting files, box 1, 5/15/75, GRFL.

14 Ford's dislike of Schlesinger: Gerald R. Ford, *A Time to Heal: The Autobiography of Gerald R. Ford* (New York: Harper and Row, 1979), p. 321.

14 Kissinger to Ford about Defense Department: National Security Advisor Memorandum of Conversations, 1973–77, box 11, folder 6/27/75—Ford, Kissinger, GRFL.

14–15 Kissinger, Schlesinger, Clements: National Security Council meeting File, box 2, 7/23/75, GRFL.

15 "Almost unprecedented occurrence": Henry A. Kissinger, *Years of Renewal* (New York: Simon and Schuster, 1999), p. 764.

15 General Brown: National Security Council meeting file, box 2, 7/23/75, GRFL.

15 Brown respected: John O. Marsh int 2/28/2005, af.

16 New instructions: National Security Decision Memorandum 302, National Security Decision Memoranda and Study Memoranda, box 1, GRFL.

16 Retirement after 1976: Ford, *A Time to Heal*, p. 99.

16 Reagan's "simplistic solutions": ibid., pp. 294ff.

16 Discussion of Reagan: National Security Council Memorandum of Conversation, 5/12/75, box 11, folder 5/12/75—Ford, Kissinger, pp. 1–2. GRFL.

16 Keep treaty from Congress: National Security Council meeting files, box 1, 5/15/75, GRFL.

16 September 2 meeting: Jorden, *Panama Odyssey*, pp. 292–294.

17 "Your politics": NYT, 7/28/75.

17 Brown's effectiveness: William D. Rogers int 2/28/2005 af.

17 George Wallace and Kissinger: NYT, 9/17/75.

18 Conservative organizations: NYT, 11/5/75.

18 M. Stanton Evans: HE, 8/30/75.

CHAPTER 3

19 "A Time for Choosing": http://www.reaganfoundation.org/reagan/speeches/rendezvous.asp, accessed 8/11/07.

19 Transformation of Reagan: Lou Cannon, *Reagan* (New York: Putnam's, 1982), p. 13.

20 Conservative attitudes on Ford: M. Stanton Evans int 3/24/06, af.

20 Not taking Reagan seriously: Ford, *A Time to Heal*, p. 294.

20 Reagan's income: Cannon, *Reagan*, p. 196.

20 "Very disappointed": Ford, *A Time to Heal*, p. 333.

21 "Popular vibrations": WP, 11/14/75.

21 Fund-raising letter: Craig Shirley files, folder Bruce Eberle.

21 Military superiority: Craig Shirley, *Reagan's Revolution: The Untold Story of the Campaign That Started It All* (Nashville, Tenn.: Nelson Current, 2005), p. 92.

21 "Buddy" system: Peter Hannaford, *The Reagans: A Political Portrait* (New York: Coward-McCann, 1983), p. 79.

21 Helms warning, research: Peter Hannaford int 3/10/05, af.

21 "False flag": Reagan to Donald M. Dozer, 4/17/67, DuVal papers, box 2, folder 1, Georgetown Library.

21 Supporters' views: Hannaford int 8/7/06, af.

22 Outraged: Lyn Nofziger, *Nofziger* (Washington, D.C.: Regnery Gateway, 1992), pp. 177–178.

22 Reagan broadcast text: Ronald Reagan Radio Commentary collection, Hoover, box 8, af.

22 Atlantic City speech: HE, 7/19/75.

22 VFW speech: NYT, 8/19/75.

22 "Marxist": HE, 9/27/75.

23 "Damn fools": *Philadelphia Inquirer*, 10/22/75.

23 Thunderous applause: *Philadelphia Inquirer*, 10/22/75.

23 Coral Springs, Arias: Hannaford, *The Reagans*, p. 77.

23 Defensive: Witcover, *Marathon*, pp. 382–385.

23 Eleventh Commandment: Cannon, *Reagan*, pp. 107–108.

23 Remarks at Exeter: Cannon, *Reagan*, p. 210.

24 Press coverage: BG, Baltimore Sun, WP, 2/11/76.

24 Reagan as extremist, Ford as conservative: Witcover, *Marathon*, pp. 383, 389.

24 Gregg prediction: Witcover, *Marathon*, pp. 393–394.

24 New Hampshire vote totals, 1972, 1976: Richard M. Scammon and Alice V. MacGillivray, *America Votes 12: A Handbook of Contemporary American Election Statistics* (Washington, D.C.: Congressional Quarterly, 1977), pp. 18, 24; vote totals, 1968, *Congressional Quarterly's Guide to U.S. Elections* (Washington, D.C.: Congressional Quarterly Press, 2001), p. 351.

24 "What a shot": Ford, *A Time to Heal*, p. 367.

CHAPTER 4

25 Delay on tarmac: Hannaford int 8/7/06, af.

25 Republicans urging: Witcover, *Marathon*, pp. 410ff.

25 Sears and Ford campaign: Cannon, *Reagan*, p. 214; Witcover, *Marathon*, p. 413; Sears int 6/25/07, af.

25 Buckley: WS, 3/22/76.

25 Kilpatrick: WS, 3/23/76.

25 Nancy Reagan on withdrawal: Sears int 6/25/07, af.

25 Nofziger and Nancy Reagan: Nofziger, *Nofziger*, pp. 179–180.

26 Sun City appearance: *Tampa Tribune*, 2/28/76; *St. Petersburg Times*, 2/28/76.

26 Sun City reaction, reasons: David A. Keene ints, 3/4/05 and 6/29/06.

26 Sears and Wirthlin: Richard Wirthlin with Wynton C. Hall, *The Great Communicator: What Ronald Reagan Taught Me about Politics, Leadership and Life* (Hoboken, N.J.: Wiley, 2004), p. 23.

26 Momentum: Sears int 6/25/07.

26 Toughened: Wirthlin with Hall, *Great Communicator*, p. 23.

26 "State Department actions": NYT, 2/29/76.

27 Minor issue: Wirthlin with Hall, *Great Communicator*, p. 23.

27 TV ad on Canal: LAT, 3/8/76.

27 Keene's blunt advice: Shirley, *Reagan's Revolution*, p. 140; Keene to author, 6/28/06, af.

28 "Santa Claus": Cannon, *Reagan*, p. 217.

28 Florida, Illinois percentages: Scammon and MacGillivray, *America Votes 12*, p. 22.

28 Mistake to ease up: Oral History Interview with Robert Teeter, 5/5/97, Gerald R. Ford vertical file, folder Teeter, Robert, p. 29, GRFL.

28 Ellis, Nancy Reagan: NYT, 3/29/76; Tom Ellis int 2/7/06, af.

28 Reagan on direct TV approach: Sears, Keene int 3/4/05, af; Sears's recollection, Sears int 6/25/07, af.

28 Editing out palms, checks: Ellis int 2/7/06, af.

29 Stations, cost: NYT, 3/29/06.

29 Reagan television speech: Audio-visual collection, GRFL. The library's copy is of a version used in Wisconsin, with a different mailing address for contributions.

29–30n "The answer was clear": Walter LaFeber, *The Panama Canal*, at page 219 in the 1978 edition and at pages 217–218 in the 1989 edition.

30 "Sally Jones": NYT, 3/25/76.

30 "Centerpiece": Charles Black int w/ Craig Shirley, 1/27/04, Craig Shirley files.

30 Emotional: Charles Black int 2/20/05, af.

30 Abandoned note cards: Paul Laxalt int 8/8/06, af.

30 "Giveaway": WP, 3/21/76.

30 "Guerilla warfare": *Charlotte Observer*, 3/20/76.

30 "We built it": Shirley, *Reagan's Revolution*, p. 170.

30 Number of ACU ads: HE, 4/3/76.

31 "Simple issue," voice: M. Stanton Evans int 3/24/06, af.

31 Ad texts: HE, 4/13/76.

31 $16,000: ACU's FEC Report, 4/76.

31 Failure: WS, 3/21/76.

32 Staring at defeat: Hannaford, *The Reagans*, p. 106.

32 North Carolina vote percentage: Scammon and MacGillivray, *American Votes 12*, p. 24.

32 "Dumbfounded": Jim Naughton int 7/10/06, af.

CHAPTER 5

33 "Reagan propelled": WP, 3/24/76.

33 "Off the ropes": CT, 3/24/76.

33 Later primaries argument: Cannon, *Reagan*, p. 219; Shirley, *Reagan's Revolution*, p. 181; Sears int 6/25/07, af.

34 $104,000: Shirley, *Reagan's Revolution*, p. 185.

34 *The Dumplings:* WP, 3/30/76.

34 Newscast audience: undated memo, President Ford Committee, Dawn Sibley File, box E4, GRFL.

34 Reagan March 31 speech: Audio-visual collection, GRFL.

34 $1.5 million: Shirley, *Reagan's Revolution*, p. 186.

34 Kissinger angered: LAT, 4/2/76.

35 Ford in Dallas: NYT, 4/14/76.

35 Bunker testimony: UPI article 4/13/76, Snyder press release 4/13/76, Richard B. Cheney files, 1974–1977, box 9, folder Panama Canal, Ellsworth Bunker Congressional Testimony, 4/8/76, GRFL.

35 Snyder telephoned Reagan: Sol Linowitz to Cyrus Vance, 5/2/77, FO3–1 Panama, JCL.

35 Midland remarks: NYT, 4/14/76.

35 Corpus Christi remarks: CBS, 4/14/76.

35 Sears on Ford-Bunker contradiction: Sears int 6/25/07.

35 Lacked "precision": NYT, 4/14/76.

35 "Off the hook": National Security Advisor, Memorandum of Conversations, 1973–77, box 19, folder 4/15/76—Ford, Kissinger, Rumsfeld, p. 3, GRFL.

35 Texas editors: WP, 4/21/76.

36 Reagan ad: Audio-Visual records, GRFL.

36 Blackmail: NYT, 4/23/76.

36 Threats: LAT, 4/22/76.

36 Boyd: CBS transcript, Interview with Aquilino Boyd (4/16/76), WHSF, box 6, folder Panama Canal Treaty negotiations 1/76–4/16/76, p. 2, GRFL.

36 "Irresponsibility": NYT, 4/22/76.

36 Goldwater in Phoenix: NYT, 4/25/76.

36 Goldwater on *Meet the Press: Facts on File*, 5/8/76.

36 Radio commercial: NYT, 5/10/76.

36 Delegate count: NYT, 5/10/76.

37 Ideological fights: Ellis int 7/17/06.

37 "Challenging the whole": John East, Oral History No. 2, Oct. 15, 1979, John East Papers, ECU.

37 "Fratricidal warfare": Hannaford, *The Reagans*, pp. 127–130.

37 "Our foreign policy": ACU, *Battleground*, August–September 1976, 109, folder 9, ACU-BYU; Stanton Evans, HE, 9/4/76.

37 Final Republican platform language: http://www.ford.utexas.edu/LIBRARY/document/platform/platform.htm, accessed 8/11/07.

38 Reagan acceptance speech: Hannaford, *The Reagans*, p. 134.

38 Reagan convention text: http://www.reaganfoundation.org/speeches/convention
.asp, accessed 8/11/07.

38 "Office seeks the man": Stu Spencer int 9/30/05, af.

38 "Destiny": Michael K. Deaver int 9/6/2005, af.

39 "Bleak": Hannaford int 8/7/06, af.

39 "All over": Paul Laxalt int 8/8/06, af.

39 "Presumptive": Cannon, *Reagan*, p. 218.

39 "Badly scarred": Richard B. Wirthlin int 8/8/06, af.

39 Did not know: Nancy Reagan to author, 1/8/2007, af.

CHAPTER 6

41 Reorganization's appeal: Peter G. Bourne, *Jimmy Carter: A Comprehensive Biography from Plains to Postpresidency* (New York: Scribner, 1997), p. 265.

41 "Decency and generosity": NYT, 6/24/76.

41 "Primacy of moral principle": Gaddis Smith, *Morality, Reason and Power: American Diplomacy in the Carter Years* (New York: Hill and Wang, 1986), p. 29.

41 More than 600: WP, 2/28/77.

41 "Full of compassion and love": LAT, 5/27/76.

41 Discrimination, King portrait: Jimmy Carter, *A Government as Good as Its People* (New York: Simon and Schuster, 1977), pp. 26–27.

42 "No Soviet domination": NYT, 10/7/76.

42 Never saw Canal, not much thought: Jimmy Carter int 7/12/06, af.

42 "Relinquishing": *Newsweek*, 5/10/76.

42 "Never give up": NYT, 10/7/76.

42 Torrijos: Jorden, *Panama Odyssey*, p. 329.

42 Eizenstat: Sol Linowitz interview by Jorden, 3/23/79, Jorden papers, box 21, LBJL.

43 Soothed Boyd: Linowitz interview by Jorden, box 21, LBJL.

43 National Guard: Jorden, *Panama Odyssey*, p. 336, and cable, Jorden to Kissinger, 11/3/76, af.

43 Robert Pastor memo: af.

43 Kissinger: memcon in Robert Pastor files, af.

43 Carter read report: Jorden, *Panama Odyssey*, p. 341.

43 "Most urgent": Jimmy Carter, *Keeping Faith: Memoirs of a President* (New York: Bantam, 1982), p. 256.

43 "Panama treaty": Time, 1/3/77; NYT, 12/28/76.

43 Meeting with members of Congress: WP, 1/13/77.

43 Pastor hired: Robert Pastor int 6/8/06, af.

44 "Convertible": Presidential Review Memorandum 1, National Security Archive, p. 32, af.

44 Cranston: Policy Review Committee minutes 1/25/77, National Security Archive, af.

44 Vance, Linowitz, Bunker: Policy Review Committee minutes, af.

44 Energy: Pastor int 6/8/06, af.

44 Resume negotiations: Jorden, *Panama Odyssey*, p. 244.

44 Torrijos strong: Cyrus Vance, *Hard Choices: Critical Years in America's Foreign Policy* (New York: Simon and Schuster, 1983), p. 145.

44 Delay invites violence: Presidential Review Memorandum 1, p. 3, af.

44 Panama first: Pastor int 6/8/06, af.

44 Opportunity: Carter int 7/12/06, af.

CHAPTER 7

45 Mideast, "treat Panama fairly": Carter int 7/12/06, af.

45 Reagan speech: box 5, folder 17, ACU-BYU.

45 Helms: Hansen, HE, 3/12/77.

45 Sikes: HE, 4/16/77.

45 *Group Research Reports*, 3/30/77, box 429, Group Research files, BLCU.

46 Thurmond letter for ACU: box 7, folder Panama Canal, Group Research files, BLCU.

46 February planning: Karen Latimer to Howard Phillips, 2/23/77, TCC files, af.

46 Thomson: TCC *Member's Report*, 9/77, af.

46 McDonald, bumper sticker: box 91, folder Conservative Caucus, Group Research files, BLCU.

46 February negotiations: Jorden, *Panama Odyssey*, pp. 341–374.

47 Logjam broken: Jorden, *Panama Odyssey*, pp. 384–385.

47 Regime of neutrality: Vance to Carter, 6/8/77, National Security Affairs, box 18, tab 7, "Evening Reports (State), 6/77," JCL.

47 Agreement: Jorden, *Panama Odyssey*, pp. 434–437.

47 Final drafting: Jorden, *Panama Odyssey*, p. 448.

47–48 Lunch, Reagan letter: Sol Linowitz to Cyrus Vance, 5/2/77, WHCF Subject File-Executive, box FO–15, "FO 3–1/Panama Canal 4/14/77–7/31/77," JCL.

48 Baker meeting: Jorden interview of James M. Cannon, 7/22/82, af; Cannon int 6/17/05.

48 Briefings: Bob Beckel int 10/19/06, af.

48 Seventy senators: I. M. Destler, "Treaty Troubles: Versailles in Reverse," *Foreign Policy*, no. 33 (Winter 1978–1979).

48 "Major effort": Joe Aragon to Hamilton Jordan and Landon Butler, 6/7/77, Chief of Staff (Jordan)-Butler files, box 118, "Panama Canal [Binder] [CF, O/A 740]," JCL.

48 Citizens' committee: Aragon to Butler, 7/9/77, COS Butler files, Chief of Staff (Jordan)-Butler files, box 118, "Panama Canal [Binder] [CF, O/A 740]," JCL.

49 "Blue-chip names": George D. Moffett III, *The Limits of Victory: The Ratification of the Panama Canal Treaties* (Ithaca, N.Y.: Cornell University Press, 1985), p. 83.

49 Telegrams, responses, "nuts": Carter, *Keeping Faith*, p. 159.

49 8 percent: WP, 8/11/77.

49 Call to Ford: WP, 8/17/77.

49 Call to Kissinger: NYT, 9/1/77.

49 Call to Reagan: NYT, 8/24/77.

49 Carter notes on Hatch, 8/25/77, Handwriting file, box 81, "Panama Canal-Status Briefing Book, 4/19/78 [2]," JCL.

49 Carter notes on Bartlett, 8/11/77, Handwriting file, box 81, "Panama Canal-Status Briefing Book, 4/19/78 [1]," JCL.

49 Carter notes on Long, 8/25/77, Handwriting file, box 81, "Panama Canal-Status Briefing Book, 4/19/78 [2]," JCL.

49 Carter notes on Morgan, 8/10/77, Handwriting file, box 81, "Panama Canal-Status Briefing Book, 4/19/78 [2]," JCL.

49 Prickly: Frank Moore and Dan Tate to Carter, 8/23/77, Handwriting file, box 45, "8/23/77 [1]," JCL.

49 Play date: Carter to Jane Frank 9/2/77, Handwriting file, box 47, "9/2/77," JCL.

50 Sunbelt: NYT, 8/11/77.

50 Mississippi, Kentucky: WP, 8/29/77.

50 Florida, Georgia: NYT, 8/31/77.

50 Goldwater to Pastor: 3/12/76, Chief of Staff (Jordan)-Butler files, box 118, "Panama Canal [Binder] [CF O/A 740]," JCL.

50 Ask Kissinger: Frank Moore to Kissinger, 9/2/77, Congressional Liaison-Nuechterlein files, box 237, "[Panama Canal Treaty-Congressional Strategy], 5/26/77–9/29/77 [CF, O/A 193]," JCL.

50 Carter's phone calls: LAT, 9/3/77.

50 Goldwater to constituents: LAT, 9/10/77.

50 Disappointment: Carter int 7/12/06, af.

50 Reagan on Joint Chiefs: NYT, 8/24/77.

50 "Giveaway": LAT, 8/25/77.

50 Reagan speech to YAF: LAT, 8/26/77.

50 Canal treaties' importance to hemisphere: Gaddis Smith, *Morality, Reason and Power*, p. 110.

50 Bad idea: Baker int by John Lindsay of *Newsweek* 2/1/78, box 14, folder 8, Howard H. Baker Jr., Papers, Baker Center, University of Tennessee.

51 Momentum: Bob Beckel int 10/18/06, af.

51 Sway public: LAT, 9/3/77.

51 Public support: NYT, 8/12/77.

51 "Reversible," "bastards": NYT, 10/13/77.

52 Carter to editors: *Public Papers of the Presidents of the United States, Jimmy Carter 1977 Book II* (Washington, D.C.: Government Printing Office, 1978), p. 1514.

CHAPTER 8

53 "It is us": Richard Viguerie int 10/17/06, af; Rhatican int 3/28/05, af.

53 Unite conservative factions: WS, 6/23/75, 6/24/75.

54 Viguerie background: Richard A. Viguerie, *The New Right: We're Ready to Lead* (Falls Church, Va.: The Viguerie Company, 1981), pp. 27–30.

54 "Poor student": ibid., p. 28.

54 First fund-raising letter: ibid., p. 30.

54 Young Americans for Freedom, set up own business: ibid., p. 32.

54 Burger, Carswell: William J. Lanquette, "The New Right: 'Revolutionaries' Out after the 'Lunch-Pail' Vote," *National Journal*, 1/21/78.

54 Nixon, Ashbrook: Viguerie, *New Right*, p. 36.

54 Wallace debt: ibid., p. 37.

54 Several million names: William C. Berman, *America's Right Turn: From Nixon to Bush* (Baltimore: Johns Hopkins University Press, 1994), p. 28.

54 Vice president: NYT, 12/4/77; WSJ, 10/6/78.

54 Reagan and Wallace: NYT, 5/23/75.

54 "Saving our nation": Viguerie, *New Right*, p. 39.

54 Meetings, participants: Viguerie int 10/17/06, af.

54 Crane mailings: Viguerie, *New Right*, p. 35.

55 Phillips in Democratic primary: Phillips int 5/31/07.

55 "Fraud": *Time*, 8/20/79.

56 "Impetus and unity": Viguerie int 10/17/06, af.

56 "Conservatives can't lose": *National Journal*, 10/8/77.

56 Phillips's view: CM, 8/22/77, Phillips int 11/14/06, af.

56 Laxalt as liaison: CBS, 9/9/77.

56 Laxalt in California: NYT, 10/3/77.

56 "Control the party": WS, 9/30/77.

56 "Grass roots conservatives": *Dayton [Ohio] Daily News*, 8/28/77.

56 "Great opportunity": Jarmin, WS, 9/30/77.

56 "Hit list": WS, 9/30/77.

56 "Conservative leaders": Steven F. Hayward, *The Age of Reagan: The Fall of the Old Liberal Order* (Roseville, Calif.: Prima Publishing, 2001), p. 547.

57 Proliferation of organizations: WS, 6/23/75.

57 Rally sponsors: Reagan, LAT, 9/3/77.

57 "Threats": Hearings, Subcommittee on Separation of Powers of the Committee on the Judiciary of U.S. Senate, part 3, 9/8/77, p. 11.

57 McDonald, John Birch Society council: NYT, 10/13/74.

57 Succeeded Welch: NYT, 9/1/83.

57 "Bipartisan treason": WP, 9/8/77.

57 "51st state", "Russian roulette": CBS, 9/7/77.

57 Whorehouses: WP, 9/8/77.

57 Crane, McClure: CT, 9/8/77.

57 Nazis: LAT, 9/8/77.

57 "All the facts": Ronald Reagan, introduction in Philip M. Crane, *Surrender in Panama: The Case Against the Treaty* (Ottawa, Ill.: Caroline House Books, 1978), pp. ix, xii.

58 100,000 copies: *New Right*, p. 68.

58 Sovereignty: Crane, *Surrender in Panama*, pp. 7, 34–40.

58 "Pathetic rabble": ibid., p. 14.

58 Torrijos, police state: ibid., p. 71.

58 American security: ibid., pp. 51–52.

58 "Descent to ignominy": ibid., p. 113

58 Reagan letter 12/7/77: box 263, folder Panama Canal, Group Research Report files, BLCU.

59 $700,000: WP, 12/20/77.

59 Laxalt, Reagan, "son of a bitch": Paul Laxalt, *Nevada's Paul Laxalt: A Memoir* (Reno, Nev.: Jack Bacon and Company, 2000), p. 232.

59 "Pretty hot Irishman": *Nashville Banner*, 12/17/77.

59 Bipartisan, "divisive": Bill Brock int 12/11/06, af.

59 Reagan advantage: Brock int 12/11/06, af.

59 $110,000, $5,000 contributors: Viguerie, *New Right*, p. 68.

59 Reporters, Viguerie on plane: WP, 1/19/78.

59 Laxalt, Garn: ABC, 1/18/78.

59 Write Chiles, Stone: *WP*, 1/19/78.

60 "Master plan," Crowe: *Miami Herald*, 1/19/78.

60 Audience size, Graham, Dole: *St. Louis Post-Dispatch*, 1/20/78.

60 "Fatally flawed": *DP*, 1/20/78.

60 "Hogwash": Weyrich, *NYT*, 1/20/78.

60 Crane, McDonald, Charlotte Kennedy: *Portland Oregonian*, 1/21/78.

60 Allott press secretary: *Knoxville News-Sentinel*, 11/7/77.

60 Afternoon meetings: Rhatican int 3/28/05, af.

CHAPTER 9

61n White House pandering: Zbigniew Brzezinski, *Power and Principle: Memoirs of the National Security Adviser, 1977–1981* (New York: Farrar, Straus and Giroux, 1983), p. 136, Gaddis Smith, *Morality, Reason and Power*, p. 114.

62 "Course of violence": HE, 9/3/77.

62 "Theories": HE, 9/10/77.

62 "When neutrality is violated," Escobar "told newsmen": HE, 9/17/77.

62 Thomson to American Legion: TCC, *Member's Report*, 9/77, af.

63 Umbrellas: *LAT*, 9/3/77.

63 150 followers, Lafayette Park: *LAT*, 9/8/77.

63 Hypocrite: *WS*, 9/8/77.

63 300,000, hundreds: *Grassroots*, TCC, 12/77, af.

63 Ads: TCC press release, 11/27/77, af.

63 Training sessions: *Democratic Congressional Campaign Committee Report*, 3/79, box 93, Group Research files, BLCU.

63 Summer camp: *LAT*, 8/30/77.

63 "Marxist dictatorship," Soviet agents: John Rees, "The Soviets Grab for Our Canal," *The Review of the News*, 8/31/77, box 92, folder 1, ACU-BYU.

63 Bumper stickers: *American Opinion*, 11/77, Howard Liebengood papers, box 26, folder 9, LOC.

63 Birch petitions: H. T. Hicks to Robert Morgan, 11/10/77, Robert Morgan papers, box 412, folder (d) ECU.

63 Buttons: *Dayton [Ohio] Daily News*, 8/28/77.

64 YAF petitions: *Democratic Congressional Campaign Committee Report*, 2/78, George D. Moffett Donated Historical Material, box 11, folder Truth Squad [1], JCL.

64 Plane, postcards: box 92, folder 3; box 49, folder 18; box 67, folder 28, ACU-BYU.

64 Attendance, 27 to 14: *Nashville Tennessean*, 11/6/77.

64 ACU Tennessee ad: *Tennessean*, 9/4/77.

65 3,600 letters: *WP*, 9/18/77.

65 "Hot brick," "brink": *WP*, 9/12/77.

65–66 Crane, Helms, Crowe, et al.: ACU infomercial transcript, box 91, folder 11, ACU-BYU.

67 209 Showings, 58,000 names, $245,000: minutes of ACU board meeting, 3/29/78, box 21, folder 24, ACU-BYU.

67 Letter totals from various groups: Viguerie, *New Right*, p. 67.

67 Greater resonance, Viguerie int 2/21/07, af.

67 Pennies: Dick Clark papers, Special Collections, University of Iowa Libraries, box 69, folder Panama Canal (second).

67 ACU postcards for Baker: box 67, folder 28, ACU-BYU.

67 *Birch Log:* Alan C. Thomaier to Thomas McIntyre, 2/20/78, McIntyre papers, MC36, box 103, folder 13, UNH.

67 $5 or $10: *CQWR*, 12/24/77.

68 "So long as I live": Dick Clark Papers, Special Collections, University of Iowa Libraries, box 69, folder Panama Canal (first).

68 4,985 letters: John Culver Papers, Special Collections, University of Iowa Libraries, box 171, folder weekly reports Feb 78.

68 "Largest net benefit": William A. Rusher, *The Rise of the Right* (New York: William Morrow, 1984), p. 299.

69 Past donors: Viguerie int 2/20/07, af.

CHAPTER 10

70 "Do everything I can": CBS, 8/16/77; NYT, 8/24/77.

70 "Without equivocation": box 14, folder 8, Baker papers, Baker Center.

71 "What if . . . ," "forefront": Hannaford int 8/6/06, af.

71 "Assuming he stays": HE, 9/3/77.

71 No time for television taping: NYT, 10/31/77.

71 Reagan testimony: Subcommittee on Separation of Powers of Committee on the Judiciary of U.S. Senate, part 3, 9/8/77, pp. 11, 21, 30.

71 "Star attraction": Frank Moore, *Weekly Reports*, 9/10/77, Walter Mondale Papers, box 154.J.8.6F, Minnesota Historical Society,

72 Press club speech: Peter Hannaford files, Hoover, box 5.

72 Panamanian resentment: William F. Buckley, Jr., *National Review*, 11/12/76.

72 Trust Torrijos: Buckley, *National Review*, 11/26/76.

72 Reagan, Buckley debating: WP, 1/15/78, 1/24/78.

72 Driveway signs: William F. Buckley, Jr., *In Overdrive: A Personal Documentary* (Garden City, N.Y.: Doubleday, 1983), p. 121.

72 Reagan on CBS: *NYT*, 2/8/78.

73 On one occasion called uncommitted senator: Hannaford to author, 5/23/07, af.

73 Called Nunn: Sam Nunn int 5/14/07, af. 122 Audience: Harry O'Connor to Pete Hannaford, 12/12/06, af.

73 Revolution, Joint Chiefs, Hoover: Reagan Subject Collection, box 8, Radio Scripts 1976–78, Folder II. The radio scripts are not precisely dated.

73 State Department: Citizens for Reagan, Hoover, box 104, folder radio scripts 1978.

73 Newspaper columns: Hannaford Collection, Hoover, box 2.

73 Chafed: author's interpretation supported by Hannaford to author, 12/3/06, af.

74 Nominated, elected, insurrection: Buckley, *In Overdrive*, p. 119.

CHAPTER 11

75 Baker's initial reaction: Howard H. Baker int 5/17/05, af.

75 Take it seriously, study issue, divided party, neither support nor opposition: Baker int 5/17/05, af.

75 "Favors Treaty": Carter's notes, Handwriting file, box 81, folder 4/19/78, Panama Canal Status Briefing Book 4/19/78 [1], JCL.

75 Kiwanis luncheon: transcript of 8/30/77 remarks, box 14, folder 5, Baker papers, Baker Center.

76 Union army majors: J. Lee Annis, *Howard Baker: Conciliator in an Age of Crisis* (Lanham, Md.: Madison Books, 1995), p. 11.

76 Photography, education: ibid., pp. 14–16.

76 Father's campaign, murder cases, Joy Dirksen: ibid., pp. 17–20.

76 "Fell swoop": Baker int 1/13/94, Clymer papers, Series 2, box 3, John F. Kennedy Library.

77 "Defeating bad legislation": *WP*, 11/14/67.

77 Subpoenas: Annis, *Howard Baker*, p. 69.

77 "What did the President know": Select Committee on Presidential Campaign Activities, Hearings, Phase I: Watergate Investigation, 6/28/73, p. 1466.

77 Press corps, White House: Jack Germond and Jules Witcover, *Blue Smoke and Mirrors: How Reagan Won and Carter Lost the 1980 Election* (New York: Viking, 1981), pp. 192–193.

77 ACU voting record: http://www.acuratings.org/, accessed 8/11/07.

77 White House fear: John F. Stacks, *Watershed: The Campaign for the Presidency, 1980* (New York: Times Books, 1981), pp. 110–111.

78 Dole: Joseph Lelyveld, "The Path to 1980," *New York Times Magazine*, 10/2/77.

78 McMahan: Ron McMahan to Baker, undated but apparently late August or early September, 1977, Liebengood Papers, box 22, folder 17, LOC.

78 Mosbacher: Rob Mosbacher to Baker, 9/9/77; Liebengood papers, box 22, folder 14.

78 Liebengood: Howard Liebengood to Baker, 9/9/77, Liebengood papers, box 22, folder 14.

78 Cannon advice, Baker reaction: James Cannon int 7/22/82 by William Jorden, af; Howard H. Baker int 6/17/05.

78 Baker at hearing: Panama Canal Treaties, Hearings before the Committee on Foreign Relations, United States Senate, First session, 95th Congress, Part 1 (Washington, Government Printing Office, 1977), pp. 7, 57.

79 Treaties in trouble: LAT, 10/12/77.

79 "Statement of understanding": Jorden, *Panama Odyssey*, p. 480.

79 Welcomed: Jorden, *Panama Odyssey*, p. 479.

79 Warned in advance: LAT, 10/12/77.

79 Torrijos reluctance: Robert Pastor int 6/8/06, af.

79 Moot court: William D. Rogers int 2/28/06, af.

80 Fontaine op-ed: WSJ, 8/22/77.

80 "Never satisfied": Roger W. Fontaine int 2/9/95 by David Welborn, af.

80 "Complexity": William D. Rogers int 11/19/93 by Welborn, af.

80 Poll, Roll analysis: "The Panama Canal Treaty Issue and Tennessee's Voters," Liebengood papers, box 14, folder 2, LOC.

80 Other national polls: NYT, 11/2/77.

80 Cannon memo: Liebengood papers, box 28, folder 3.

81 Annoyance: CSM, 10/25/77.

81 Tasked: notes on Dec. 20, 1977 meeting, Liebengood papers, box 21, folder 13.

81 Rogers, Fontaine, recommendations: Liebengood papers, box 20, folder 1.

81 Amendment: Liebengood and Montgomery to Baker, 1/2/78, Liebengood papers, box 20, folder 1.

81 See for himself, Torrijos and changes: Cannon int 7/22/82 with Jorden, af.

CHAPTER 12

82 Zoo: NYT, 1/9/78.

82 "Convinced": CT, 8/21/77.

82 "Mistake": LAT, 8/20/77.

82 Panamanians do not care: Lelyveld, "The Path to 1980."

82 Sabotage encouraged, "military man": *Meet the Press* transcript, 8/21/77, af.

83 "Technician," "rankled": Robert C. Byrd, *Robert C. Byrd, Child of the Appalachian Coalfields* (Morgantown: West Virginia University Press, 2005), p. 385.

83 "Exceedingly vulnerable": Brzezinski to Byrd, 11/8/77, National Security Affairs, Brzezinski material, JCL.

84 Opinion shifting: *LAT*, 11/9/77.

84 "Political price": Jorden, *Panama Odyssey*, p. 483.

84 Softening image: *WP*, 11/12/77.

84 "Grilled": Jorden, *Panama Odyssey*, p. 485.

84 White House advice: Metzenbaum, "Report on the Visit Made By Senator Robert C. Byrd and the Group of U.S. Senators," 11/77, transmitted by Jorden to Vance and Carter, William J. Jorden papers, box 23, LBJL.

84 Sarbanes: "Report of the Visit . . . ," LBJL.

84 "Somewhat reassuring": ABC, 11/10/77.

85 Dinner, fiddle, neckties: Jorden, *Panama Odyssey*, p. 486; Memorandum, Howard Liebengood to Howard Baker, 11/19/77, Liebengood papers, box 14, folder 3.

85 Jorden concluded: *Panama Odyssey*, p. 487.

85 Abolish martial law, "positive step": *LAT*, 11/13/77.

85 Senate approval: *NYT*, 12/4/77.

86 "Both of us": Jorden, *Panama Odyssey*, p. 481.

86 Lofton: HE, 1/21/78.

86 Hamlet: WS, 1/6/78.

86 Baker-Jorden conversation: Cran Montgomery notes (handwriting identified by him 3/28/07), Liebengood papers, box 14, folder 12.

86 Colon: *NYT*, 1/9/78.

86 Reduce fees: Liebengood draft of report on trip, Liebengood papers, box 29, folder 6.

87 Impatient: Roger Fontaine int with David Welborn, 2/9/95, af.

87 Upstairs: Baker int 5/15/05.

87 Sent for interpreter: Baker int with Edward Annis, 3/9/90, Annis papers, Baker Center.

87 Defend canal, head of line, forty years: James Cannon notes, undated, box 14, folder 3, Baker Papers, Baker Center, Cannon to author, 2/16/2007, af; Cannon int 2/25/07, af.

87 Pressed Torrijos: Baker int with John Lindsay of *Newsweek*, 2/1/78, box 14, folder 8, Baker Papers, Baker Center.

87 Torrijos on Baker comments, Baker response: *NYT*, 1/5/78.

87 Advisers: CT, 1/6/78.

87 *Critica:* Jorden, *Panama Odyssey*, p. 493.

87 Noriega briefing: Montgomery int with Wellborn, 9/1/92, af; Fontaine int with Welborn, 2/9/95, af; cable Jorden to Vance, 1/11/78, af.

88 Noriega-Baker exchange: Jorden to Vance, 1/11/78, af.

88 "Candid and friendly": Jorden to Vance, 1/11/78, af.

88 Baker to press: U.S. Embassy transcript, box 23, folder 9, Liebengood papers, LOC.

88 Ahead of himself: Baker int with Lindsay, 2/1/78, box 14, folder 8, Baker papers, Baker Center.

88 Support treaty: *Tennessean*, 1/7/78.

88 Byrd and Baker talked January 12: *Tennessean*, 1/14/78.

88 Byrd press conference: NYT, 1/14/78.

89 Byrd-Baker strategy: LAT, 1/26/78.

89 Byrd testimony: Hearings before the Committee on Foreign Relations, United States Senate, Second session, 95th Congress (Washington, D.C.: Government Printing Office, 1978), 1/26/78, pp. 4–5.

89 Battle not over: Hearings before the Committee on Foreign Relations, 1/26/78, p. 33.

CHAPTER 13

90 Taft withheld: American Law Institute, *Third Restatement of the Foreign Relations Law of the United States* (St. Paul, Minn.: American Law Institute Press, 1987), vol. 1, p. 163.

91 Gutted: NYT, CT, AC, 3/8/1912.

91 "Sell": *Public Papers of the Presidents of the United States, Jimmy Carter 1977 Book II* (Washington, D.C.: Government Printing Office, 1978), p. 1514.

91 Twenty-five times: Bernard Roshco, "The Polls: Polling on Panama—Si; Don't Know; Hell, No," *Public Opinion Quarterly* 42, no. 4 (Winter 1978): 551.

91 Gallup question: Gaylord Nelson papers, M80–626, box 73, folder Panama Canal, 8/26/80, Wisconsin State Historical Society.

91 *Times/CBS* News: iPoll, Roper Center for Public Opinion Research, af.

92 Caddell: "Panama Canal: Summary of Public Opinion," 2/78, Office of Congressional Liaison files Beckel, box 227, folder "Panama public opinion" JCL.

92 *Times/CBS* follow-ups: iPoll, af.

92 Harris, Roper, NBC: Roshco, "The Polls . . . ," p. 562.

92 Trend: Roshco, "The Polls . . . ," p. 562.

93 State Department speakers: *WP*, 2/26/78.

93 Pastor explained: Beckel int 2/1/05, af; Pastor int 6/8/06, af.

93 Town meetings: *NYT*, 2/1/78.

93 Theodore Roosevelt: *NYT*, 2/2/78.

93 Polling claims: *NYT*, 2/1/78.

93 "Snaky feeling": Hamilton Jordan int 3/16/06, af.

93 Herman C. Selya to Carter, Lowell Thomas, Jr., to Carter: WHCF Executive FO 3–1, box 18, JCL.

93 "Elites," "firewall": Jordan int 3/16/06, af.

94 1930s: John Wayne statement, attached to Wayne to Carter, 10/12/77, WHCF, COS Jordan subject files, box 50, folder Panama Canal Treaties 1977, JCL.

94 Wayne-Torrijos exchange: Jorden, *Panama Odyssey*, p. 487.

94 McGowan: Jorden, *Panama Odyssey*, p. 487.

94 Wayne backing treaties: *NYT, LAT*, 9/21/77.

94 "Somebody else's collar": October statement, Wayne to Carter, 10/12/78, WHCF, COS Jordan subject files, box 50, folder Panama Canal Treaties 1977, JCL.

94 Pastor's help: Pastor int 6/8/76, af.

94 Op-ed: *WP*, 10/25/77; *LAT*, 10/28/77.

94 Persuade: Wayne to Reagan, 11/11/77, Liebengood papers, box 27, folder 2, LOC.

95 "You've been had": John Lofton Jr., "An Open Letter to John Wayne: Dear Duke, You've Been Had," *Battle Line*, 12/77, box 209, folder 10, ACU-BYU.

95 Wayne op-ed: *CT*, 2/5/78.

95 Wayne with senators: Jorden, *Panama Odyssey*, p. 502.

95 Church newsletter: FCC, box 49, folder 2.

95 Hatfield: Bill Smith, Bob Thomson, Dan Tate and Bob Beckel to Walter Mondale, 3/28/78, Mondale papers, Minnesota Historical Society.

95 Cranston and Baucus: Max Baucus int 7/8/07.

95 Cartoon: *CT*, 12/30/77.

95 Weaken presidency argument: Robert Beckel Session, Carter Presidency Project, White Burkett Miller Center of Public Affairs, University of Virginia, 11/13/81, p. 30.

95 Stone: *Miami Herald*, 2/7/78; *CSM*, 2/13/78.

96 San Francisco State College: *NYT*, 12/3/68, 12/4/68, 1/9/69.

96 "Stole it": *NYT*, 2/14/77; *Time*, 8/22/77.

96 Weakness: S. I. Hayakawa to Carter, 4/13/78, Handwriting files, box 80, "4/14/78," JCL.

97 Hayakawa conversations with Mondale, Carter: Walter F. Mondale int 3/14/06, af.

97 Semantics book: Carter, *Keeping Faith*, p. 175.

97 "Carter would not": Beckel int 2/1/05, af.

97 Dams: Mondale int 3/13/06, af.

97 "No overt offers": Moore to Carter 2/28/78, Office of Congressional Liaison files Beckel, box 227, JCL.

97 Desalinization plant: Carter, *Keeping Faith*, p. 172.

97 Matsunaga: Moore to Carter, 8/23/77, Handwriting files, box 45. "8/24/77," JCL.

97 Redwoods: Robert Thomson and Beckel to Moore, 12/12/77, WHCF, Chief of Staff Jordan subject files, box 50, folder Panama Canal Treaties 1977, JCL.

97 Shipbuilding, Amtrak: Beckel int 10/18/06, af.

97 "Lists of demands": Moffett, *Limits of Victory*, p. 236.

98 Copper: NYT, 3/14/78.

98 Farm legislation: NYT, 3/14/78.

98 *Let's Make a Deal*: NYT, 3/15/78; WSJ, 3/16/78.

98 "Our side": DP, 3/16/78.

98 "Quietly changed": NYT, 3/14/78.

98 "Pet proposal": "Carter's Panama Triumph – What It Cost," U.S. *News and World Report*, 3/27/78.

98 No "trade-off": Talmadge papers, Series II, box 64, folder 33, RBRUGA.

98 Howard Hjort: NYT, 3/14/78.

98 "Less objectionable": handwriting file, box 76, folder 3/11/78, JCL.

98 Talmadge announcement: NYT, 3/15/78.

99 "Hold nose": Panama Canal Status Briefing Book 4/19/78 [3], handwriting file, box 81, folder 4/19/78, JCL.

99 Slump: NYT, 11/6/77.

99 Five times as much: WP, 4/14/78.

99 250,000 tons: NYT, WSJ, 9/29/77.

99 DeConcini pressure: Beckel int 2/1/05, af.

99 Copper stockpiling: Moore, Beckel and Thomson to Carter, 2/10/78, Office of Congressional Liaison files Beckel, box 227, "Panama Treaty Status Reports, 1/25/78–9/19/78 [CF, O/A 425]," JCL.

99 DeConcini told Radcliffe: WP, 4/14/78.

100 "Killer amendment": WP, 2/27/78; NYT, 2/28/78.

100 Seventy-seven amendments: LaFeber, *The Panama Canal*, p. 182.

100 Simplify, Talmadge, Long: Sam Nunn int 5/14/07, af.

100 Warren Christopher: Moffett, *Limits of Victory*, p. 237.

100 Hodges: ibid., p. 237.

100 Final wording: NYT, 3/17/78.

100 More copper: Beckel int 2/5/05, af.

101 Mondale et al.: NYT, 3/16/78; Kevin Gottlieb int 3/9/07, af.

101 Crude offer: WP, 3/15/78.

101 Cannon: Newsweek, 3/27/78.

102 Randolph: Newsweek, 3/27/78.

102 Baker's influence: NYT, 3/19/78.

102 Ad campaigns: CBS, 3/26/78; NBC, 4/4/78; Frank Moore weekly legislative report, 4/3/78, Handwriting file, box 79, Folder 4/4/78, JCL.

102 "Can't afford": Time, 4/3/78.

102 Panamanian anger: Jorden, Panama Odyssey, p. 558.

102 "Internal Panamanian activities": consent, CR 95:II, pp. 7147f, 3/16/78.

102 Torrijos's allies: Jorden, Panama Odyssey, p. 558.

102 Torrijos to Carter: Jorden, Panama Odyssey, p. 562.

102 "Senate has insulted": NBC, 4/13/78.

103 Haskell, Metzenbaum, Moynihan: DP, 4/14/78.

103 Recall: CBS, 3/22/78.

103 Stronger provision: NYT, 4/12/78.

103 Lewis efforts: Jorden, Panama Odyssey, pp. 565–588.

103 Byrd taking charge: NYT, 4/14/78.

103 Meeting at Capitol: Jorden, Panama Odyssey, pp. 602–604.

103 "Dignified solution": Jorden, Panama Odyssey, p. 607.

103 Liberals: Jorden, Panama Odyssey, p. 613.

103 Enjoyed: CBS, 4/12/78.

103 Mocked: NYT, 4/13/78; WP, 4/13/78.

103 "Military force": Jorden, Panama Odyssey, p. 613.

104 Forty-five minutes: Paul Sarbanes int by Jorden, 3/28/79, Jorden papers, box 21, LBJL.

104 "It has to be": Thomas M. Franck and Edward Weisbrand, Foreign Policy by Congress (New York: Oxford University Press, 1979), p. 283.

104 DeConcini announces language: CBS, 4/17; NBC, 4/18/78.

104 Attack on Canal: CT, LAT, NYT, WP, 4/19/78; LAT, 4/20/78, 4/22/78; Omar Torrijos int by William J. Jorden, 4/28/79, Jorden papers, box 21, LBJL.

104 Ready: NYT, 4/20/78, Intelligence Memorandum, CIA National Foreign Intelligence Center, 4/13/78, WHCF COS Jordan box 36, Folder Pan Canal Treaties 1978, JCL.

104 "Most impressive": Charles O. Jones, The Trusteeship Presidency: Jimmy Carter and the United States Congress (Baton Rouge: Louisiana State University Press, 1988), p. 155.

104 "Political suicide," willing to compromise: Robert A. Strong, "Jimmy Carter and

the Panama Canal Treaties," *Presidential Studies Quarterly* (Spring 1991): 282, 283.

104 Admired Wilson: Carter, *Keeping Faith*, pp. 19, 142.

104n Possibility of compromise: Robert A. Pastor, "The United States: Divided by a Revolutionary Vision," in Robert A. Pastor, ed., *A Century's Journey: How the Great Powers Shape the World* (New York: Basic Books, 1999), p. 213.

105 Comparison to debate on Treaty of Versailles: J. Michael Hogan, *The Panama Canal in American Politics: Domestic Advocacy and the Evolution of Policy* (Carbondale: Southern Illinois University Press, 1986), p. 7.

105 Phillippi, "badges": CR 95:II, p. 7185f, 3/16/78.

105 "Big boy": CR 95:II, p. 2733, 2/8/78.

105 Measure of strength: CR 95:II, p. 10533, 4/18/78.

105 "Raised money," rallied troops: *Newsweek*, 4/24/78.

CHAPTER 14

106 Anderson's primary: NYT, 2/16/78, 3/22/78.

106 Republican, "heart": Gordon Humphrey int 9/19/05, af.

106 Massachusetts, outdoors, Senate: Humphrey int 9/19/05, af.

107 "Good-looking": Bernard Fagelson int 10/5/2005, af.

108 Organizer: Howard Phillips int 5/3/05, af.

109 August Conservative Caucus meeting: CM, 8/22/77.

109 "Peoples' Democratic Republic": MUL, 1/7/78.

109 January rally: CM, 1/14/78; Manchester, N.H., NHSN, 1/15/78.

109 February rally: MUL, 2/15/78; NHSN, 2/18/78.

109 Kennedy, Ford, Eisenhower: Niall A. Palmer, *The New Hampshire Primary and the American Electoral Process* (Westport, Conn.: Praeger, 1997), p. 2.

109 Carter: MUL, 3/14/78.

109 Smith, McGovern: Eric P. Veblen, *The Manchester Union Leader in New Hampshire Elections* (Hanover, N.H.: University Press of New England, 1975), pp. 3, 46.

109 Loaded pistol: James Doyle int 11/24/05, af.

110 "Invincible": Humphrey int 9/19/05, af.

110 Lesser office, "upstart": Gerald P. Carmen int 10/6/06, af.

110 "Hello, my name is": CM, 2/27/78.

110 Major, decorations: *Congressional Directory, 88th Congress, 1st Session* (Washington, D.C.: Government Printing Office, 1963), p. 95.

110 "Hero": Gerald Carmen int 8/23/05, af.

110 Frugal, taciturn: Larry Smith int 9/1/06, af.

110 Vietnam, Johnson: NYT, 8/10/92.

110 "Vote with you": Walter F. Mondale int 3/13/06.

110 "Lose my seat": Elizabeth Webber int 9/15/06, af.

110 "Best guarantee": McIntyre papers, UNH, MC36, box 103, folder 18.

110 Thurmond resolutions: 1974, CR 94:2, pp. 8833, 8847 3/29/74; 1975, CR 95:I, pp. 5070–5071, 3/4/75.

111 Study issue, threats: 9/6/77 press release, McIntyre papers, Series IV, box 15, folder 1, UNH.

111 "Publicly censured": McIntyre papers, Series III, box 104, folder 2, UNH.

111 Fifty-dollar prize: MUL, 2/4/78.

111 Questions answered: CM, 2/14/78.

111 "Aspirant," "disgust": MUL, 2/18/78.

111 "Most strategically important:" CM, 2/27/78.

112 "Hard study": CR, 95:2, 3/1/78, p. 5132.

112 Radical right: CR 95:2, 3/1/78, pp. 5132–5135.

113 "Traditional conservatives," "common ground": CR 95:2, p. 5134, 3/1/78.

113 "Loutish primitivism": CR 95:2, p. 5135, 3/1/78.

113 "Armchair warrior": CR 95:2, p. 5134, 3/1/78.

113 Thomson might run: MUL, 3/16/78.

113 Thomson will not run: CM, 4/21/78.

113 Poll: CM, 4/22/78.

113 "Boorish behavior": CM, 3/3/78.

113 "Emotional stability": MUL, 3/3/78.

113 Ignored wishes: MUL, 4/20/78.

113 "Keep the focus": CM, 6/1/78.

114 "Whistling": CM, 6/5/78.

114 Spending: CM, 7/3/78.

114 Capital gains: MUL, 7/13/78.

114 Mail: Jeffrey Kelley int 9/13/78.

114 "Man on the street": MUL, 2/3/78, 3/3/78, 6/5/78, 6/7/78, 7/7/78, 8/9/78; NHSN, 3/5/78.

114 Market Opinion Research: MUL, 8/9/78.

114 National Republican Senatorial Committee: Mary Lukens int 9/13/06, af.

114 "Small portion": CM, 8/31/78; MUL, 9/1/78.

114 Humphrey on Jacobson: MUL, 8/21/78.

114 Endorsement: MUL, 7/20/78.

114 Humphrey married: CM, 10/28/78; Humphrey int 9/19/05, af.

114 Assistant editor: Phillips int 5/3/05, af.

114 Conservative vote: Carmen int 10/6/06, af.

114 "Stand-in": CM, 8/31/78.

114 Vote totals: Richard M. Scammon and Alice V. MacGillivray, *America Votes 13* (Washington, D.C.: Congressional Quarterly, 1979), p. 233.

115 Dolan, advice: Humphrey int 9/19/05; CM, 10/28/78.

115 Staffers from NCPAC: CM, 10/28/78.

115 No votes to be changed: *Carroll County Independent*, Center Ossipee, N.H. 11/1/78.

115 Canal ad: Craig Shirley int 3/21/05, af.

115 Opinions of New Hampshire voters: MUL, 10/23/78.

115 Weakened defense: CM, 10/17/78.

115 "Free the American Spirit" flyers: af.

115 Florida condominium: MUL, 10/30/78, 11/6/78.

115 Antiabortion leafleting: MUL, 10/17/78.

115 Humphrey wrote flyer: CM, 12/28/78.

115 Reagan et al.: CM, 10/9/78.

115 Seriously: Jeffrey Kelley int 9/13/06, af; Dotty Lynch int 8/28/06, af; Larry Smith int 9/1/06, af.

115 "Gentlemen": CM, 9/28/78.

115 "Windsock": Ned Helms int 9/20/06.

115 "Could not believe": John Gorman int 8/31/06, af.

115 Interviewers: Lynch int 8/28/06, af.

116 Advice: Lynch int 8/28/06, af; Joseph A. Millimet letters, McIntyre papers, box 47, folder 12, UNH.

116 "Frame of reference": Dave LaRoche int 9/28/06.

116 Sound trucks: Gerald Carmen int 8/23/05, af; Kelley int 9/13/06, af.

116 30,000 votes: WP, 12/31/78.

116 Poll of 600: CM, 10/27/78.

116 Tibbetts's prediction: NHSN, 11/5/78.

116 Two or three dozen: WP, 11/9/78.

116 Vote totals: Scammon and MacGillivray, *America Votes 13*, p. 228.

116 Taxes: MUL, 11/9/78.

116 "Greater role": CM, 11/8/78.

116 "Pivotal": Humphrey int 9/19/05.

CHAPTER 15

117 Africa: WP, 11/9/78.

117 Feared Panama vote: Dick Clark int 1/26/05.

117 10,000 letters: Clark to Alice Lynch, 3/31/78, Dick Clark papers, box 69, folder Panama Canal (first), Special Collections, University of Iowa Libraries.

118 Iowa Poll: DMR, 4/15/78.

118 "Best interests": Dick Clark to Dan Duncan, 4/18/78, Clark papers, box 69, folder Panama Canal.

118 Flansburg dismissed: DMR, 3/19/78.

118 Eight minutes: DMR, 4/1/78.

118 Social Security: DMR, 5/15/78.

119 "Horrible": Cedar Rapids Gazette, 3/9/78.

119 "Major issue": Omaha World Herald, 3/10/78.

119 "Pay $50,000,000": Jepsen to Dear Friend, 3/23/78, Clark papers, box 82, folder 1978 Senate Race (May).

119 "Anybody in Iowa": Cedar Falls Record, 3/18/78.

119 Defenses: Quad City Times, Davenport, Iowa, 4/10/78.

119 Farmers: Daily Gate City, Keokuk, Iowa, 5/30/78; Quad City Times, 4/78.

119 "Does what he knows is right": DMR, 4/23/78.

119 Constitutional amendment: Times-Democrat, Davenport, Iowa, 5/9/78.

119 Antiabortion flyers: Des Moines Tribune, 6/22/78.

119 "Emotional issues": DMR, 5/14/78.

119 Viguerie efforts: Cedar Rapids Gazette, 5/26/78.

119 "Politics of hate": DMR, 6/3/78.

119 Ray: Oskaloosa [Iowa] Daily Herald, 5/22/78.

119 100,000 conservatives: Cedar Rapids Gazette, 6/1/78.

119 Thomson letter: 5/16/78, Clark papers, box 82.

119 Weyrich sent aide: Paul Weyrich int 1/8/2007, af.

120 Gun Owners, Senior Citizens: DMR, 5/26/78.

120 Brushed off: DMR, 6/4/78.

120 Viguerie one of many: DMR, 5/14/78.

120 Money to Viguerie: Ottumwa Courier, 5/31/78.

120 Jepsen on Thomson's letter: Cedar Rapids Gazette, 6/1/78.

120 "Choice in 1978": DMR, 4/4/78.

120 "For real": Cedar Rapids Gazette, 4/9/78.

120 Iowa Primary results, counties: Summary of Official Canvass of Votes Cast In Iowa Primary Election June 6, 1978, compiled by Melvin D. Synhorst (Des Moines: State of Iowa, 1978), af.

120 Hart survey: Clark papers, box 85, folder polls.

120 Vote rating flyer: Clark papers, box 82.

120 Right to Work: *CT*, 11/3/78.

120 Reagan ad: *WSJ*, 10/30/78.

120 Reagan in Ames: DMR, 9/15/78.

121 Tax cut: *WP*, 10/23/78.

121 Jepsen drops Viguerie: DMR, 8/16/78.

121 Jepsen uses Viguerie for debt: *Quad City Times*, 3/16/79.

121 Liberal votes: Clark papers, box 72, folder political affairs and DMR, 9/22/78,
   9/24/78, 10/4/78.

121 Pro-communist: *Review of the News*, 8/30/78.

121 Thousands of copies: WS, 12/12/78.

121 "Rightwing creep": DMR, 11/12/78.

121 Dilley: DMR, 6/21/78.

121 Canal, Alaska, Texas flyer: Clark papers, box 69, second folder Panama Canal.

121 Weyrich, Curtis: Weyrich int 1/8/07.

121 Iowa Republican platform: DMR, 7/2/78.

121 Treaty cost, radio ad: Jepsen int 11/1/06; DMR, 11/8/78.

121 Radio ad on national defense: HE, 11/4/78.

121 New Jepsen flyer: Box 72, folder PA 4, Clark papers; DMR, 9/22/78.

121 Jepsen used Canal frequently: DMR, 10/29/78.

121 Call-in program: *Baltimore Sun*, 11/1/78.

121 "All the time": Clark int 1/26/05.

121 Thompson's role: DMR, 6/8/78.

121 Right to Life convention: NYT, 7/3/78.

122 Three pro-abortion votes: *Des Moines Tribune*, 8/31/78.

122 "Unrestricted abortion policy": DMR, 10/1/78.

122 Clark dismisses antiabortion groups: DMR, 10/22.

122 Clark opposes abortion: DMR, 10/2/78.

122 Mid-July poll: DMR; 7/23/78.

122 Early September poll: DMR, 9/17/78.

122 Hart October poll: Box 85, folder polls, Clark papers.

122 Final *Register* poll: DMR, 11/5/78.

122 Politicians' consensus: DMR, 10/29/78.

122 Hart: *Baltimore Sun*, 11/1/78.

122 "Going good": DMR, 10/25/78.

122 300,000 antiabortion flyers: WP, 11/9/78; NYT, 11/13/78.

122 "See Why": WSJ, 11/24/78.

122 Windshields, churches, Clark flyers: DMR, 11/6/78.

122 Iowa Senate vote totals: Scammon and MacGillivray, *America Votes 13*, p. 128.

122 National press: *WP*, 11/9/78; *NYT*, 11/13/78; *WSJ*, 11/24/78.

123 "Study": *DMR*, 11/8/78.

123 Hart resurvey: *WSJ*, 2/8/79.

123 "Victory has a hundred fathers": *Public Papers of the Presidents of the United States, John F. Kennedy. 1961* (Washington, D.C.: Government Printing Office, 1962), p. 312.

123 "Best Man Lost": *DMR*, 11/9/78.

123 Phillips insists: Phillips int 5/3/05, af.

123 Joined McGovern: *DP*, 4/13/78.

124 "American folklore": *DP*, 2/1/78.

124 "Yielding control": *DP*, 3/15/78.

124 "No bargain": *DMR*, 10/4/78.

124 Attacked Haskell: *DMR*, 10/4/78.

124 "Big spending": *DP*, 1/14/78.

124 Evans and Novak: *DP*, 10/5/78.

124 Running on inflation: *Rocky Mountain News*, Denver, 11/5/78.

124 Most important issue: Armstrong to author, 10/9/06, af.

124 "Fringe group": *DP*, 10/7/78.

124 Telegram: *Rocky Mountain News*, 11/8/78.

124 Colorado vote totals: Scammon and MacGillivray, *America Votes 13*, p. 68.

124 Veterans: William S. Cohen int 4/29/05, af; *Maine Sunday Telegram*, 4/23/78.

125 Rogers: *Bangor Daily News*, 4/19/78; campaign press release 6/17/78, box 10, William S. Cohen papers, Raymond H. Fogler Library, University of Maine.

125 Veterans of Foreign Wars: *Bangor Daily News*, 6/12/78.

125 "Went a bit easy": Cohen int 4/29/05.

125 "Long before": campaign press release 9/21/78, Cohen papers.

125 "Serious reservations": William S. Cohen, *Maine Sunday Telegram*, 12/11/77.

125 "Evaluating": Cohen to Mr. and Mrs. Willard Smart, 3/15/78, Cohen to David S. Logan, 3/17/78, Correspondence 1978, Jan-April folder, Cohen papers.

125 "Voted against": Cohen to Morris Day, 5/4/78, Correspondence 1978, May-July folder, Cohen papers.

125 Radio ad: Cohen papers, box 11, folder "news clippings."

125 Maine Senate vote totals: Scammon and MacGillivray, *America Votes 13*, p. 155.

125 New Right support for Gahagan: *WP*, 9/8/78.

125 Excited conservatives: *Group Research Reports*, Vol. 17, No. 6, 6/27/78.

125 Bell's issues, television appearance, elite attitude: Jeff Bell int 2/05, af.

125 State polls: *NYT*, 4/2/78.

126 "Millions of voters": CBS, 6/2/78.

126 New Jersey primary results: Scammon and MacGillivray, *America Votes 13*, p. 240.

126 "Astonishing upset": HE, 7/8/78.

126 Angelo: NYT, 8/8/78.

126 New Jersey Senate vote totals: Scammon and MacGillivray, *America Votes 13*, p. 234.

127 Bunker Hill Day: BG, 6/18/78.

127 Liabilities: BG, 5/16/78.

127 Probate judge: BG, 6/16/78.

127 District attorney: WS, 8/1/78.

127 "Widespread reputation": WS, 8/31/78.

127 Primary vote results: Scammon and MacGillivray, *America Votes 13*, p. 176.

127 Nelson damaged Brooke: Edward W. Brooke III int 4/18/07, af.

127 Tsongas margin: Scammon and MacGillivray, *America Votes 13*, p. 167.

127 "Much closer": Joe Rogers, Tom Griscom int 2/10/05, af.

127 Presidential candidate: LAT, 11/1/78.

127 Goldwater: CBS, 4/19/78.

128 Endorsement: *Tennessean*, 10/22/78.

128 Represent people: Memphis *Press-Scimitar*, 8/5/78.

128 Tellico Dam: *Tennessean*, 10/22/78.

128 Literature, polling, "myth": *Atlanta Journal*, 11/3/78.

128 Tennessee Senate vote totals: Scammon and MacGillivray, *America Votes 13*, p. 320.

128 Cover, expect "no votes," 20 percent, signs: Nunn int 5/14/07.

128 McDonald backs out: AC, 5/2/78.

128 "Chomping": AC, 10/19/78.

128 $6,000: AC, 11/5/78.

128 16.9 percent: Scammon and MacGillivray, *America Votes 13*, p. 89.

129 Facing a strong opponent: Nunn int 5/14/07, af.

129 Cheney: Cheney int with Craig Shirley, 6/9/04, Shirley files.

CHAPTER 16

130 PAC growth numbers: Edwin M. Epstein, "Business and Labor under the Federal Election Campaign Act of 1971," in Michael J. Malbin, ed., *Parties, Interest Groups and Campaign Finance Laws* (Washington, D.C.: American Enterprise Institute, 1980), p. 115.

130 Labor effectiveness: CIO PAC, Frank J. Sorauf, "Political Action Committees in American Politics, An Overview," in Twentieth Century Fund Task Force on

Political Action Committees, *What Price PACS?* (New York: Twentieth Century Fund, 1984) p. 33.

130 Non-Partisan League: Arthur M. Schlesinger, Jr., *The Politics of Upheaval* (Cambridge, Mass.: Riverside Press, 1960), pp. 592–94; NYT, 4/2/36, 4/12/36.

131 Government contractors, company funds: Robert E. Mutch, *Campaigns, Congress and the Courts: The Making of Federal Campaign Finance Law* (New York: Praeger, 1988), pp. 164–166.

131 Business and labor PAC growth: Sorauf, "Political Action Committees," p. 37.

131 Twice as much: ibid., p. 46.

131 "Liberals": Viguerie, *The New Right*, p. 23.

131 "Tough conservative": Paul Weyrich, "The New Right and Coalition Politics," in Malbin, ed., *Parties, Interest Groups*, p. 96.

131 Four dollars: Common Cause, *Interest Group and Political Party Contributions to Congressional Candidates 1976 Vol. I* (Washington, D.C.: Common Cause, 1977), p. viii.

131 "Too stupid": *Conservative Digest*, 12/79.

132 Disc jockey: *Norfolk Virginian-Pilot*, 6/2/82.

132 Reporter, press secretary Coors, Heritage, "After a year": *Knoxville News-Sentinel*, 11/7/77.

133 $42,000: Americans for Democratic Action, *A Citizens' Guide to the Right Wing* (Washington, D.C.: Americans for Democratic Action, 1978), p. 8, af.

133 $194,000: Curtis letter quoted in *DCCC Report*, 12/77, box 5, folder publicity, Weyrich files, American Heritage Center, University of Wyoming.

133 $245,259, winners and losers, contributions: Common Cause, *Interest Group*, p. 651.

133 Quayle, Roush: *Practical Politics*, Oct–Nov '77, Weyrich files, box 5, folder CSFC, Inc. Correspondence May.

133 "Conservative Register": *Richmond Times-Dispatch*, 10/31/77.

133 "Chamber of Commerce": *Time*, 10/3/77.

133 Questionnaire, hopeless: *Knoxville News-Sentinel*, 11/7/77.

133 Campaign schools: Weyrich, "The New Right and Coalition Politics," in Malbin, ed., *Parties, Interest Groups*, pp. 73–74.

134 Required lesson: *DCCC Report*, 12/77, Weyrich files, box 5, folder publicity.

134 "Kasten Method": Weyrich int 5/29/07, af.

134 $71,431: Bob Biersack to author 6/4/07, af.

134 International Paper, UAW, National Committee for an Effective Congress: Biersack to author, 6/5/07, af.

134n "Kool-Aid": Russ Evans int 6/5/07.

135 Ten visits, values, $250: author's analysis of committee's FEC reports.

135 Daniel Crane race: *WP*, 11/9/78.

135 Daniel Crane vote total: Scammon and MacGillivray, *America Votes 13*, p. 121.

135 18 Visits, values, $1,000: author's analysis of committee's FEC reports.

135 David Crane–David Evans 1976 vote totals: Scammon and MacGillivray, *America Votes 13*, p. 126.

135 Precincts: *Indianapolis Star*, 11/3/78.

135 Crane ads: *Indianapolis Star*, 11/8/78.

135 1978 vote totals: *American Votes 13*, p. 126.

136 Thorsness image: Peter Stavrianos int 6/6/07, af.

136 Evangelicals: Weyrich int 5/29/77, af.

136 "Liberal incumbents": Paul Weyrich, "Conservative Issue Groups," *Conservative Digest*, 11/79.

136 Demonstration: *Sioux Falls Argus-Leader*, 10/15/78.

136 Thorsness ads: Stavrianos int 6/6/07, af; *Argus-Leader*, 11/4/78, 11/8/7.

136 Seven visits, values, salaries, contribution: author's analysis of committee's FEC reports.

136 139 votes, 14 vote margin: South Dakota Secretary of State, *Official Election Returns by Counties for the State of South Dakota, General Election, November 7*, 1978, p. 3, af.

136 "Newer special interest groups": Weyrich, "The New Right," p. 80.

136 Special elections: *CQWR*, 12/24/78, p. 2652.

136 93 percent: *Winston-Salem Journal*, 10/31/77.

137 Spent heavily: *Atlanta Journal-Constitution*, 8/13/78.

137 Campaign attacks: *Atlanta Journal-Constitution*, 8/27/78.

137 $2,000, five visits: author's analysis of committee's FEC reports. August 29 vote total, Scammon and MacGillivray, *America Votes 13*, p. 98.

138 Necessity for direct mail: Weyrich, "The New Right," pp. 72–73.

CHAPTER 17

140 Comfortable: Sorauf, "Political Action Committees," p. 54.

140 Mickey Mouse: Larry J. Sabato, *PAC Power: Inside the World of Political Action Committees* (New York: Norton, 1984), p. 96.

140 "Fear": ABC, 10/13/80.

140 "Destruction": NYT, 8/8/80.

140 "Stupid law": *WP*, 8/10/80.

141 "Groups like ours": *WP*, 8/10/80.

141 Founders: Sabato, *PAC Power*, p. 99.

141 "Dirty tricks": NYT, 6/13/73, 8/26/74.

141 Dolan family: Anthony Dolan int 12/14/06, af.

141 Terry Dolan's attitudes, Nixon: Anthony Dolan ints 3/6/07, 6/13/07, af.

141 Young Americans for Freedom: *WP*, 12/31/86.

141 NCPAC prospectus: "Democratic Congressional Campaign Committee Report," 8/78, George D. Moffett Donated Historical Material, box 11, folder Truth Squad [1], JCL.

142 Virginia legislative candidates: *WP*, 9/30/75.

142 $343,867: Common Cause, *Interest Group*, p. 658.

142 Asked Reagan, $800,000: Charles Black int 2/10/05.

142 Reagan letter: Box 237 folder National Conservative Political Action Committee, Group Research files, BLCU.

142 NCPAC activities: Charles Black int 6/7/07, af; Roger Stone int 5/24/07, af.

142 Seven candidates: *Democratic Congressional Campaign Committee Report*, 8/78, JCL.

142 Television ad, "obnoxious": *WP*, 10/25/76.

142 Newspaper ad: *WP*, 10/27/76.

142 Spellman percentages: Scammon and MacGillivray, *America Votes 12*, p. 167.

142 Anti-Howell ads: *WP*, 10/18/77, 10/19/77, 10/2–0/77, 10/22/77.

142n "Prospect" for Reagan: Ann Stone int 6/4/07.

143 Campaigns' own inaccurate charges: *WP*, 11/8/77.

143 Dalton margin: Richard M. Scammon and Alice V. MacGillivray, *America Votes 14* (Washington, Congressional Quarterly, 1981), p. 393.

143 Godwin: NYT, 9/25/77.

143 Larsen campaign: Don Todd int 9/20/06, af.

143 Candidate the issue, "leftover postage": Don Todd int 9/20/06, af.

144 10,000 letters: IS, 1/23/79.

144 Republican reaction: IS, 1/28/79.

144 Golder commercial: FCC, MS 56, series 5.6, box 1, folder 1.

144 Titan missiles: NYT, 10/27/80.

144 $15, news use of ad: Don Todd int 6/13/07.

145 "Dangerous": IS, 8/18/79.

145 Convinced Dolan, Finkelstein, several liberals at once: Roger Stone int 5/11/07, af.

145 Adopting Todd's approach: Todd int 9/20/06 af; Stone int 5/11/07, af; Anthony Dolan int 3/6/07.

145 Absorbing ABC: "The ABC Informant," 8/79, FCC, MS 57, series 5.7, box 2, folder 71.

145 NCPAC spending against McGovern: NCPAC 4/79 FEC report.

145 Newspaper advertisement: *WP*, 4/10/79.

145 Targets: *WP*, 8/17/79.

145 Eagleton: NCPAC 6/80 FEC report.

145 "We picked 'em": Terry Dolan int with Rod Gramer, FCC, MS 173, box 1, Folder 52.

145 Importance of Canal issue: Terry Dolan int with Rod Gramer, FCC, MS 173, box 1, Folder 52.

145 Verna Smith scripts, Globetrotters (Culver, McGovern), baloney (Cranston): FCC, MS 56, series 5.6, box 1, folder 1.

146 Baloney, gas, Cranston: Kanter 02400.

146 Baloney Church: Kanter 44135; baloney Culver: Kanter 44137; baloney McGovern: Kanter 44134.

146 Anti-Eagleton: Kanter 44131.

146 Culver and Carter: Kanter 44132.

146 Grassley over Culver ad: box 57, folder 26, ACU-BYU.

146 Dolan letter: Culver papers, box 97, Folder 5, Special Collections, University of Iowa Libraries.

146 Pay raise ad: *IS*, 7/27/80.

146 McGovern, press conferences: Brent Bozell to author 5/30/07, af.

147 Finkelstein, Cunningham: *CQWR*, 11/15/80.

147 Fay, Quayle: *CQWR*, 11/15/80; Quayle: *WP*, 11/12/80.

147 NCPAC studies: Michael J. Robinson, "The Media in 1980: Was the Message the Message?" in Austin Ranney, ed., *The American Elections of 1980* (Washington, D.C.: American Enterprise Institute for Public Policy Research, 1981), pp. 188ff.

148 Independent expenditures total: Biersack to author, 6/15/07.

148 Advertising purchases: author's analysis of NCPAC's FEC reports for 1979 and 1980.

148 Anti-McGovern effort: author's analysis of NCPAC's FEC report filed in February 1980.

148 Kennedy Truth Squad ad: *WP*, 11/7/79.

149 $247,918: Biersack to author, 6/15/07.

149 $23,616.90: NCPAC November 1979, FEC report.

149 Anti-Kennedy spending as fund-raising device: Richard Viguerie int 5/11/07, af; Roger Stone int 5/11/07.

150 "Cagers": Stone int 5/11/07.

150 $1,859,168 for Reagan: Biersack to author, 6/15/07.

150 $209,990, mostly in South: author's analysis of NCPAC's FEC reports for 1980.

150 Rafshoon, text of "Why Not the Best?" ad: Kathleen Hall Jamieson, *Packaging the Presidency: A History and Criticism of Presidential Campaign Advertising* (New York: Oxford University Press, 1984), p. 423.

150 "Damaging," "promises": ibid., p. 423.

153 Americans for Change: ibid., pp. 421–422.

153 Americans for an Effective Presidency: ibid., pp. 425–426.

153 Fund for a Conservative Majority: Craig Shirley int 6/15/07, af.

153 Alabama, Mississippi margins for Reagan: *American Votes* 14, p. 19.

153 "We went south": Jamieson, *Packaging the Presidency*, p. 424.

CHAPTER 18

154 Contributors as members: M. Stanton Evans int 3/24/06.

154 325,000: ACU press release 11/17/78, ACU at BYU, box 91, folder 7.

154 Pressure: ACU press release 6/23/79, box 91, folder 10, ACU-BYU.

154 SALT II film: HE, 8/18/79.

154 Speaker's bureau: HE, 10/27/79.

154 "More of the same": HE, 11/10/79.

155 Financial trouble: ACU board minutes 7/15/79, box 21, folder 28, ACU-BYU.

155 $3 million: Lee Edwards, *The Conservative Revolution: The Movement That Remade America* (New York: Free Press, 1999), p. 215.

155 Television donors, "boon," "letdown": David Keene int 5/21/07, af.

155 Affiliate activity: Becky Norton Dunlop int 4/24/07, af.

155 County organizations: box 64, folders 1–3, ACU-BYU.

155 Mr. Peanut: *Miami Herald*, 3/2/80.

155 Texas: Dunlop memo 5/14/80, box 49, folder 16, ACU-BYU.

155 Books wrong: ACU board minutes 7/15/79, box 21, folder 30, ACU-BYU.

155 82 cents: Becky Norton Dunlop memo to state ACU leaders, 11/26/80, box 1, folder 16, ACU-BYU.

156 Bonsib judgment: Curtis Herge to ACU directors, 11/14/80, box 21, folder 33, ACU-BYU.

156 CPAC date: Dunlop to Robert Heckman, 8/22/80, box 49, folder 18, ACU-BYU.

156 Annual ratings, *Battle Line*: *Baltimore Sun*, 10/31/80.

156 Fund-raising, staff cuts: Becky Norton Dunlop memo, 11/26/80, box 1, folder 16, ACU-BYU.

156 Reagan mailgram: 9/12/80, box 44, folder 6, ACU-BYU.

157 Abortion, equal rights amendment: *WP*, 10/7/80.

157 "Mr. Speaker": *NYT*, 10/4/80.

157 "Tough": *WP*, 1/3/80.

157 Not close to problem: *Baltimore Sun*, 10/31/80.

157 Charges: *NYT*, 10/4/80.

157 Weyrich reaction: *WP*, 10/7/80.

157 Bauman's legislation about gays: *NYT*, 10/4/80.

157 Bauman resigned: David Keene to author, 5/23/07, af.

157 Edwards elected: *WP*, 11/20/80.

157 Tension: Dunlop int 5/24/05, af.

158 "Collar-ad": Germond and Witcover, *Blue Smoke and Mirrors*, p. 94.

158 Crane's ambition: *NYT*, 7/20/78.

158 Talking publicly: *CT*, 7/14/78, 7/30/78; *NYT*, 7/20/78.

158 Youth, "very good chance": *NYT*, 7/20/78.

158 "Ten and a half": Hannaford, *The Reagans*, p. 176.

158 Assured Reagan: *CT*, 8/3/78.

158 Risk: *MUL*, 7/26/78.

158 Starting early, age: *CT*, 8/3/78.

158 "Commitment to future," policy: CBS, 8/2/78.

159 Attacked Carter: *NYT*, 8/3/78.

159 Cooling, "activists": CBS, 8/2/78.

159 Drinker, womanizer, editorial: *MUL*, 3/8/79.

159 Conservative Movement candidate: *HE*, 5/5/79.

159 Finkelstein focus: *HE*, 5/26/79.

160 Weyrich's departure: *HE*, 5/26/79; Weyrich int 5/29/07, af.

160 Arlene Crane's role: *HE*, 5/12/79, 5/19/79, 5/26/79; *CT*, 7/1/79.

160 Crane debt: *NYT*, 4/12/79.

160 Viguerie quit: *NYT*, 8/8/79.

160 Mail, conservatism: *NYT*, 8/28/79.

160 Connally not best conservative: *HE*, 8/18/79.

160 Crane vote percentages: Scammon and MacGillivray, *America Votes 14*, p. 38.

160 Too little attention: Beckel int 2/1/05, af; Jorden, *Panama Odyssey*, p. 659.

161 "Project Mayday": TCC *Member's Report*, 12/78–1/79, af.

161 Court test: *Conservative Digest*, 11/79.

161 191 supporters of discharge, constitutional argument: TCC *Member's Report*, 3–4/79, af.

161 Carter administration and Murphy bill provisions: *NYT*, 5/18/79.

161 TCC mailgrams: 5/23/79, af.

161 House passage: *WP*, 6/22/79.

162 "Decisive vote": TCC *Member's Report*, 6–7/79, af.

162 Startled: NYT, 9/21/79.

162 Carter at fault: NYT, 9/22/79.

162 Murphy on shutdown, Bauman on continued operation: CR 94: I, p. 26327, 9/26/79.

162 "Parrot," "guts": CR 94: I, pp. 26329f, 9/26/79.

162 "Given away": CR 94: I, p. 26334, 9/26/79.

162 "Probably 30 members": CR 94:I, pp. 26334f, 9/26/79.

163 Published roll call, switchers: TCC, *Grassroots*, 1/80, af.

163 $1 million, 12.5 million households: TCC press releases, 9/25/79, 9/27/79, af.

CHAPTER 19

164 "He's dead": CBS, 4/19/78.

164 Canal not determining issue: *Tennessean*, 4/20/78.

164 "Catechism," "15 short months": WP, 5/4/78.

165 Easton meeting: NYT, WP, 2/4/79.

166 SALT II and Baker campaign: WP, 11/2/79.

166 Resigning: Germond and Witcover, *Blue Smoke and Mirrors*, pp. 103–104.

166 13 percent: NYT, 11/6/79.

166 Maine straw poll: NYT, WP, 11/4/79.

166 Fifty reporters: WP, 11/5/79.

166 Register college students: Josie Martin int 6/19/07, af.

166 "Remember all that stuff": WP, 11/4/79.

167 Occasionally challenged on Canal: Tom Griscom int 6/19/05.

167 "The president said": NYT, 2/29/80. See also WP, 11/19/79; NYT, 12/16/79.

167 Reagan in Japan: Hannaford, *The Reagans*, p. 164; Hannaford int 3/10/05; Richard V. Allen int 8/2/06.

167 "It is no secret": Associated Press, 4/18/78.

168 "I hope it's over": *Face the Nation* transcript, 5/14/78, af.

168 "Get the canal back": LAT, 5/19/80.

168 "Step over the line": NYT, 3/29/80.

168 "Never say never": *Detroit News*, 10/23/80.

168 "Hypothetical questions": NBC, 10/23/80.

168 "There you go again": NYT, 10/29/80.

169 "Anathema": HE, 6/14/80.

169 Dunce cap: *Conservative Digest*, 6/80.

169 Two dunce caps: Viguerie int 4/18/05.

169 Prevented Baker, "Bush Blunder": *Conservative Digest*, 8/80.

169 Liked Baker, unimpressed as campaigner, not intimidated: Richard B. Wirthlin int 6/8/07.

169 Bush fought on: Cannon, *Reagan*, p. 266.

169 Reagan did not like Bush: Cannon, *Reagan*, p. 263; Germond and Witcover, *Blue Smoke and Mirrors*, p. 169.

169 Bush strong where Carter weak: Germond and Witcover, *Blue Smoke and Mirrors*, pp. 169–170.

169 Never intimidated: Hannaford to author, 6/25/07; Wirthlin int 6/25/07.

169 Baker not being considered: Hannaford, *The Reagans*, p. 273.

170 Call to Reagan: Cannon int 3/5/06, af.

170 Told aides: Cannon int 3/5/06; Tom Griscom int 6/19/07, af.

170 "My political landscape": Face the Nation transcript, 6/29/80, af.

170 Told Reagan of hope for majority: Cannon int 3/5/06, af.

CHAPTER 20

171 62 percent: Scammon and MacGillivray, *America Votes 14*, p. 292.

171 Well-regarded: Robert Morgan int 6/21/06, af.

171 Thurmond resolution: CR 94:I, pp. 5070f, 3/4/75.

171 "I can see no reason": Robert Morgan to Voit Gilmore, 3/18/75; Morgan papers, box 411, folder h, ECU.

171 Trip to Panama, told Carter: Morgan int 6/21/06, af.

173 "Our relationship with Panama": speech to North Carolina State Bar Association, 10/28/77, af.

173 "Solid and substantial," Morgan's Canal vote crucial: John P. East Oral History Interview (#OH0171), 10/1/79, ECU.

174 Plato, Cicero: RNO, 11/9/80.

174 Negative campaign: East Oral History int 10/1/79.

174 "Rapid erosion", Panama Canal: East for U.S. Senate press release, 1/26/80, box 64, folder 15, ACU at BYU.

174 Letters, $2 million, independent expenditures: Carter Wrenn int 6/20/07, af.

174 $252,000: RNO, 10/19/80.

174 Few knew of wheelchair: RNO, 9/28/80; Time, 5/4/81.

174 Polio: RNO, 11/9/80.

174 Outspent Morgan three to one: Bill Arthur, "I Can't Go On," *Washingtonian*, 9/90.

175 90 percent, "people calling me": Wrenn int 2/7/06, af.

175 Four or five spots: Tom Ellis int 2/7/06, af.

175 Carrier: RNO, 10/16/80.

175 Reagan and East bumper stickers: *Charlotte Observer*, 9/17/80.

175 Liberal parade: RNO, 9/28/80.

175 Helms group helped pay: RNO, 9/4/80.

175 "Marxist government of Nicaragua": RNO, 9/28/80.

175 "Mafia-type figure": Steve Suitts, "Southern Republicans for a Change," *Southern Changes* 3, no. 1 (1980).

175 Morgan issued defense: *Charlotte Observer*, 9/16/80; "White Paper Facts related to charges by the Congressional Club," af.

175n "Pick up the tapes": Morgan memo, 1/5/04, af.

176 "Incomplete and misleading": RNO, 10/3/80.

176 "Clichés and half-truths": *Charlotte Observer*, 11/9/80.

176 Flyer Carter and Morgan, Reagan and East: af.

176 Pictured with Kennedy, "typical of the McGoverns": RNO, 9/28/80.

176 Defend votes: RNO, 10/21/80, 11/3/80.

176 "Private club," "innuendo": Remarks at 6/21/80 press conference, Morgan papers, box 376, folder b, ECU.

176 "Master of deceit": RNO, 10/16/80.

176 Andrew Young: RNO, 11/2/80.

178 Ku Klux Klan: "Campaign Issues 1980," Morgan memo 11/1/99, af; Wayne Greenhaw, *Elephants in the Cottonfields: Ronald Reagan and New Republican South* (New York: Macmillan, 1982), chapter 16.

178 "Far Left votes": Robert W. Lee, "Robert Morgan," *Review of the News*, 10/8/80.

178 Christian in Senate: Morgan papers, unprocessed accession 20, ECU.

178 Separate church and state: Morgan speech, NC District Council of Assemblies of God, Charlotte, 5/7/80, Morgan papers, box 376, folder a, ECU.

178 52 to 32 percent: RNO, 10/27/80.

178 "Dead heat": RNO, 11/1/80.

178 Vote totals: Scammon and MacGillivray, *America Votes* 14, p. 292.

179 "Impossible": Ellis int 2/7/06.

179 "Only one": RNO, 10/29/80.

CHAPTER 21

180 Uncomfortable with Carter: Leroy Ashby and Rod Gramer, *Fighting the Odds: The Life of Senator Frank Church* (Pullman: Washington State University Press, 1994), p. 533.

181 Cuba trip: ibid., pp. 534–535.

181 Count on support: FCC, series 2.2, box 48, folder 14.

181 Cost him reelection: Bethine Church int 8/21/06, af.

181 Slammed phone: Ashby and Gramer, *Fighting the Odds*, p. 540.

181 "Back in 1903": CR 94: II, p. 2723f, 2/8/78.

182 "Magnificent": McCullough to Church, 2/8/78, FCC, series 2.1, box 48, folder 14.

182 Newsletters: Ashby and Gramer, *Fighting the Odds*, p. 544.

182 Letters exchanged with Cameron Fuller: LeRoy Ashby collection, MS 173, box 17, folder 18, Boise State University.

182 Childhood hero: Ashby and Gramer, *Fighting the Odds*, pp. 11, 96.

182 European wars, "sucker": ibid., p. 14.

182 Lyndon Johnson and Borah: ibid., p. 194.

182 Prestige: Jill Buckley to Peter Fenn 10/25/79, FCC, series 5.6, box 1, folder 1; NYT, 6/9/79.

182 Tarrance poll: Symms papers, Robert E. Smylie archives, Albertson College of Idaho, Caldwell, Idaho, box 1.41.

183 Hart poll: FCC series 5.7, box 1, folder 8.

183 Resisted advice: Bethine Church int 8/21/06, af.

183 Discussed Canal often: WP, 7/12/80; WSJ, 8/28/79.

183 "Maintained a strip": Lewiston, Idaho speech March 5, 1979, marked "also delivered in Soda Springs, Burley, Coeur d'Alene and other Idaho communities," Ashby collection MS 173, box 13, folder 12.

183 Television commercial on Canal: Peter Fenn int 3/4/05, af.

184 "Every town he'd go in": Associated Press, 12/5/79.

184 "Negative, anti-Church campaign": Bill Barlow, Idaho Committee for Positive Change, to Baine Evans, 6/14/79, Carl Burke collection, manuscript 57, box 2, folder 68, Boise State University.

184 Union bosses: Burke collection, manuscript 57, box 2 folder 41.

184 "These politicians": Burke collection, box 2, folder 68.

184 Baby Killers: *Time*, 8/20/79.

184 Church on abortion: Ashby and Gramer, *Fighting the Odds*, p. 584.

184 "Big lie": *Lewiston Morning Tribune*, 8/15/79.

185 Soviet combat brigade: Ashby and Gramer, *Fighting the Odds*, pp. 591–599; WP, 10/12/79.

185 Mikva, Wald: WP, 10/12/79.

185 "Weak and vacillating": Symms papers, box 1.41.

185 Wilderness legislation: Ashby and Gramer, *Fighting the Odds*, pp. 588–590; Marines, "The Idaho Compass," p. 600.

185 Apples: Michael Barone, Grant Ujifusa, and Douglas Matthews, *The Almanac of American Politics 1980* (New York: Dutton, 1979), p. 228.

186 Oil industry: *WP*, 7/11/80.

186 Silver, do-nothing: Church mailing to "Fellow Idahoan," 9/80, FCC Series 5.6, box 1, folder 4.

186 "Up for grabs": Church mailing to "Fellow Idahoan," 9/80, FCC Series 5.6, box 1, folder 4.

186 Lieutenant General Graham: *IS*, 7/27/80.

186 McClure: ABC, 10/13/80; NYT, 10/27/80.

186 *Christian Citizens News*: FCC, series 5.67, box 6, folder 9; Rev. Hoffman, *WP*, 10/12/80.

187 Thousands of copies: *Twin Falls Times-News*, 10/16/80.

187 "One of the secrets": *Review of the News*, 7/8/80.

187 "Heavy hitter": *IS*, 6/28/80.

188 Debate: *IS*, 10/24/80.

188 Effectiveness: Hart report on October 134–16 telephone poll, FCC series 5.7, box 1, folder 13.

188 At least eighteen: Symms papers, box 1.21.

188 "Whose Leadership?": *Idaho Register* (a Catholic diocesan newspaper published in Boise), 10/24/80.

188 Blizzard: All ads cited are from the *Lewiston Morning Tribune*: Buckley, McClure, 10/28/80; Zero accomplishments, 10/29/80; gun control, 10/30/80; veterans, 10/31/80; too many laws, 10/28/80; Symms votes no, 11/2/80.

188 Last commercial: Todd int 10/20/06; *WS*, 10/19/80.

189 Vote totals: Scammon and MacGillivray, *America Votes 14*, p. 19, p. 119.

CHAPTER 22

190 Denounced: AC, NYT, 10/12/79; CR 96:1, pp. 27767–27789, 10/11/79.

191 Caddell's firm: Cambridge Survey Research, "An Analysis of Political Attitudes in the State of Georgia," 10/80, Herman E. Talmadge Collection, T. Rogers Wade Files, Series I, box 2, folder 5, RBRUGA.

191 Goldwater, IBM, eighteen months: Mattingly int with Manay Tanneeru, WXIA-TV, Atlanta 12/25/05, http://11alive.com.news/news_article.aspx?storyid=73724, accessed 6/17/07.

191 FEC filing: campaign press release 9/28/79, Mack F. Mattingly Collection, Series VI, box 2, folder 8, RBRUGA.

191 "Defense posture": AC, 2/4/80; B–1, Mack Mattingly int 4/3/07, af.

191 Absenteeism: *Thomasville, Ga., Times-Enterprise*, 10/2/80.

191 SALT II, Panama: James A. Rose to Talmadge, 10/25/79, Herman E. Talmadge Collection, Series VII, box 13, folder 3, RBRUGA.

191 Mattingly ad: Kanter 31169.

192 Twenty-three questions, Dalton headquarters: *Chattanooga News-Free Press*, 10/1/80.

192 Small-town papers: *Winder News*, 10/1/80; *Vidalia Advance*, 10/9/80; *Newnan Press-Herald*, 10/16/80; *Tattnall Journal*, 10/16/80; *Hahira Gold-Leaf*, 10/16/80.

192 "Thorn": Mattingly int 4/3/07, af.

192 "Cold water": T. Rogers Wade int 3/29/07, af.

192 "5 to 10 percent": Sam Nunn int 5/14/07, af.

192 Georgia vote totals: Scammon and MacGillivray, *America Votes 14*, p. 102.

192 Q & A: George McGovern int 4/17/06, af.

192 Attacked in flyers: NYT, 10/20/80.

192 Abdnor ads: *Watertown Public Opinion*, 11/1/80; Kanter 31759.

193 McGovern flyer: McGovern papers, box 487, Seeley G. Mudd Manuscript Library, Princeton University.

193 LaRocque commercial: Kanter 40144.

193 NCPAC focus: People for an Alternative to McGovern, press release, 3/80, McGovern papers, box 485.

193 "I'm always answering": NYT, 6/2/80.

193 Abdnor sued: NYT, 11/5/80.

193 Schumaker, anti-family: NYT, 10/13/80.

193 Twenty years away: Mitchell, S.D., *Daily Republic*, 5/29/80.

194 South Dakota results: Scammon and MacGillivray, *America Votes 14*, p. 357.

194 Hart Poll: "A Survey of Voter Attitudes in the State of Iowa, November, 1979," John Culver papers, Special Collections, University of Iowa Libraries, box 98, folder 4.

194 Tarrance poll: "A Survey of Voter Attitudes in the State of Iowa, August 1980," af.

194 Committee for Another: ACU at BYU, box 57, folder 26.

194 Dolan letter: Culver papers, box 97, folder 5.

194 "Searched the Scripture," opposed abortion and SALT II: NYT, 10/24/80.

195 Iowa vote totals: Scammon and MacGillivray, *America Votes 14*, p. 149.

195 40,824: ibid., p. 411.

195 Spring and summer, small business: Robert W. Kasten int 1/8/07, af.

195 Kasten television ad, videotape: Gaylord Nelson papers, Wisconsin Historical Society, M80–626, box 10.

195 "Hurt Gaylord": David Obey int 1/9/07, af.

195 "Eventual return": *Madison Capital Times*, 10/20/80.

195 Indiana results: Scammon and MacGillivray, *America Votes 14*, p. 139.

195 Time for a change: *WP*, 10/19/80.

195 "Another million dollars": Birch Bayh int 10/11/06.

195 Gunter used Canal: *NYT*, 10/7/80.

195–196 Florida runoff primary result: Scammon and MacGillivray, *America Votes 14*, p. 103, general election, p. 97, Reagan margin, p. 19.

CHAPTER 23

197 "Roll over and play dead": CBS, 11/8/80.

198 Baker, McMahan, Cannon, and Laxalt: James Cannon int 5/8/07, af.

199 "Counted votes": Baker int 6/27/07, af.

199 "All of us": Ronald Reagan, unpublished diaries, 9/25/81, courtesy of Douglas Brinkley, af.

199 "Great present": Ronald Reagan, *The Reagan Diaries*, edited by Douglas Brinkley (New York: HarperCollins, 2007), p. 3, 2/6/81.

199 "Never let you do that again": Howard Baker int 6/26/07, af.

199 Tax bill more sweeping than under Long: Bob Dole int 6/22/07, af.

200 Nancy Reagan, Deaver, Spencer: James A. Baker III int 7/11/07, af.

200 Senators unimpressed: Cannon int 5/8/07, af.

200 "Sound" advice: *The Reagan Diaries*, p. 14, 4/23/81.

200 Social Security benefit: ibid., p. 31, 7/18/81.

200 Tax increases: ibid., p. 96, 8/4/82.

200 Not appreciate Senate majority: Howard Baker int 6/26/07, af; Bob Dole int 6/22/07, af.

200n "Who's going to tell": Howard Baker int 6/27/07, af.

201 "Made all the difference": James Baker int 7/11/07, af.

201 "Disastrous": *Reagan Diaries*, p. 108.

201 "These people represent": NBC, 11/14/80.

201 "Disassociate ourselves": Howard Phillips "What Is to Be Done," *Conservative Digest*, 12/80.

201 "It's mind-boggling": Reagan under attack, *NYT*, 1/25/81.

202 "A compromise is never": *Reagan Diaries*, p. 86.

202 "Viguery held press conference": ibid., p. 72, 2/26/82.

202 Richard Richards: *LAT*, 4/28/81; *NYT*, 6/2/81.

202 Kennedy aides: Adam Clymer, *Edward M. Kennedy: A Biography* (New York: William Morrow, 1999), p. 328, citing an interview with Jack Leslie, 4/9/92, available in Clymer papers at the John F. Kennedy Library in Boston.

202 Democratic Senatorial Campaign Committee: Ted Waller, to "All Democratic Senators running in 1980," 7/30/81, People for the American Way library, folder NCPAC.

202 NCPAC sued: NYT, 12/16/81.

202 Ship in Canal: Kanter 44145.

CHAPTER 24

204 Never mentioned Canal: Howard Baker int 6/2/07, af.

204 Reagan met Panama's president: NYT, 10/1/82.

204 Threat to Canal: *Public Papers of the Presidents of the United States, Ronald Reagan, 1986 Book I* (Washington, D.C.: Government Printing Office, 1988), p. 353.

204 Shah to Panama: Hamilton Jordan, *Crisis: The Last Year of the Carter Presidency* (New York: Putnam's, 1982), pp. 75–87.

205 Panamanian approval: CBS News Poll, conducted with Belden and Russonello, 1/5/90, af.

205 Counternarcotics center: NYT, 12/11/99.

206 Changed date: CSM, 12/14/99.

206 "I frankly don't know": memorandum of Clinton-Moscoso discussion in Albright to American Embassy, 10/28/99, af.

206 Carter urged Clinton: Carter int 6/12/06, af.

206 State Department: NYT, 12/11/99.

206 American ambassadors: author's conversation with Thomas Dodd, ambassador to Costa Rica, 2/9/00.

206 Albright and Berger argued: NYT, 12/12/99.

206 Albright-Moscoso conversation: Christopher Webster memorandum, 12/13/99, af.

206 "Ten-foot pole": Maria Echeveste int 4/7/2005, af.

206 Jennings: ABC, 12/14/99.

206 Avila: NBC, 12/14/99.

207 Snubbed: NYT, 12/11/99; CBS, 12/14/99.

207 "No big names": NYT, 12/11/99.

207 "Ode to Joy," locomotives: NYT, 12/15/99.

207 Carter remarks: Jimmy Carter, "Transfer of the Panama Canal, 12/14/99," Vertical File, box 93, "Panama Canal–1990-," JCL, af; NYT, 12/15/99; "It's Yours," PBS NewsHour with Jim Lehrer, 12/14/99, http://www.pbs.org/newshour/nn/latin_america/panamacanal/canal_12–14.html, accessed 7/10/07.

207 Horns, fireboats: CNN, 12/14/99.

207 Dozen soldiers: NewsHour, 12/14/99.

207 Actual transfer: NYT, 1/1/2000.

207 Crane: Philip Crane int 2/05.

207 Laxalt: Paul Laxalt int 8/8/06.

207 Bush: diplomatic source int 6/20/07.

208 Monarchy, whipping: Jamieson, *Packaging the Presidency*, pp. 5, 6.

208 Club for Growth, misleadingly: FactCheck.org, "A Half-True Attack on McCain," 8/31/05, http://www.factcheck.org/elections–2006/a_half-true_attack_on_mccain.html, accessed 7/11/07.

208 MoveOn.org, inaccurately: FactCheck.org, "MoveOn.org PAC: They've Got the Wrong Guys," 2/9/07, http://www.factcheck.org/iraq/moveonorg_pac_theyve_got_the_wrong_guys.html, accessed 7/11/07.

209 "Make anybody vulnerable": WP, 8/20/07.

209 2003–2004 outside spending: Stephen R. Weissman and Ruth Hassan, "527 Groups and BCRA," in Michael J. Malbin, ed., *The Election after Reform: Money, Politics, and the Bipartisan Campaign Reform Act* (Lanham, Md.: Rowman and Littlefield, 2006), pp. 104–105.

209 Efforts by Swift Boat Veterans: *Electing the President 2004: The Insiders' View*, ed. Kathleen Jamieson (Philadelphia: University of Pennsylvania Press, 2006), p. 194.

209 46 percent: National Annenberg Election Survey press release, 8/27/04, af.

210 "Godfather": Jamieson to author 7/11/07, af.

210 Willie Horton ad: Bush campaign, NYT, 11/3/88.

210 NCPAC in South: Jamieson, *Packaging the Presidency*, p. 424.

210 Published polling: Jamieson, *Electing the President 2004*, p. 212.

211 "Vandenberg was right": NYT, 2/4/79.

211 "We've made a difference": Reagan farewell address, 1/11/89, *Public Papers of the Presidents of the United States, Ronald Reagan. 1988–89* (Washington, D.C.: Government Printing Office, 1991), p. 1719.

212 "Man is not free": ibid., p. 1721.

212 "Era of big government": *Public Papers of the Presidents of the United States, William J. Clinton. 1996* (Washington, D.C.: Government Printing Office, 1997), p. 79.

AN ESSAY ON SOURCES

The original research for this book was conducted with interviews and at various archives. The interviews, along with other materials designated "af" in the notes, will be deposited at the Jimmy Carter Library in Atlanta. The Carter Library is the most important resource for information about the development of the treaties, and especially for information about the efforts to win Senate approval. The collections of Hamilton Jordan and Landon Butler are especially rich, as is President Carter's handwriting file with its notes on his own talks with senators about the pacts.

The Gerald R. Ford Library in Ann Arbor, Michigan, provides valuable accounts of how the treaty policy developed in Ford's brief presidency, especially through the collections of National Security Council minutes and memorandums of conversations. The Ford Library also has extensive material, including television tape recordings, on the 1976 presidential primary campaign between Ford and Reagan in which the Canal was a major issue. Comparable material in the Ronald Reagan Library in Simi Valley, California, has not yet been made available for research. Some Reagan materials from that campaign are housed at the Hoover Institution on War, Revolution and Peace at Stanford University in Palo Alto, California.

The Lyndon B. Johnson Library in Austin has telephone tape recordings of President Johnson discussing rioting in the Canal and ways of resolving the issue in 1964, and also materials relating to the development of the failed 1967 treaties. But the most valuable resource there is the collection of papers, and especially interviews, conducted by William J. Jorden, the Johnson adviser who later served as ambassador to Panama under Presidents Nixon, Ford, and Carter.

The quality of archiving and access at the presidential libraries is a tough standard for custodians of senatorial papers to match. For that matter, the actual papers collected by senators and sent to research institutions vary widely. In the case of senators who were defeated, as opposed to those who voluntarily retired, papers may have been boxed and shipped to home-state university or other archives in a rush, with little thought as to who would pay the cost of organizing them for research. And materials on the campaign a senator lost are sometimes located in those files and sometimes not. The same can be said for material on the campaign a senator waged to win his seat for the first time, for he was not actually a senator at the time and campaign staffs are not reliable record keepers.

With those handicaps acknowledged, the most useful of the senatorial collections I used were those of Senators Howard Baker at the Baker Center of the University of

Tennessee in Knoxville, Tennessee, and Frank Church at Boise State University, Boise, Idaho. The Baker papers (and those of aide Howard Liebengood at the Library of Congress) reveal how his position developed and his courageous disregard for the personal political consequences. The Frank Church Collection at Boise, along with the papers of Carl Burke, a longtime aide, and Leroy Ashby and Rod Gramer, Church's biographers, provide insights into the treaty fight on the Senate floor and Church's 1980 campaign and the New Right more generally. The papers of Church's 1980 conqueror, Steve Symms, at Albertson College in Caldwell, Idaho, are especially rich in newspaper clippings describing the campaign.

Senator Tom McIntyre's papers at the University of New Hampshire in Durham illuminate his handling of the Canal issue and his revulsion at the New Right. But Senator Gordon Humphrey's papers at the New Hampshire State Archives in Manchester have nothing on the 1978 campaign; they begin with his taking office in 1979. Senator Dick Clark's papers at the University of Iowa in Iowa City have well-organized material on the treaties and on the 1978 campaign. Roger Jepsen's papers at the State Historical Society of Iowa, a few blocks away, are notable mainly for clippings on the 1978 campaign.

At East Carolina University in Greenville, North Carolina, the papers of Senator Robert Morgan are useful on his attitudes on the treaty issue in 1977 and 1978 but thin on his 1980 loss to John P. East. Still, they provide more material than East's uncataloged papers at the same institution, which, except for two oral histories, appear to deal almost exclusively with his time in the Senate and not how he got there. At the University of Georgia in Athens, the papers of Senator Herman E. Talmadge (and associate T. Rogers Wade) and Senator Mack Mattingly both deal usefully with the 1980 campaign, in Mattingly's case because of clippings showing how his race was run. The papers of Gaylord Nelson at the Wisconsin Historical Society in Madison are illuminating and thorough on the 1980 campaign; they convinced me the Canal was not at issue then. Similarly, the papers of Senators William Hathaway and William Cohen at the University of Maine in Orono showed how the Canal mattered there in 1978, but also how other issues were much more important in a one-sided race.

The best archive on a conservative organization is the American Conservative Union papers at Brigham Young University in Provo. It contains political material (including some from other organizations), board minutes, and revealing correspondence, dating back to the founding of the ACU in 1964. The archive also includes a brief history, compiled at the archives, of the organization through 1980. The University of Wyoming's American Heritage Center in Laramie has extensive records of Paul Weyrich and the Committee for the Survival of a Free Congress; these do not, however, go back to 1974, when the organization was founded, but are chiefly from the 1980s. Records of The Conservative Caucus are still retained by the Conservative Caucus Foundation in Vienna, Virginia, and there does not appear to be any substantial collection of records from the National Conservative Political Action Committee. The Rare Book and Manuscript Library at Columbia University Butler Library has a valuable but little-used collection of the papers of Wes McCune's *Group Research Reports*, a watchdog effort to keep track of conservatives. The Georgetown University library has an excellent collection of materials on the Canal, especially its early days.

Two television archives provided important material. The Julian P. Kanter Political Commercial Archive at the University of Oklahoma Political Communication Center in the Department of Communication at Norman has a large collection of political commercials dating back to 1936 for radio and 1950 for television. Its online catalog enables researchers to see if commercials from a particular campaign are available. The Vanderbilt Television News Archive at Heard Library of Vanderbilt University, Nashville, has tapes of evening television news broadcasts dating back to 1968 and an accessible online catalog. While researchers have long used major newspapers to learn about past events, the Vanderbilt Archive allows access to the news as presented to much larger audiences, and also ensures precise, accurate quotation, which as a retired newspaper reporter, I know the print press cannot always guarantee.

The books used in this research fall into several categories: the history of the Canal and the Canal Zone themselves, the 1977–1978 treaty debate, Ronald Reagan, Gerald Ford, Jimmy Carter, conservative organizations, and particular senators. In any of these areas, there are dozens of books I did not consult; this discussion is confined to the ones I used.

For the history of the Canal up until it opened for traffic, no work approaches—either in compelling prose or in dedicated research—David McCullough's *The Path between the Seas: The Creation of the Panama Canal, 1870–1914* (New York: Simon and Schuster, 1977). The updated edition of Walter LaFeber's *The Panama Canal: The Crisis in Historical Perspective* (New York: Oxford University Press, 1989) is a clear account of the treaty issues and the development of the legal relationship between the United States, Panama, and the Canal. John Major's *Prize Possession: The United States and the Panama Canal, 1903–1979* (New York: Cambridge University Press, 1993) covers the period from the revolution from Colombia to the end of the Canal Zone as a separate entity. A vigorous but partisan assertion of the arguments against the treaty is available in Philip M. Crane's *Surrender in Panama: The Case against the Treaty* (Ottawa, Ill.: Caroline House Books, 1978).

For the treaties and their ratification, the most thorough account is in William J. Jorden's *Panama Odyssey* (Austin: University of Texas Press, 1984). Jorden, a former *New York Times* reporter, gives a highly readable account, from the perspective of a diplomat scornful of the politics that made ratification difficult. Unfortunately, while his book draws on cables in his possession and a fine set of interviews, it does not indicate the sources of particular facts. A useful companion is George D. Moffett III, *The Limits of Victory: The Ratification of the Panama Canal Treaties* (Ithaca, N.Y.: Cornell University Press, 1985). Moffett worked on the citizens committee that supported ratification, but the book is a straight, well-sourced account. J. Michael Hogan's *The Panama Canal in American Politics: Domestic Advocacy and the Evolution of Policy* (Carbondale: Southern Illinois University Press, 1986) covers much the same ground. Each deals with public opinion, Moffett more fully, but the definitive discussion of it came in an article by Bernard Roshco, the State Department's expert on polling, in "The Polls: Polling on Panama—Si; Don't Know; Hell, No," *Public Opinion Quarterly* 42, no. 4 (Winter 1978): 551–562. Charles O. Jones, in *The Trusteeship Presidency: Jimmy Carter and the United States Congress* (Baton Rouge: Louisiana State University Press, 1988), saw Carter's success as emblematic of the president's view that he had to be resolute on tough political issues because Congress was weak and swayed by special interests. An important work on the overall subject of the congressional role in international affairs is *Foreign Policy by Congress* (New York: Oxford University Press, 1979), by Thomas M. Franck and Edward Weisbrand. Jorden's history of negotiations also tells how the Johnson administration, the first to promise Panama the Canal, approached the issue, but the most thoughtful examination of that episode is Mark Atwood Lawrence's "Exception to the Rule? The Johnson Administration and the Panama Canal," in *Looking Back at LBJ: White House Politics in a New Light*, edited by Mitchell B. Lerner (Lawrence: University Press of Kansas, 2005).

Gerald Ford has not been subject to anything like the extensive examination directed at presidents before and after him. One important book is James Cannon's *Time and Chance: Gerald Ford's Appointment with History* (New York: HarperCollins, 1994), from a respected former journalist turned political aide who knew and admired Ford, but Cannon's book does not go into much detail after Ford's pardon of Richard Nixon. The best summary of Ford's entire administration is John Robert Greene's *The Presidency of Gerald R. Ford* (Lawrence: University Press of Kansas, 1995). Ford's own memoir, *A Time to Heal: The Autobiography of Gerald R. Ford* (New York: Harper and Row, 1979), deals with many of the issues of his administration and gives unvarnished opinions about Reagan and others. Stephen E. Ambrose, *Nixon: Ruin and Recovery 1973–1990* (New York: Simon & Schuster, 1991), gives some sense of White House thinking behind the selection of Ford to be vice president. Yanek Mieczkowski's *Gerald Ford and the Challenges of the 1970s* (Lexington: University Press of Kentucky, 2005) gives a general look at Ford's approach to foreign policy. None of these books says much about the Canal except as an issue in the 1980 campaign. The most detailed writing on the Ford administration's Canal policy can be found in Henry Kissinger's *Years of Renewal* (New York: Simon & Schuster, 1999).

With respect to Ronald Reagan, for a quarter of a century Lou Cannon's *Reagan* (New York: Putnam's, 1982) has remained the definitive biography of the fortieth president, through his first year in office. No journalist covered Reagan for so long or as well, and his many books (covering the days before and after *Reagan*) convey Reagan brilliantly. Peter Hannaford's *The Reagans: A Political Portrait* (New York: Coward-McCann, 1983) gives a personal sense of Reagan through the eyes of one of his most important aides from 1975 to 1980. Lyn Nofziger's *Nofziger* (Washington, D.C.: Regnery Gateway, 1992) gives a brisk account of Reagan from the eyes of his sometimes aide and longtime supporter. Paul Laxalt's *Nevada's Paul Laxalt: A Memoir* (Reno, Nev.: Jack Bacon & Company, 2000) is devoted largely to an account of Reagan from the perspective of someone who was a friend and a contemporary. *The Great Communicator: What Ronald Reagan Taught Me about Politics, Leadership and Life* (Hoboken, N.J.: Wiley, 2004), by Richard Wirthlin with Wynton C. Hall, has the perspective of a pollster and friend. Finally, Ronald Reagan's own book *The Reagan Diaries*, edited by Douglas Brinkley (New York: HarperCollins, 2007), gives quick, authentic looks at how Reagan as president viewed the events of the day.

A few books stand out as accounts of particular presidential elections. For 1976, Jules Witcover's *Marathon: The Pursuit of the Presidency 1972–1976* (New York: Viking, 1977) is the best general account. Craig Shirley's *Reagan's Revolution: The Untold Story of the Campaign That Started It All* (Nashville, Tenn.: Nelson Current, 2005) is a superior account of the 1976 insurgency, and Shirley is completing work on an account of the 1980 campaign. Witcover joined with Jack Germond to write the best published account of the 1980 race: *Blue Smoke and Mirrors: How Reagan Won and Carter Lost the 1980 Election* (New York: Viking, 1981). Austin Ranney edited *The American Elections of 1980* (Washington, D.C.: American Enterprise Institute for Public Policy Research, 1981), a compendium of thoughtful essays on that contest. Cannon's *Reagan* is strong on both the 1976 and 1980 elections, too.

On President Carter, his own memoir, *Keeping Faith: Memoirs of a President* (New York: Bantam, 1982), discusses the Canal fight proudly. And detail on the Carter administration's considerations and actions can be found in Zbigniew Brzezinski's *Power and Principle: Memoirs of the National Security Adviser, 1977–1981* (New York: Farrar,

Straus and Giroux, 1983) and in Cyrus R. Vance's *Hard Choices: Critical Years in America's Foreign Policy* (New York: Simon and Schuster, 1983). Gaddis Smith's *Morality, Reason and Power: American Diplomacy in the Carter Years* (New York: Hill and Wang, 1986) is a thoughtful analysis that stands up after two decades. More generally on Carter, Witcover's *Marathon* is the best account of his election in 1976. Carter's own *Why Not the Best?* (Nashville, Tenn.: Broadman Press, 1975) and *A Government as Good as Its People* (New York: Simon and Schuster, 1977) show what kind of a candidacy he was projecting. Burton I. Kaufman's *The Presidency of James Earl Carter Jr.* (Lawrence: University Press of Kansas, 1993) summarizes Carter's administration, with brief attention to the treaties.

On the conservative movement, no one volume stands out, but there are important ideas in William C. Berman's *America's Right Turn: From Nixon to Bush* (Baltimore: Johns Hopkins University Press, 1994); Lee Edwards's *The Conservative Revolution: The Movement That Remade America* (New York: Free Press, 1999); Steven F. Hayward's *The Age of Reagan: The Fall of the Old Liberal Order* (Roseville, Calif.: Prima Publishing, 2001); and William A. Rusher's *The Rise of the Right* (New York: William Morrow, 1984). Clear-cut advocacy, along with plenty of valuable information, is presented in Richard A. Viguerie's *The New Right: We're Ready to Lead* (Falls Church, Va.: Viguerie Company, 1981).

Few biographies of current and recent senators are available. The one I found most useful was Leroy Ashby and Rod Gramer, *Fighting the Odds: The Life of Senator Frank Church* (Pullman: Washington State University Press, 1994), though some would find it too pro-Church. Not much has been written about one of the major figures in American politics and government for a third of a century, Howard H. Baker Jr. J. Lee Annis's *Howard Baker: Conciliator in an Age of Crisis* (Lanham, Md.: Madison Books, 1995) is an important book and deals thoughtfully with the Canal. Robert C. Byrd's autobiography, *Robert C. Byrd, Child of the Appalachian Coalfields* (Morgantown: West Virginia University Press, 2005), gives a sense of an equally complex lawmaker and how the Canal issue helped him prove himself to skeptical Washington, but it also often reads like a compendium of pork-barrel projects he obtained for West Virginia.

The changes in campaign finance rules, the role of political action committees, and the history of political commercials are addressed in Michael J. Malbin, ed., *Parties, Interest Groups and Campaign Finance Laws* (Washington, D.C.: American Enterprise Institute, 1980); Robert E. Mutch, *Campaigns, Congress and the Courts: The Making of Federal Campaign Finance Law* (New York: Praeger, 1988); Larry J. Sabato, *PAC Power: Inside the World of Political Action Committees* (New York: Norton, 1984); and Kathleen Hall Jamieson, *Packaging the Presidency: A History and Criticism of Presidential Campaign Advertising* (New York: Oxford University Press, 1984).

ACKNOWLEDGMENTS

This book profited from the generous help of many people. First of all, Caroline Herron, the best editor I ever had in twenty-six years at the *New York Times*, read the manuscript and offered wise counsel on matters small and large. I can't imagine a book I would have been proud of coming together without her.

Personal interviews formed a major part of my research, and I am grateful to many who took the time to talk to me, from Presidents Carter and Ford, who talked about the major diplomatic and political questions of Panama Canal policy, to Bernard Fagelson, a longtime member of the Alexandria Democratic Committee in Virginia, who remembered Senator Gordon Humphrey before he became a Republican. The subjects are listed in the endnotes, but I want to single out those who responded frequently when I called back about a detail that had come up since we first talked. The multiple interviewees include Howard Baker, Charles Black, James Cannon, Lou Cannon, Tom Ellis, Peter Hannaford, David Keene, Robert Pastor, Howard Phillips, Craig Shirley, Richard Viguerie, Paul Weyrich, Richard Wirthlin, and Carter Wrenn.

I am particularly grateful for access to interviews conducted by others before I became involved in this project. In many cases they were conducted years ago, when memories were fresher, and with some participants in this story who have died since the interviews. Some of the most valuable are already in libraries, such as William Jorden's talks with Omar Torrijos and others at the Lyndon Baines Johnson Library (although Ambassador Jorden also gave me access to still more he had not deposited there). Rod Gramer's interview of Terry Dolan in 1980 is at the Boise State University library, and John Lindsay's 1978 interview of Howard Baker is at the Baker Center at the University of Tennessee. Additionally, David Welborn made available interviews he had conducted with associates of Senator Baker, Lee Annis allowed me to listen to interviews he had done with Baker as he prepared his biography, *Howard Baker: Conciliator in an Age of Crisis*, and Craig Shirley gave me access to interviews and other materials gathered as he researched his book, *Reagan's Revolution: The Untold Story of the Campaign That Started It All*. Nothing can be more frustrating to a researcher than finding a citation to an interview with no idea of how to find it, so I am depositing my interviews and other materials collected for this book at the Jimmy Carter Library, where they will be available to researchers.

While most of the documents cited are from library collections, several individuals made material from their personal or organizational files available to me. They include Robert Pastor, Howard Phillips, and Senator Robert Morgan. Douglas Brinkley provided access to unpublished material from Ronald Reagan's diaries, which he had edited into a fascinating, just-published book. Burton I. Kaufman shared his research on the sea-level canal project and related issues.

The list of librarians and curators who provided assistance in using research collections is so long that I fear I will leave some out. The various collections at the Library of Congress were invaluable, especially the newspapers on microfilm. Individuals include Jan Boles, at the Albertson College Library in Caldwell, Idaho; Alan Virta and Mary Carter at the Frank Church Collection at Boise State University; James V. D'Arc and Irene Adams at the L. Tom Perry Special Collections at Brigham Young University; Robert Bohanan and Sara Saunders at the Jimmy Carter Library, along with Pamela Coleman Nye, who did research for me there; Jennifer Govan at the Gottesman Libraries at Teachers College, Columbia University; Jonathan Dembo and Martha Gay Elmore at Special Collections in the J. Y. Joyner Library at East Carolina University; David Haight at the Dwight D. Eisenhower Library; Nicholas Scheetz at the Panama Collection at Georgetown University; William McNitt and Nancy Mirshah at the Gerald R. Ford Library; Rob Christensen and Peggy Neal at the *Raleigh News and Observer*; Rena Tutten at the Richard B. Russell Library for Political Research and Studies at the University of Georgia; Carol Leadenham and Brad Bauer at the Hoover Institution of War, Revolution and Peace, and Jenny Fichmann, who conducted research among its collections for me; Kathryn Hodson at Special Collections and University Archives at the University of Iowa; Deborah L. Miller and Steve Nielsen at the Minnesota Historical Society; Paige Lilly at the Fogler Library of the University of Maine; Bill Ross at the Milne Special Collections and Archives, University of New Hampshire Library; Barclay Walsh at the *New York Times*; Lewis Mazanti and Christen Walker at the Julian P. Kanter Political Commercial Archive at the University of Oklahoma Political Communication Center; Carol Keys at the library of People for the American Way; Daniel J. Linke at the Seeley G. Mudd Manuscript Library at the Princeton University Library; Allen Lowe and Bobby Holt at the Baker Center of Public Policy, University of Tennessee, Knoxville; Greg Harnett at the U.S. Senate Library; John Lynch at the Vanderbilt Television News Archive, Heard Library, Vanderbilt University; Eddy Palanzo at the *Washington Post*; Jennifer Graham at the Wisconsin Historical Society; Shannon Bowen at the American Heritage Center at the University of Wyoming. Jack Siggins, the librarian of George Washington University, not only made books and electronic resources available but also provided an office where I began the book.

I also received important help from Richard Baker, the Senate Historian; Bob Biersack and Patricia Young of the Federal Election Commission; Regalle Asuncion of the Associated Press; Rebecca Carr of Cox Newspapers; Phyllis Collazo, Marjorie

Connelly, Steve Crowley, and Ron Skarzenski of the *New York Times*; Kathleen Frankovic of CBS News; Catherine Gwin of the Nuclear Threat Initiative; David Broder and Bob Woodward of the *Washington Post*; Kim Cumber of the North Carolina State Archives; David Yepsen of the *Des Moines Register*; Kent Cooper of Political Moneyline; and Mary Lukens of Ann Arbor, Michigan.

Nor could this book have gone forward without encouragement from Dean Eleanor Miller of the University of Vermont; my agents, David Black and David Larabell; and, of course, Fred Woodward, Susan McRory, Susan Schott, and Susan Ecklund of the University Press of Kansas.

Finally, my wife, Ann Fessenden Clymer, cheered the work on and put up with the hectic accumulation of books and papers, repeatedly filed away and then returned to piles cluttering the study of our apartment.

INDEX

windsock, 115
Winter, Tom, 54, 57, 61
Wirthlin, Richard, 26, 27, 39, 201
Witcover, Jules, 127, 158
Women's Campaign Fund, 151
World Affairs Council, 23
Wrenn, Carter 174, 175
Wright, Jim, 162

Xerox Corporation, 42

yellow fever, 1, 181
Young, Andrew, 94, 150, 176, 178
Young Americans for Freedom (YAF), 50,
    54, 63–64, 141, 156, 158

Zorinsky, Edward, 101